HOW TO PLANT A GARDEN

Royal Horticultural Society

HOW TO PLANT A GARDEN

Design tips, ideas and planting schemes for year-round interest

MATT JAMES

MITCHELL BEAZLEY

KEY TO ABBREVIATIONS

Sp. (singular) or spp. (plural):
Species. A group of plants that share similar characteristics and, while they can interbreed freely, whose offspring are more-or-less the same. For example Common beech (*Fagus sylvatica*) – a species of beech.

Cvs: Cultivars [**culti**-vated **var**-ieties] – plant varieties created or selected for particular characteristics, which differ to the species (for example,

larger flowers or multi-coloured leaves) and are maintained through cultivation. For example, weeping beech (*Fagus sylvatica* 'Pendula') – a weeping cultivar of common beech.

H&S: Height and spread. (Note: the sizes given here are at maturity and don't factor in the effects of different soil types or competition from neighbours, for example, so use them as a rough guide only.)

Contents

Introduction

I know very few garden-makers who find it difficult not to get seriously excited about plants. There are just so many to choose from, in every single size, shape and colour you can possibly think of. And as for the different ways they can be used in creative combinations, well, they're seemingly endless!

Such choice can overwhelm both new and accomplished gardeners alike. Add in changing trends, horticultural jargon, Latin names and hardiness ratings and, at times, gardening can be a little bewildering.

Although planting a garden isn't easy at times (if it was you wouldn't be reading this book) I do know one thing – each and every one of us can do it, with beautiful results (teaching professional planting design for more than 10 years now has certainly taught me that). All it takes is the enthusiasm to make the most of your garden's potential, and the desire to transform it from the ordinary to the truly extraordinary. A little research and reading also help enormously. That's where this book comes in.

If you are seeking a brand new look perhaps start by feasting your eyes on the hundreds of gorgeous images for inspiration, (particularly in Chapter 4), to help you make some decisions. Experienced gardeners might want to jump straight to Chapters 5 and 6. Both look at design details like colour, form and scent but, importantly, also concentrate on tried-and-tested techniques that can be used to arrange plants in pleasing combinations. Those seeking advice on how to solve common garden problems with plants should head straight to Chapter 3 – 'Plants with a Purpose'.

New gardeners, or those who want to think in the way professional planting designers think, should start from Chapter 1. Together we'll follow a logical journey through the planting design process, from analysing your space to choosing an appropriate design style. Then we'll get down to detail and look closely at what to consider and the best ways to put your planting together. Finally, there are plans to copy or simply add into a creative melting pot of your own design, then I'll show you how to get your new scheme 'off' – or I should say 'into' – the ground.

Whether you have a tiny courtyard garden or an hectare-sized patch, and whether you know little about plants or have enjoyed tinkering in the garden for years, my aim is to demystify the planting design process and to help you choose and use plants, and create beautiful planting schemes with confidence, just like the professionals.

Opposite: Sensational show gardens – and yes you will see some in this book – certainly astound with their complex planting designs, but all good designers at heart know that simple is hard to beat.

1.

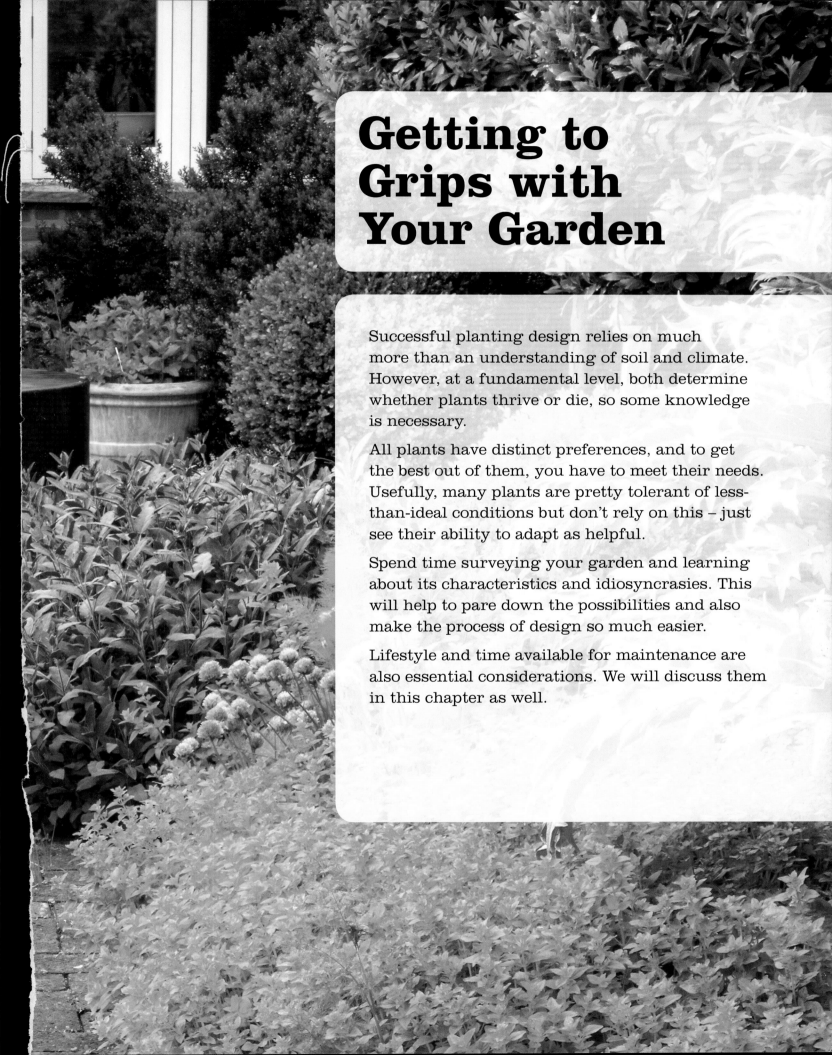

Getting to Grips with Your Garden

Successful planting design relies on much more than an understanding of soil and climate. However, at a fundamental level, both determine whether plants thrive or die, so some knowledge is necessary.

All plants have distinct preferences, and to get the best out of them, you have to meet their needs. Usefully, many plants are pretty tolerant of less-than-ideal conditions but don't rely on this – just see their ability to adapt as helpful.

Spend time surveying your garden and learning about its characteristics and idiosyncrasies. This will help to pare down the possibilities and also make the process of design so much easier.

Lifestyle and time available for maintenance are also essential considerations. We will discuss them in this chapter as well.

Climate & microclimates

The regional climate (including rainfall frequency, sunlight hours/intensity, prevailing wind direction and temperature) impacts on gardens at a local level and must be studied. But every garden also has numerous mini microclimates within it too. Aspect, the orientation of walls and fences, topography, trees, buildings, natural pools and watercourses all have a big effect, as does soil type. By the coast, gardens also have salt-laden winds to contend with; it'll also be wetter than normal there (but usually not cold).

Look closely around the garden and identify the different microclimates. Some will be more hospitable than others, but view them all as opportunities for creative planting design. There are plenty of plants to choose from, for every situation.

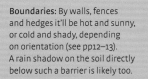

Trees: Large trees provide shelter but the soil beneath them might be dry and infertile. Evergreen trees and conifers, especially those with a low canopy, exacerbate these conditions still further. Only tough plants tolerant of dry shade thrive there.

Boundaries: By walls, fences and hedges it'll be hot and sunny, or cold and shady, depending on orientation (see pp12–13). A rain shadow on the soil directly below such a barrier is likely too.

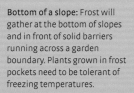

Bottom of a slope: Frost will gather at the bottom of slopes and in front of solid barriers running across a garden boundary. Plants grown in frost pockets need to be tolerant of freezing temperatures.

Top & above: Gardens with high water tables and thick clay soils will be naturally boggy in low-lying areas, so species tolerant of waterlogged soil are essential. The availability of sun or shade is another deciding factor in the different planting options.

Manipulating microclimates

It is possible to influence a microclimate by, for example, lifting the crown of a spreading tree to let in more light. Hedges and freestanding trelliswork could be introduced to temper strong winds. As trees or built structures cast shade, consider the impact of such features at the drawing board stage if you're planning a complete redesign – not just remodelling beds and borders. Hardscape features and larger plants may create new microclimates around them, whether you intend them to or not.

Hardiness zones & ratings

Hardiness ratings are helpful when identifying appropriate plants for your particular region, especially if you're a beginner gardener in the early stages of learning all about plants. The American USDA (United States Department of Agriculture) system is the most common throughout the world, but in the UK the simple 'snowflake' system is a good guide too. You'll find that, where necessary, this book features both, written thus: *Taxus baccata* (yew; ❊❊❊ Z7–8). For all the specific details, see pp278–279.

Buildings: Depending on their orientation, the prevailing wind direction and natural topography, buildings can provide shelter or, close together, funnel strong, drying gusts. The northerly and easterly sides will be shady and cold. The southerly and westerly ones will be warm by day and night (masonry absorbs heat, releasing it slowly like a storage radiator after dark). The eaves will also cast a rain shadow on the soil directly below, which will be dry.

Below: In a garden exposed to strong salt-laden winds, chosing the right plants to cope with conditions is key. Be mindful that some 'salt-tolerant' plants can cope with full exposure; others need protection, such as planted windbreaks, polypropylene webbing or woven hazel hurdles.

Lawns: Open areas such as lawns are typically hot and may be windy. At the top or the middle of a slope, the soil could also be quite dry.

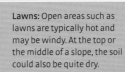

Right: Balconies and roof terraces that are open to prevailing winds are the urban equivalent of a clifftop garden. Robust, wind-tolerant plants are essential to cope with strong gusts and provide shelter for people.

Aspect & orientation

Your garden's aspect determines how windy it will be and, in particular, how much light it'll receive. A compass will help here. Do remember that the different seasons have an impact. In winter the sun follows a lower arc, so areas in summer that might have received an hour or two of sunlight might now get none. Check too if trees or buildings block the sunlight during the day. Offices covered in glass might even reflect more light into the garden (the albedo effect). Walls and fences have a huge impact on the amount of wind and sunlight, especially in small gardens. Note the orientation of each barrier, so you can choose plants accordingly.

WEST-FACING

- similar conditions to south-facing gardens but without the extremes;
- slow to warm in early morning;
- the 'kindest' aspect for plants – ideal for more tender species;
- depending on soil type, most plants will thrive here (except those that require shade).

Examples: *Actinidia, Azara, Clematis, Dahlia, Eremurus* (foxtail lily), *Euphorbia mellifera* (honey spurge), *Lilium* (lily), *Magnolia, Nicotiana* (tobacco plant), *Rosa* (rose), *Salvia* (sage)

SOUTH-FACING

- warm in winter, hot in summer;
- high, often intense light levels;
- with sandy soil or south-facing slopes, plants should be selected with drought-tolerance in mind;
- plants that require full sun (that is, six hours of sunlight per day) grow well here.

Examples: *Abutilon, Agapanthus* (African blue lily), *Amaryllis belladonna, Callistemon* (bottlebrush), *Campsis* (trumpet vine), *Ceanothus* (California lilac), *Chimonanthus* (wintersweet), *Cistus* (rock rose), *Cytisus battandieri* (pineapple broom), *Hebe, Hoheria, Leptospermum* (tea tree), *Passiflora* (passion flower), *Wisteria*

Soil

This is made up of the mineral particles sand, silt and clay, plus organic matter, air spaces and water. The proportion of each determines how soil acts when it comes to drainage, nutrient availability, water-holding potential and temperature, as well as the method and timing of cultivation techniques. The ideal soil for gardeners is a 'loam', which has an even balance of the three mineral particles, being crumbly, dark, moist (but not waterlogged) and free-draining. It smells 'sweet', has a high earthworm population and won't bake hard or crust over in summer. Unfortunately, few of us start with the perfect soil, so careful plant selection and some remedial work are often necessary.

SANDY SOILS

- drains easily but is prone to drying out – sand particles are large and so are the spaces between them;

- well aerated;

- infertile – poor nutrient-holding capacity;

- early warming – good for seeds and spring growth;

- easy to dig, unlikely to become compacted;

- high in silica, so often acidic (see p16).

SILTY SOILS

- good water retention;

- can suffer from compaction;

- highly susceptible to wind and water erosion;

- prone to 'capping' – a surface crust that prevents seedlings emerging.

CLAY SOILS

- moisture retentive, but can waterlog in winter and bake hard in summer;

- very fertile;

- often difficult to dig;

- susceptible to wind and water erosion;

- prone to compaction – never use machinery (especially a rotavator) or walk directly on a clay soil when wet, as this will ruin its structure. Surface puddling and a sulphurous smell are signs of compaction;

- cold in winter and slow to warm in spring.

Topsoil & subsoil

The topsoil is the fertile uppermost layer and usually dark in colour, being rich in humus (organic matter); most plant roots grow in this area. The subsoil below is generally paler and may contain stones or coarse particulates. Topsoil is of greatest value for plants – this is where they get most food and water needed for growth. If you're digging out an area or undertaking major earthworks, avoid mixing topsoil with subsoil, as it will lower fertility levels.

CHALKY SOILS

- light brown/white colour;
- often very thin topsoil;
- free-draining, but doesn't dry out quickly;
- light and fairly easy to dig, but can be full of stones;
- low nutrient retention;
- high pH because of calcium carbonate content (see p16).

PEATY SOILS

- infertile;
- high water retention;
- easy to dig;
- early warming – good for growth;
- can be very acidic (see p16).

ASSESSING SOIL TYPE

Add water to a small soil sample and rub it between thumb and forefinger. Clay soil feels sticky and will mould into a ball, or even a ring if the clay content is high. Sandy soil is gritty and won't hold any shape. Individual irregular-sized grains might also be visible to the naked eye. Silty soils lie between the two – particle-size-wise – and feel silky and soapy. When rubbed close to the ear, they sometimes 'squeak'.

Soil pH

As well as identifying your soil's texture, you should also record its pH. Simply, pH is how acid or alkaline the soil is, as measured on a scale ranging from pH1 (very acid) to pH14 (very alkaline). A pH of 7 is known as neutral (neither acid nor alkaline). Most plants prefer a pH of 6–7 – even plants that have a distinct preference normally thrive in this range.

Plants that prefer alkaline soils are called calcicoles, and they usually grow on soils over limestone or chalk. Those that prefer acidic soils are called calcifuges, and they hate lime. Soil pH has a direct effect on nutrient availability, and plants with a specific pH preference (acid-lovers are most fussy) will show signs of nutrient deficiencies when grown in less-than-ideal conditions; these deficiencies will manifest themselves as stunted growth and discoloured leaves. As a temporary solution they can be remedied with the appropriate fertiliser – depending on the specific deficiency – but it is much better if true acid-lovers are never grown on very alkaline soil, and vice versa.

pH CHART

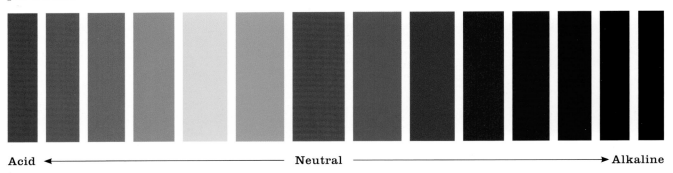

Acid ◄———————————————— Neutral ———————————————► Alkaline

Acid

Acer palmatum 'Sango-kaku' (Japanese maple)

Enkianthus campanulatus

Deschampsia cespitosa 'Goldtau' (tufted hair grass)

Fothergilla major Monticola Group

Sorbus pseudohupehensis 'Pink Pagoda' (Hubei rowan)

Hamamelis × intermedia 'Glowing Embers' (witch hazel)

Calluna vulgaris 'Athene' (Garden Girls Series) (Scots heather)

Magnolia 'Elizabeth'

Determining soil pH

Healthy plants in neighbouring gardens can also indicate your soil's likely pH – rhododendrons growing well would mean their soil is acidic. However, for accuracy, use a soil pH testing kit. For a genuine reading, scrape away mulch or leaf litter before collecting a sample 10cm (4in) deep. Watch out for sand or cement spillages and other construction detritus – this will affect the results. In large gardens take samples in all areas you plan to plant; soil pH can vary over a relatively short distance.

Amending pH

Lime will make acidic soil more alkaline, while aluminium sulphate, iron sulphate and organic matter will acidify all but chalky soil (where the concentration of calcium carbonate is too high). But you can't realistically change soil pH long term. Additives need reapplying regularly, and it's cheaper to work with, rather than fight, your soil's natural pH. If you do want to grow acid-lovers on an alkaline soil, for example, plant them in large pots filled with ericaceous compost.

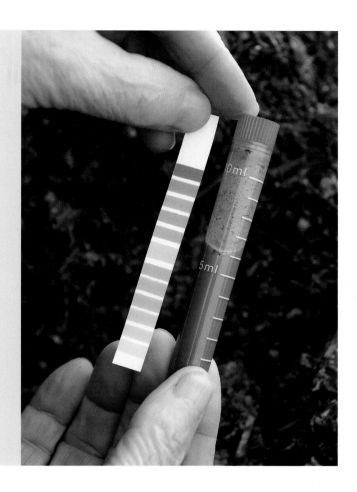

Alkaline

Philadelphus 'Virginal' (mock orange)

Salvia nemorosa 'Ostfriesland' (Balkan clary)

Syringa pubescens subsp. *microphylla* 'Superba' (lilac)

Ceanothus 'Cynthia Postan' (California lilac)

Iris 'Sable'

Aster × *frikartii* 'Jungfrau' (Michaelmas daisy)

Achillea 'Fleur van Zonneveld' (yarrow)

Stipa splendens (feather grass)

Managing soil

There are two broad strategies for managing soil. Conventional advice is to enrich it with organic matter such as composted green waste, then apply fertiliser regularly to support a broader plant palette. Contemporary thinking looks to choose plants that naturally thrive in such conditions in the wild, thereby minimising maintenance in the process. With long-term sustainability and a 'sense of place' in mind, it's always best to work with what you've got. But ameliorants such as well-rotted manure improve soil structure and background fertility levels, so are particularly helpful to young plants establishing on nutrient-poor, compacted soil.

Above: Raised beds are ideal if your garden soil is particularly poor – you can fill them with the perfect soil tailored to match your plants if need be. Designers also use raised beds like this to define or separate one garden space from the next.

Left: Garden compost is so easy to make – everyone should do it. Just aim for a healthy mix of browns (such as prunings and sawdust from pet cages) and greens (such as vegetable peelings and grass clippings). Turn the contents of the heap occasionally for the best results.

PROBLEM	LIKELY SOIL TYPE	STRATEGIES & SOLUTIONS
soil is dusty and dry	sandy and silty	• Incorporate organic matter; this soaks up water like a sponge. • Cultivate lightly in spring before the weather warms. • Spread organic mulches around plants in summer after rainfall, to stop evaporation. • In sun, choose plants such as lavender (*Lavandula*); in shade, barrenwort (*Epimedium*) and Oregon grape (*Mahonia*) – all have naturally adapted to dusty dry conditions.
soil is difficult to dig, wet and waterlogged	clay	• Dig in organic matter as this improves 'workability' and drainage. Fine grit is a permanent solution to waterlogged soil but can be expensive. • Cultivate in autumn and early winter when conditions are dry, to avoid damaging soil structure. • Postpone planting until mid-spring when the soil temperature is warmer than in the winter months. • Choose woody plants and perennials that don't need to be disturbed. • Direct-sown seed will struggle; use plug plants instead. • Dig a wider hole than normal and plant on a slight mound, to avoid waterlogging. • Make raised beds to assist drainage. • With some clay soils, lime can 'bind' clay particles together into larger crumbs (called flocculation), but this needs to be applied carefully. • Choose plants such as hemp agimony (*Eupatorium*) and *Astilbe*, which have adapted to waterlogged soil. Big borders are necessary as many grow big, so need suitable space.
soil is strewn with builder's detritus	'new-build'	• Dig deeply over the planting areas, removing rubble in the process. • Incorporate organic matter to improve soil structure and fertility. • If the soil is full of rubble, buy small plants rather than large specimens, as they're much easier to plant physically. Smaller plants will establish more readily too. • In heavily polluted soils with a high pH choose calcicoles such as *Buddleja* and lilac (*Syringa*). • Grow plants in raised beds or containers filled with a suitable growing medium.
'dead' soil	soil once covered with concrete	• Work in organic matter to improve soil structure. • Apply general fertiliser in spring and early summer while plants establish. • Replace the topsoil, after having considered costs carefully.
topsoil is too thin, often infertile and 'loses' nutrients and water	potentially all, but notably chalk	• Dig in organic matter. • Mulch regularly. • If the soil layer is very thin, grow plants in raised beds and containers. • Choose low-growing, shallow-rooting plants; large trees and shrubs in particular are not suitable, as there simply isn't the necessary depth of topsoil for them to establish well or to 'anchor' themselves firmly.

Existing plants

With garden design it's often unnecessary to start from scratch so, before you plan new displays, survey the condition and position of existing plants. Are they diseased or awkwardly placed, and therefore warrant removal, or could they be kept and included? For new homeowners who've inherited a garden it pays to note plant performance and what comes up – perennials, bulbs and weeds, for example – throughout the first growing season before making changes; hopefully you'll find some pleasant surprises.

Maturity

You might have to be ruthless but remember that mature plants aren't easy or cheap to replace with others of a similar size. Perhaps those with distinctive form could become a fine focal point, or the backbone to a new planting design, after pruning them hard to give them a new lease of life. Keep any trees if you can. Cutting one down may expose an ugly eyesore or a gap that'll be hard to fill.

If a tree casts too much shade or dwarfs the garden, surgery can reduce, thin or lift the canopy. Do discuss this with neighbours, though, and check with your local authority that no restrictions apply.

In a small garden, suckering shrubs such as stag's horn sumach (*Rhus*), spreading perennials and running bamboo are always tricky to tame. Remove problem plants early, unless you've space to extend borders to accommodate them.

Climbing high

Overgrown climbers can be problematic. But removing one depends on their vigour, year-round performance and whether they're swamping other plants. Mature grapevines (*Vitis*), climbing roses, large-flowered *Clematis* and *Wisteria* are assets to embrace, so wherever possible simply provide additional support rather than cutting them back hard. Hyper-vigorous climbers such as Russian vine (*Fallopia baldschuanica*) aren't easily controlled; consider eradicating any of these straight off.

Re-home?

Healthy plants of a manageable size in the wrong place can be moved. In temperate climates, small deciduous trees, shrubs and roses can be lifted bare root in autumn/late winter. For everything else it's necessary to 'rootball' the roots to minimise transplanting shock. Taller trees and shrubs are tricky to manage without experience; perennials, ferns and ornamental grasses are easy to re-home – many can be split into numerous clumps before replanting (see p52).

Neighbouring plants

Plants that overhang from adjacent gardens can be 'borrowed' to make a garden feel bigger or bring maturity to a new scheme in front of them. Don't be too quick to chop them back to your boundary line. With trees in particular, hard pruning could leave behind an ugly 'face' of bare branches that'll be impossible to hide.

Left: Beautiful as they may be, vigorous spreading perennials and prolific self-seeders such as Mexican fleabane (*Erigeron karvinskianus*) can be a nuisance in the wrong place and may swamp other plants. They should be removed before implementing a new scheme, or else diligently kept under control.

Opposite: Mature trees, even those overhanging from adjacent gardens like this great white ornamental cherry (*Prunus* 'Tai-haku'), are an asset. Don't be too quick to remove or prune them back hard without careful consideration.

Who's it for?

How you lead your life, or plan to in the future, impacts on plant selection and the long-term success of a planting scheme.

Wants & needs

Don't kid yourself; honesty is essential, so spend time carefully considering specific things you might like and require from both your planting and the garden as a whole. Now prioritise the list into those that are most important, to those that, while desirable, you can live without – the characteristics of your garden and budget will have an influence here. This process of reflection brings clarity and direction to your design process, honing your thoughts down to a brief, which you can then use to dictate, direct and ultimately support any design decisions you might make.

Below: Water presents all manner of exciting planting opportunities. However, wherever possible in small gardens, water features should be integrated into other features (here a terrace and wooden boardwalk) to make the best use of space.

Key questions to consider

When and at what times of day are you at home to enjoy the garden?
Daytimes, or only evenings and weekends? If you're away over summer, plan for peaks in spring and autumn. Likewise, plants that save their scent until dusk are a good choice for those out at work during the day.

Who uses the garden?
Particular people often have specific requirements. For young children, for example, scented and soft-leaved plants are welcome, so too are quick colourful growers that tolerate overenthusiastic picking. Thorny and poisonous plants should be avoided at all costs.

Are there any problems?
Issues such as privacy will dramatically affect how you use the garden. With your lifestyle in mind, examine the space to identify where changes are necessary. Plants could help here (see pp72–85).

What's the 'design vision'? Do you have a 'big idea' or concept in mind?
Do you favour a particular style? Think about atmosphere too. Do you crave somewhere to eat and entertain in lively company, or a place to rest and relax quietly? Consequently, what might the planting look like? Functional concepts from sustainability to encouraging wildlife are also invaluable and again hone down the design options. Use words or images to describe or translate your ideas. A metaphor might be useful: the 'seashore', 'secret garden' and 'orchard glade', for example, conjure imagery that could help you conceive design ideas (we'll look at this more in Chapter 4).

How long do you plan to live where you are?/ Are you impatient?
If you plan to relocate soon, fast-growing perennials and ornamental grasses are a better option than lots of slower-growing shrubs. Similarly, large, semimature specimens might satisfy requirements for instant impact, but they're not cheap – and could you justify the expense?

Opposite, above: A generous lawn is essential in a family garden. As needs change over time, existing beds and borders can be enlarged, or new ones created easily with just a spade and edging iron – without doubt the cheapest form of redesign.

Opposite, below: A hybrid of sleek hardscape and naturalistic meadow or prairie-like planting is *de rigueur* in garden design today, a juxtaposition that works well anywhere given some space.

Above: On balconies and roof terraces where access is tricky and space for storing tools is limited, low-maintenance shrubs, conifers and ornamental grasses are the perfect planting option.

Right: Cottage-style plantings typically feature extensive collections of annuals, biennials, traditional perennials, roses (here *Rosa* 'Pink Grootendorst', *R.* 'Buff Beauty' and *R.* 'Gruss an Aachen'), fruit and vegetables. It's a beautiful style that taps into our bucolic beginnings, but is inappropriate for busy lives.

Time to tend

Maintenance has a significant effect on the long-term success of a planting scheme: how much time can you commit? Some plants need virtually no work while others require a lot, so once more an honest appraisal is necessary. Also consider the family. Can you rely on others for help?

While low maintenance isn't a key component of everyone's ideal garden, it's a sensible starting point, especially if you're new to gardening, work full time, aren't very mobile or are raising a family. You can always add 'high-maintenance' plants to the mix, but at least with 'low maintenance' in mind you stand more chance of creating a sustainable scheme that won't weigh heavily on your shoulders.

Cutting down on the upkeep

For many people, nurturing plants is one of the best aspects of gardening. However, few of us have the time to tend them every day. Here are 10 key ways to keep maintenance at a manageable level.

- **Match** the right plant to the right place. This approach will often point to the most appropriate style or theme too.

- **Keep** the planting simple. The more involved the plant palette, the more work there will be. The way in which you arrange plants matters too. Large drifts (see pp188–189), for example, are easier to maintain than intermingled plants (see pp190–191).

- **Choose** plants that like the same conditions or grow in a similar way, so that you can deal with them altogether.

- **Select** reliable plants rather than short-lived or tender ones. Grasses, most shrubs, conifers, shrub roses, ground cover and many bulbs need little attention once established. Free-climbers such as climbing hydrangea (*Hydrangea anomala* subsp. *petiolaris*) require little pruning or training. Avoid perennials that need staking or deadheading regularly.

- **Consider** plant vigour and size at maturity, allocating space accordingly. Don't partner thuggish plants with delicate ones either; there'll be only one winner.

- **Choose** an appropriate design style. A cottage garden sounds idyllic, but needs more work than a minimalist garden.

- **Always** ensure the soil is weed-free before starting to plant; this is essential. Minimise the need to weed thereafter with mulches and groundcover plants.

- **Go easy** on the edibles. Evergreen herbs are the exception – generally these need little work.

- **Cut back** on containers or choose big ones that don't dry out too quickly.

- **Buy** robust, healthy, pest- and disease-free plants in the first place. Look for the RHS Award of Garden Merit symbol. Plant them properly and at the right time of year.

2.

The Plant Palette

Armed with the knowledge of the characteristics of your garden that will influence what plants you select, and with some initial thoughts about maintenance, it's time to consider the plants themselves. Before we look at how plants can create or enhance an already established style or theme, it's necessary to understand the plant palette available in order to draw conclusions about what's appropriate. What groups are on offer? How and where do they grow? And, of course, what part might they play in planting design? Specific focus on the problems common to many gardens and how plants can help solve them is given on pp74–85.

One thing to note: in this chapter there's reference to the importance of the right soil type, pH or climate only when it's particularly pertinent. As discussed in Chapter 1, all plants will struggle in conditions they're not happy with, and that includes competition from weeds. Right plant, right place is the motto that applies to all.

Roles & responsibilities

Trees bring all-important height and help to structure a garden. Use them to frame views and vistas or filter views from one 'room' to the next. Those with distinctive characteristics – columnar, fastigiate and weeping habits, palm-shaped leaves or brightly coloured bark, for example – are also invaluable focal points. On the flip side, trees with less distinctive characteristics – simple green leaves and amorphous shapes – make good backdrops, particularly when grouped together.

Left: This tidy Chinese dogwood (*Cornus kousa* var. *chinensis*) is a stunning spectacle in spring and autumn. Here it's also used to 'ceiling' the seating area underneath, making for a more intimate experience.

Trees
No matter the size, or style there's a tree for every garden. Deciduous species lose their leaves in autumn, while evergreen ones shed them gradually throughout the year. Most trees have a single clear stem or trunk. However some – particularly those with attractive bark – look good grown as multistemmed trees with three or four trunks. Others, including birch (*Betula*), fastigiate hornbeam (*Carpinus*) and many conifers, have branches (known as 'feathers') from the bottom of the trunk. Both multistemmed and feathered trees take up more space on the ground and restrict room for planting or sitting underneath; consider this fact carefully in a small garden.

Above: Many trees burst into the spotlight in autumn with awesome autumn colour. Stag's-horn sumach (*Rhus typhina*) is one of the best. Box (*Buxus*) balls and green *Hakonechloa macra* tolerate the shady conditions underneath.

Opposite: Cherries are popular garden favourites with a long season of interest. *Prunus* 'Shirofugen' here has gorgeous, double, white flowers that fade to pink, while the leaves are deep coppery brown when young and turn orange in autumn.

Seasonal changes

Trees have a big impact so choose one with as many seasons of interest as possible, especially for a small garden. Trees with colourful autumn leaves, fruit or winter stems are particularly invaluable. Crab apples (*Malus*), many ornamental cherries (*Prunus*), hawthorn (*Crataegus*) – a favourite for wildlife, snake-bark maples (*Acer capillipes*, *A. davidii* and *A. rufinerve*) and white-stemmed birch (like *Betula papyrifera*) all fit the bill.

Evergreens have year-round presence and are ideal for screening eyesores (see pp76–77). Unlike deciduous trees, which lose their leaves almost all at once, evergreens don't change dramatically with the seasons and can be visually oppressive if used en masse (rather like deciduous trees with purple foliage). Conditions underneath evergreen trees, particularly conifers, can be tricky to work with – only a limited number of plants tolerate such dry, shady conditions.

Some of the best… trees

EVERGREEN TREES FOR SMALL GARDENS – H&S: 5–15M (16–50FT)

- *Arbutus unedo* (strawberry tree; ✲✲✲ Z8–9) and cvs
- *Eriobotrya japonica* (loquat; ✲✲ Z8–11)
- *Eucryphia × nymansensis* 'Nymansay' (✲✲✲ Z8–9)
- *Ilex aquifolium* 'J C van Tol' (English holly; ✲✲✲ Z7–9)
- *Laurus nobilis* (bay laurel; ✲✲ Z8–11)
- *Magnolia grandiflora* (bull bay; ✲✲ Z7–9) and cvs
- *Olea europaea* (olive; ✲✲ Z8–10)
- *Trachycarpus fortunei* (Chusan palm; ✲✲ Z8–11)

TIDY DECIDUOUS TREES FOR TINY GARDENS – H&S: <5M (16FT), WITH TWO OR MORE SEASONS OF INTEREST

- *Acer griseum* (paper-bark maple; ✲✲✲ Z4–8)
- *Amelanchier canadensis* (✲✲✲ Z3–7) and cvs
- *Cercis chinensis* (Chinese redbud; ✲✲✲ Z6–9) and cvs
- *Cornus kousa* (Chinese dogwood; ✲✲✲ Z5–8) and cvs
- *Malus × scheideckeri* 'Red Jade' (crab apple; ✲✲✲ Z4–8)
- *Morus alba* 'Pendula' (weeping white mulberry; ✲✲ Z4–8)
- *Prunus* 'Amanogawa' (fastigate Japanese cherry; ✲✲✲ Z6–8)
- *Sorbus vilmorinii* (vilmorin rowan; ✲✲✲ Z6–8)

TIDY DECIDUOUS TREES FOR SMALL GARDENS – H&S: 5–10M (16–33FT), WITH TWO OR MORE SEASONS OF INTEREST

- *Amelanchier lamarckii* (juneberry; ✲✲✲ Z5–9)
- *Betula albosinensis* (Chinese red birch; ✲✲✲ Z5–8) and cvs
- *Cercis siliquastrum* (Judas tree; ✲✲✲ Z6–9) and cvs
- *Crataegus laevigata* (Midland hawthorn; ✲✲✲ Z5–8) and cvs
- *Magnolia × loebneri* (✲✲✲ Z5–9) and cvs
- *Malus floribunda* (Japanese crab apple; ✲✲✲ Z4–8)
- *Malus × robusta* 'Red Sentinel' (crab apple; ✲✲✲ Z4–8)
- *Sorbus aria* 'Lutescens' (whitebeam; ✲✲✲ Z4–5)
- *Sorbus cashmiriana* (Kashmir rowan; ✲✲✲ Z5–7)
- *Stewartia sinensis* (Chinese stewartia; ✲✲✲ Z5–8)

GROWING SUCCESS

- **Size at maturity:** Spread is just as important as height, with trees. Where space is tight, choose top-worked, weeping trees (those that look like an umbrella), fastigiate trees such as the cherry *Prunus* 'Amanogawa' and pleached trees (essentially hedges on 'stilts').

- **Vigour:** Big, fast-growing woodlanders such as sycamore (*Acer pseudoplatanus*) and poplar (*Populus*) suit only large gardens. Small- to medium-sized, fast growers such as honey locust (*Gleditsia tricanthos*) and perhaps *Robinia pseudoacacia* 'Bessoniana' (although it does have brittle branches) are also worth considering, as they won't grow to monstrous proportions.

- **Root run:** Large, vigorous trees typically have aggressive roots. Common ash (*Fraxinus excelsior*), poplar (*Populus*), weeping willow (*Salix* × *sepulcralis* var. *chrysocoma*), sycamore (*Acer pseudoplatanus*) and silver maple (*A. saccharinum*) can lift paving and on thick clay soil contribute to subsidence, if planted too close to the house. Wild cherry (*Prunus avium*) and gum (*Eucalyptus*) may be less tall (cider gum/*E. gunnii* is the notable exception, reaching 25m/80ft), but both have shallow root systems; again, avoid these in a small garden.

- **Protection & support** are required for a tree to establish properly. Small trees need a thin cane or stake plus a tree shelter, whereas semimature trees should be triple-staked or guyed with wire. Remember that large trees cosseted on nursery beds will suffer if suddenly plonked on a windy hillside or cliff top – in such a site, the smaller the tree when planted, the better.

- **Shade:** Small or narrow leaves let in more sunlight. Large ones and a dense crown create deeper shade. Consider how much shade is cast as the tree matures too. Eventually you'll need to replace sun-loving plants underneath with those that tolerate more shade.

- **Maintenance:** All trees drop some debris but lots of big leaves might be annoying to clear up. Avoid fruit trees over seating areas – fallen fruit can stain surfaces and attract wasps.

- **Pruning:** Most trees require little pruning once established, particularly if you purchase pre-trained trees, where the formative pruning has already been done on the nursery field. Small transplants – 'whips' – are cheaper, but you'll need to prune and train them into the desired shape.

- **People friendly:** Thorny trees and poisonous ones such as *Laburnum* and false acacia (*Robinia*) should be avoided in gardens where young children play, or positioned out of reach.

Opposite: Where there is acid soil and a sheltered sunny spot, *Magnolia* are ideal garden trees and require little maintenance or pruning once established. Some, such as *M.* × *soulangeana* 'Alba Superba', however, have a broad spreading habit and therefore need space to stretch out.

Left: Many trees such as this field maple (*Acer campestre*) can be pleached into tidy shapes. These add a formal note and help divide one space from the next. Because pleached trees are tall but thin and don't take up much room, they're also useful to help provide privacy in small gardens.

Shrubs

Shrubs are different from trees, having multiple woody stems, rather than (usually) just the one. There's an enormous range of evergreen and deciduous species for every aspect and in every size and shape, from conical cultivars reaching 4m (13ft) or more to carpeting shrubs such as prostrate rosemary (*Rosmarinus officinalis* Prostratus Group) growing to only 30–40cm (12–16in).

Like trees, shrubs are important structural plants bringing 'body' and – if you buy a few large specimens to start with – a sense of maturity to young gardens. Shrubs with strong characteristics are important 'key' or theme plants too, used to punctuate the planting and dictate or emphasise the desired style or theme.

Note: Roses are technically shrubs, but because of their popularity they are dealt with separately on pp46–49.

First positions

In traditional beds and borders, shrubs form the backdrop to multilayered mixed plantings. With borders backed by walls or fences, they also make the transition height-wise to ankle-high ground cover. But, when positioned upfront, squat shrubs such as rock roses (*Cistus*) and smaller *Hebe* species also work as a structural – often flowering – foil to foreground perennials and ornamental grasses. Alongside taller, back-of-border species, designers will also plot these early on in the design process to help break down a mixed planting into more manageable parts.

Clipped topiary and tidy evergreen subshrubs (smaller shrubs that don't get very woody), including common sage (*Salvia officinalis*) and wormwood (*Artemisia* 'Powis Castle'), are particularly useful here. All provide reliable contrasting form and colour year-round. With carpeting junipers (*Juniperus*) and purple gromwell (*Lithodora*), weed control is a bonus.

Left: *Pittosporum tenuifolium* 'Silver Queen', *Hydrangea arborescens* and juneberry (*Amelanchier lamarckii*), all underplanted with sweet woodruff (*Galium odoratum*), make a wonderful informal contrasting foil to the crisp limestone stepping stone path and raised deck.

Choices, choices

With shrubs, the tendency is to focus on foliage texture and its colour – particularly with evergreens. But, being such a big group, there's lots more on offer. Shrubs such as lilac (*Syringa*) and pineapple broom (*Argyrocytisus battandieri*) have large heavily scented flowers in summer while those of wintersweet (*Chimonanthus*) and shrubby honeysuckle (*Lonicera fragrantissima*) usefully punch out perfume in late winter. Deciduous species including *Enkianthus campanulatus* and winged spindle (*Euonymus alatus*) have fiery autumn colour. Shrubs with attractive bark – try dogwood (*Cornus*) – or brilliantly coloured berries – beauty berry (*Callicarpa bodinieri* var. *giraldii* 'Profusion') is amazing – are cherished in the depths of winter.

Opposite: Small-leaved shrubs such as burkwood osmanthus (*Osmanthus × burkwoodii*) can be easily clipped into various shapes, just like box (*Buxus*) – which features alongside in this scheme. Together these domes bring a formal structural note to this modern Mediterranean planting containing acid-yellow spurge (*Euphorbia*) and deep blue alkanet (*Anchusa azurea* 'Loddon Royalist').

Right, above: Delavay osmanthus (*Osmanthus delavayi*) is a tidy, back-of-the-border favourite with white, highly scented spring flowers.

Right, below: Common lilac (here, *Syringa vulgaris* 'Zhemchuzhina') is another fragrant spring sensation; just give plants space to spread. A neutral to alkaline soil is essential too.

Top: The spindle (here, *Euonymus europaeus* 'Red Cascade') is cherished in autumn for its scarlet flowers and beautiful pink fruits that open to reveal bright orange seeds. It is an ideal choice for the natural garden.

Above: Shrubby dogwoods – here, *Cornus sanguinea* 'Anny's Winter Orange' – are renowned for their colourful winter stems. Prune all shoots back to 2–3 buds from the ground each spring, to intensify the colour. (Such a pruning technique is called coppicing.)

Opposite: This sculptural Mediterranean evergreen shrubbery revels in every shade of green. It is certainly an exception to the rule 'easy on the evergreens'!

GROWING SUCCESS

- **Size-wise:** Consider size at maturity carefully. Regular hard pruning to control size should be avoided. Done at the wrong time it might adversely affect flowering. With conical evergreens (and conifers – see pp36–37), drastic pruning will ruin the natural shape too.

- **Bigger borders?** A common mistake is to plant big shrubs in narrow borders where they quickly outgrow their space, affecting proportional harmony. Any shrub that grows to 2–3m (6½–10ft) tall could spread a similar distance. If height is important but space is tight, choose columnar and fastigiate forms, wall-trained shrubs (see pp42–45) or clipped topiary.

- **Seasonal interest:** Hardworking shrubs with a long flowering period or more than one season of interest – spring flowers with autumn berries for example – are important in smaller gardens. Those with larger gardens can be slightly more laissez-faire, having more room to accommodate one-season wonders such as *Forsythia*.

- **Time:** Unless you buy big, shrubs will take time to reach maturity. But don't overplant or you'll need to keep cutting back or remove a few plants later on. Instead fill in gaps temporarily with fast-growing annuals, biennials or short-lived perennials such as purple top (*Verbena bonariensis*).

- **Easy on the evergreens:** Evergreens are the most useful structural plants but too many dark ones can look gloomy. How many? In mixed borders one or two larger types every 6–8m (20–25ft) or so – partnered with two or three smaller evergreen or deciduous shrubs (including roses and topiary) around or in front – is plenty.

- **Subtlety isn't a bad thing:** While shrubs with interesting shapes such as Japanese snowball bush (*Viburnum plicatum* f. *tomentosum* 'Mariesii') are invaluable, those shrubs that are seemingly innocuous, such as burkwood osmanthus (*Osmanthus* × *burkwoodii*), complement through contrast the more showy starlets grown around them, so also have an important role. Many often flower in spring or berry in autumn, just when we need them most. Of course evergreen shrubs (and trees) with small leaves and stubby stem growth can be clipped into topiary to make them more visually appealing through the summer.

- **Pruning:** Choose plants wisely so pruning should be needed only to improve flowering or winter stem colour. Leave evergreens and conifers alone, removing only dead, diseased or damaged wood. Late summer shrubs such as *Buddleja*, which flower on new growth, should be cut back hard in spring. Shrubs such as mock orange (*Philadelphus*), lilac (*Syringa*) and *Weigela* flower on the previous season's growth in late spring/early summer; prune these – removing a third of the old growth – after flowering. Shrubs grown for bright stems such as dogwood (*Cornus*) and white-stemmed bramble (such as *Rubus cockburnianus*) should be cut back hard to 20–30cm (8–12in) from the ground each spring.

Some of the best… shrubs

SMALL SHRUBS/SUBSHRUBS – H&S: 0.5–1.5M (1½–5FT)

- *Deutzia* × *rosea* (❀❀❀ Z6–8)
- *Genista lydia* (Lydian broom; ❀❀❀ Z6–9)
- *Hebe* 'Great Orme' (❀❀ Z9–11)
- *Lavandula angustifolia* (lavender; ❀❀❀ Z9–11) and cvs
- *Perovskia* (❀❀❀ Z6–9)
- *Philadelphus* 'Manteau d'Hermine' (mock orange; ❀❀❀ Z5–8)
- *Skimmia japonica* (❀❀❀ Z7–9) and cvs
- *Syringa meyeri* (Korean lilac; ❀❀❀ Z4–7) and cvs

MEDIUM–LARGE SHRUBS/SUBSHRUBS – H&S: 2M (6½FT) OR MORE

- *Corylopsis pauciflora* (winter hazel; ❀❀❀ Z6–9)
- *Enkianthus campanulatus* (❀❀❀ Z5–8)
- *Euonymus alatus* (winged spindle; ❀❀❀ Z4–9) and cvs
- *Hamamelis* × *intermedia* (witch hazel; ❀❀❀ Z5–9) and cvs
- *Magnolia stellata* (star magnolia; ❀❀❀ Z5–9)
- *Paeonia ludlowii* (tree peony; ❀❀❀ Z3–8) and cvs
- *Viburnum* × *burkwoodii* (burkwood viburnum; ❀❀❀ Z5–8) and cvs

Conifers

Much loved by the Victorians and once the darling of 1970s' island beds and borders, conifers slipped from favour following overexposure, nightmarish stories of thuggish Leyland cypress (× *Cuprocyparis leylandii*) and trends in prairie-like planting design. But they're tough, with many originating from harsh alpine and arid habitats. Most are evergreen, giving a year-round presence. And there's every size and shape imaginable, from carpeting ground cover to graceful trees with sculptural foliage, attractive cones and, sometimes, autumn colour. Of course tall dense species, including western red cedar (*Thuja plicata*), Lawson's cypress (*Chamaecyparis lawsoniana*), Monterey cypress (*Cupressus macrocarpa*) and yew (*Taxus baccata*), can be clipped into formal hedges (see p39). With such a huge range of conifers available, it's likely you'll find one suitable for every garden.

Opposite: Conifers with a sculptural shape such as Irish yew *(Taxus baccata 'Fastigiata')* are particularly invaluable and make fine focal points. Here they help structure this contemporary summer border edged in box (*Buxus*) and frame views to a white foxtail lily (*Eremurus* 'Joanna') behind.

Some of the best… 'border' conifers

- *Abies koreana* 'Silberlocke' (Korean fir; ❋❋❋ Z5–6)
- *Cupressus sempervirens* (Italian cypress; ❋❋❋ Z7–9) and cvs
- *Chamaecyparis lawsoniana* 'Green Globe' (Lawson's cypress; ❋❋❋ Z5–9)
- *Chamaecyparis obtusa* 'Nana' (Hinoki cypress; ❋❋❋ Z4–8)
- *Cryptomeria japonica* 'Vilmoriniana' (Japanese cedar; ❋❋❋ Z6–9)
- *Juniperus communis* 'Green Carpet' (common juniper; ❋❋❋ Z2–6)
- *Juniperus scopulorum* (Rocky Mountain juniper; ❋❋❋ Z3–7) and cvs
- *Picea abies* 'Little Gem' (Norway spruce; ❋❋❋ Z3–8)
- *Picea glauca* var. *albertiana* 'Conica' (Alberta spruce; ❋❋❋ Z2–6)
- *Picea mariana* 'Nana' (dwarf black spruce; ❋❋❋ Z2–6)
- *Pinus mugo* (dwarf mountain pine; ❋❋❋ Z3–7) and cvs
- *Pinus parviflora* 'Adcock's Dwarf' (Japanese white pine; ❋❋❋ Z6–9)
- *Pinus sylvestris* Fastigiata Group (fastigiate Scots pine; ❋❋❋ Z3–7)
- *Taxus baccata* 'Fastigiata' (Irish yew; ❋❋❋ Z7–8)
- *Thuja occidentalis* 'Hetz Midget' (white cedar; ❋❋❋ Z2–7)

Right: Shrubby junipers (*Juniperus*) with seas of lavender (here, *Lavandula angustifolia* 'Munstead') contained in a box (*Buxus*) parterre make a wonderful neutral foil to the armillary sphere in the centre.

GROWING SUCCESS

- **Mixed up:** A giant cedar of Lebanon (*Cedrus libani*) or giant redwood (*Sequoiadendron giganteum*) is a joy to behold but few gardens can accommodate plants of this size. In smaller gardens 'border' or 'dwarf' conifers are best. However don't create kitsch collections; instead use plants to anchor mixed plantings featuring ever-changing arrangements of perennials and bulbs.

- **Green is good:** While conifers come in many colours, for most designs nowadays variegated cultivars and those with overly fancy foliage are dated. Instead army-greens and glaucous greys work better in contemporary gardens.

- **Focus in:** Conifers with strong fastigiate form such as Irish yew (*Taxus baccata* 'Fastigiata'), sentinel pine (*Pinus sylvestris* Fastigiata Group) and pencil junipers (*Juniperus scopulorum* 'Skyrocket' or *J. communis* 'Compressa'), which grow no taller than 2m (6½ft) in 10 years, are useful focal points. Dwarf pines such as dwarf mountain pine (*Pinus mugo*) are also popular, again for their shapely form, natural colouring and attractive, needle-like foliage; they associate really well with clipped topiary.

- **Topiary substitute:** Globose varieties are perfect for pots and useful alternatives to clipped box (*Buxus*) balls in sunny beds and borders. Colorado spruce (*Picea pungens* Glauca Group 'Globosa'), Norway spruce (*P. abies* 'Little Gem') and Lawson's cypress (*Chamaecyparis lawsoniana* 'Green Globe') stay tight and compact and, unlike topiary, need no trimming.

- **Size-wise:** Many conifers grow very big so choose carefully. Dwarf doesn't always mean small either. Many dwarf conifers grow slowly but might outgrow their space after 10–15 years or so. Conifers don't respond well to pruning but if you must prune, never cut back into old wood, as new leaves and shoots will never regrow from there. Yew (*Taxus*) is the only exception.

Hedges

This invaluable group can be divided into formal and informal hedges. Both can be evergreen or deciduous and almost any height, from low-growing lavender (*Lavandula*) to tall Portugal laurel (*Prunus lusitanica*). Formal hedges are clipped into a regular shape. Blowsy informal hedges – where you can often see the outline of each individual plant – are made using flowering shrubs such as rosemary (*Rosmarinus officinalis*), Japanese rose (*Rosa rugosa*) and flowering currant (*Ribes sanguineum*) and are pruned accordingly.

Style guide

Hedges are bold garden features and impact dramatically on the aesthetic. Clipped yew (*Taxus*) or box (*Buxus*) hedging implies sophistication and control – perfect for classic formal design (see pp90–93). Informal hedges are more relaxed and romantic, ideal for cottage gardens (see pp94–97). In country settings native mixed hedges with plants such as hawthorn (*Crataegus monogyna*), English holly (*Ilex aquifolium*) and hazel (*Corylus avellana*) will honour the surrounding landscape. However hedges don't have to feature in long lines. Columns, pillars or blocks – particularly of tidy box, yew, hornbeam (*Carpinus*) and beech (*Fagus*) – have a bold architectural quality. Modern planting designers, especially those who favour a more naturalistic approach, position them to contrast with billowing grasses and perennials.

Right: In natural settings native hedges such as hazel (*Corylus avellana*) are best. Here they mark the boundary, yet seamlessly blend the garden into the wider landscape beyond. Other English natives including elder (*Sambucus nigra*), foxgloves (*Digitalis purpurea*) and teasel (*Dipsacus fullonum*) help too.

Shape up

Almost any plant that can be trimmed into a formal hedge can be shaped into topiary balls, cones, cubes – even unusual animal shapes. Perfect for pots or to punctuate planting, topiary is like living sculpture adding a tailored, eye-catching presence year-round. In recent years 'cloud'-pruned topiary trees have been popularised by designers including Chelsea Flower Show stalwarts such as Tom Stuart-Smith, but these aren't cheap and training them yourself will take years.

Left: Formality on a grand scale! This extensive planting of box (*Buxus*), cubed common hornbeam (*Carpinus betulus*) trees, backed by a dark green yew (*Taxus baccata*) hedge, looks amazing but everything will need regular clipping to maintain the crisp shapes.

Roles

Defining garden boundaries while offering shelter, privacy and security are certainly the most common roles for hedges, but they are also important structural plants. Designers use them to divide garden space into different 'rooms', to frame views, to reinforce strong design geometry and to line circulation routes to propel you forward from one space to the next. Darker hedges (yew being the favourite) are also the ideal background foil to colourful planting. And let's not forget that the berry-bearing hedges of guelder rose (*Viburnum opulus*), English holly or spiky firethorn (*Pyracantha*) support wildlife too.

Below: Shrub roses such as *Rosa* 'De Resht' (a Portland rose) make ideal informal hedges, here kept low enough so as not to obstruct the view.

Some of the best… hedges

SMALL HEDGES – H&S: 0.3–0.9M (1–3FT)

- *Berberis microphylla* 'Pygmaea' (dwarf box-leaved barberry; ❋❋❋ Z6–9) – formal
- *Buxus microphylla* (box; ❋❋❋ Z6–9) and cvs – formal
- *Ilex crenata* (box-leaved holly; ❋❋❋ Z5–7) – formal
- *Lavandula angustifolia* (lavender; ❋❋❋ Z5–8) and cvs – informal/formal
- *Lonicera nitida* (shrubby honeysuckle; ❋❋❋ Z6–9) and cvs – formal
- *Rosmarinus officinalis* (rosemary; ❋❋ Z8–11) and cvs – informal
- *Santolina chamaecyparissus* (cotton lavender; ❋❋ Z6–9) and cvs – informal/formal

MEDIUM–LARGE HEDGES – H&S: 0.9–1.8M (3–6FT)

- *Crataegus monogyna* (common hawthorn; ❋❋❋ Z5–7) – formal
- *Fagus sylvatica* (common beech; ❋❋❋ Z4–7) – formal
- *Ilex aquifolium* (English holly; ❋❋❋ Z7–9) and cvs – formal
- *Rosa* 'Roseraie de l'Haÿ' (rose; ❋❋❋ Z4–9) – informal
- *Spiraea* 'Arguta' (bridal wreath; ❋❋❋ Z4–9) – informal
- *Taxus baccata* (yew; ❋❋❋ Z7–8) – formal
- *Thuja plicata* (western red cedar; ❋❋❋ Z6–8) and cvs – formal

GROWING SUCCESS

- **Evergreen or deciduous?** Evergreens are best for year-round presence but usually need trimming twice a year. Conifer hedges might need cutting three times a year (yew is the exception). Deciduous hedges should be pruned only once or twice, depending on the species and shape. They aren't as dense as evergreen hedges and in winter let in more light.

- **Formal or informal?** Informal hedges need space to spread. With a row of low lavender, this generally isn't a problem but with a taller hedge, it might be. In small gardens clipped formal hedges are a better choice. But of course this does mean more work.

- **Access:** Allow space for trimming – don't plant borders right up to the hedge – leave a decent gap or you'll trample all over the planting in front. Hedges – particularly coniferous ones – do make life difficult for plants growing close by – another reason to leave a gap.

- **Cost:** Long hedge runs can cost. 'Instant' hedges are available, but they're not cheap. Instead most hedges are made using young bare-root transplants (see p270) or 'whips' planted at the appropriate spacing to keep costs down. Evergreen hedges generally cost more, as plants typically come supplied in pots.

- **Tolerance to clipping:** Small-leaved species are better than large; they're easier to trim and pruning cuts are less noticeable. Cherry laurel (*Prunus laurocerasus*) and broadleaf (*Griselinia*) are popular hedges, particularly by the coast. But both have larger leaves so try to trim with secateurs; avoid powered hedge cutters, as these slash the leaves, which looks awful afterwards.

- **Hedge your bets?** Box is the most popular plant for low hedging and topiary but box blight – a nasty fungal disease – can be a problem nowadays. While cultural controls may help, and regular foliar feeding during the growing season to keep the plants strong and healthy can help, there is no real cure. For long low hedge runs consider hardy, disease-free alternatives including Japanese holly (*Ilex crenata*), small-leaved *Euonymus*, even Christmas box (*Sarcococca ruscifolia* var. *chinensis*). Like box, all tolerate some shade.

Left: Hedges can be used to divide a garden into rooms, in turn making the whole space feel bigger. Here a living 'wall' of common beech (*Fagus sylvatica*) also piques one's interest about what's on the other side of it.

Climbers & wall shrubs

These plants add colour and scent to the garden while occupying the minimum of ground space. Use them as 'wallpaper' over ugly sheds and outbuildings, as a background foil to mixed borders or partially to obscure decrepit garden boundaries (in turn making the garden seem bigger than it actually is). Growing well-behaved cultivars through trees, shrubs and hedges can bring two seasons of interest from the same spot.

Climbers are particularly useful in small gardens dominated by tall boundaries; here some vertical thinking is essential.

Climbing high

Understanding the methods by which climbers grow upwards helps determine where they'll work best, what support is required and how much maintenance is necessary.

- **Self-clinging:** Plants such as ivy (*Hedera*) and climbing hydrangea (*Hydrangea anomala* subsp. *petiolaris*) grow upwards using their sticky adventitious roots, which grow from the stems. Virginia creeper (*Parthenocissus*) species (including Boston ivy/*P. tricuspidata*) free-climb using little adhesive pads (essentially modified tendrils). Ideal for covering large, out-of-reach areas, all need little maintenance once established. While no self-clingers need support, free climbers will exacerbate problems with crumbling brickwork; therefore don't grow them on walls.

- **Tendrils:** *Clematis*, flame nasturtium (*Tropaeolum speciosum*) and everlasting pea (*Lathyrus*) use tendrils (modified stems or leaves) to climb. These struggle with thick trellis; instead use thin wire supports.

- **Stem twiners:** Honeysuckle (*Lonicera*) and *Wisteria* climb using twining stems, as do many really vigorous plants, including golden hop (*Humulus lupulus* 'Aureus') and Russian vine (*Fallopia baldschuanica*). Be sure to position fast-growing stem twiners carefully, as they can soon swamp a garden.

- **Ramblers:** While not technically climbers, ramblers scramble up supports using long whippy stems and sometimes curved thorns, to hook onto their host. Rambling roses are perhaps the most common group here and they need to be tied in regularly.

- **Wall shrubs:** Although not true climbers, many shrubs benefit from being grown against a wall for protection or support. Gardeners' favourites like silk-tassel bush (*Garrya elliptica* 'James Roof'), holly-leaved sweetspire (*Itea ilicifolia*), winter jasmine (*Jasminum nudiflorum*) and Japanese quince (*Chaenomeles*) need to be tied into sturdy supports.

Left: Tidy climbers such as flame nasturtium (*Tropaeolum speciosum*) can be grown through hedges, doubling the season of interest. Just don't choose a vigorous species and make sure that the host can tolerate the shade cast by its partner.

Opposite: Almost anything can be used as a support for twining climbers. Here, wire bedsprings provide the perfect quirky climbing frame for alpine clematis (*Clematis alpina*).

Garrya elliptica 'James Roof'

Clematis cirrhosa var. *balearica*

Agyrocytisus battandieri

Trachelospermum jasminoides

Ceanothus 'Puget Blue'

Hedera helix 'Glacier'

Pileostegia viburnoides

Ceanothus 'Concha'

Below right: Loved for their showy, pea-like, fragrant flowers, *Wisteria* are vigorous twining climbers and need a sturdy support. A sunny wall is also essential.

Opposite: In more traditional, cottage-inspired designs rustic hazel wigwarms are perfect to support sweet peas such as *Lathyrus odoratus* 'Henry Eckford'. This is an easy way to introduce height to the middle of beds and borders too.

Some of the best… climbers & wall shrubs

- *Akebia quinata* (chocolate vine; ❀❀❀ Z5–9)
- *Campsis radicans* (trumpet vine; ❀❀ Z5–9) and cvs
- *Clematis* (❀❀–❀❀❀ Z4–11, depending on spp)
- *Eccremocarpus scaber* (Chilean glory flower; ❀❀ Z11–15)
- *Garrya elliptica* 'James Roof' (silk-tassel bush; ❀❀ Z8–11)
- *Hedera helix* (English ivy; ❀❀❀ Z5–11) and cvs
- *Itea ilicifolia* (holly-leaved sweetspire; ❀❀ Z7–9)
- *Jasminium officinale* (common jasmine; ❀❀ Z9–10)
- *Lathyrus odoratus* (sweet pea; ❀❀❀ zone not applicable) and cvs
- *Lonicera periclymenum* (common honeysuckle; ❀❀❀ Z5–9) and cvs
- *Passiflora caerulea* (blue passion flower; ❀❀ Z6–9) and cvs
- *Trachelospermum jasminoides* (star jasmine; ❀❀ Z9–10)
- *Vitis coignetiae* (crimson glory vine; ❀❀❀ Z5–9)
- *Wisteria floribunda* (Japanese wisteria; ❀❀❀ Z5–9) and cvs

GROWING SUCCESS

- **Type of support:** Vigour is an important consideration when choosing how to hold up a climber or wall shrub. Put supports in place early, not when plants are almost collapsing.

- **Wire:** A sturdy wire support is essential for fast-growing, heavy twiners and ramblers such as *Wisteria*, rambling roses, kiwi (*Actinidia*) and crimson glory vine (*Vitis coignetiae*), which quickly break delicate timber trellis. Use thick wire strung through vine eyes or eye screws, which hold the wire 5–8cm (2–3½in) off the wall. Start 30cm (12in) from the ground then space each horizontal wire 30–45cm (12–18in) apart, unless you're creating a fan shape.

- **Trellis:** For less vigorous climbers, and where looks count, use wooden trellis. If the horizontal and vertical timber strips are flush with each other, mount the panel on 4–5cm (1½–2in) wooden battens so it's not tight to the wall. This way twining stems can grip properly. Fix trellis 30cm (12in) above soil level to prevent rotting.

- **Mesh & wire rope:** Metal mesh or marine-grade stainless steel wire rope trellis kits suit contemporary design. For tendril twiners such as summer-flowering *Clematis* that can't cope with thick trellis, they're the ideal support.

- **Arches & obelisks:** In protected gardens freestanding wood or metal arches and obelisks made from hazel withes, thick bamboo canes or even rusty steel poles can provide support for less vigorous climbers. Freestanding, post-and-wire screens or post-and-trellis panels laden with climbers could be used to divide up the garden into 'rooms'.

- **The microclimate by walls & fences** is more extreme than usual so it's vital to match the right plant to the right aspect.

- **The soil at the base of walls** is usually poor, plus the wall casts a rain shadow on the soil directly below. Don't plant close in. Dig in lots of well-rotted compost or manure and position plants 30cm (12in) away from the structure. Then train the plant back to the wall along a thick bamboo cane. Tie in shoots to help the plant find its way.

- **Key aim:** Create a strong framework from the bottom of the plant. After planting, train in the main shoots, or leaders, and hard prune sideshoots to 10cm (4in). Then, 2–3 months later, train new shoots along their supports as low as possible so the plant is bushy from the base up.

Roses

Although they are loved by gardeners for their big, sometimes heavily scented blooms in summer, roses do have the reputation of being time-consuming, disease-prone plants, which sulk anywhere that's not ideal (sun and thick, fertile yet free-draining soil is preferable for most). While this may be true in some cases, plant-breeding programmes in recent years by rose growers including Peter Beales (UK), Griffith Buck (USA), Ralph S Moore (USA), W Kordes & Sons (Germany) and, most famously, David Austin (UK) have resulted in lots of tougher, tidier plants, which makes selection and success easier than ever.

GROWING SUCCESS

- **Position:** Most roses like a warm sunny spot and shelter from strong winds. Some shrub roses such as Japanese rose (*Rosa rugosa* and cvs) (see p48) and ramblers including *R.* 'Albéric Barbier' are a notable exception however, as they tolerate semishade and a northerly aspect.

- **Soil type:** Roses are deep rooted and prefer a heavy but well-drained soil. On light sandy or very thin soils, dig in plenty of well-rotted organic matter when planting or grow species roses such as red-leaved rose (*R. glauca*). As a group, species roses don't mind drier conditions (see p48). Spread thick mulch (ideally 8–10cm/3½–4in deep) around plants in spring, and again in summer if need be. This will not only top up background fertility levels and improve soil structure, but also conserve water and keep weeds down.

- **Feeding:** Modern bush, modern shrub, patio and miniature roses (see p48), especially repeat-flowering cultivars, are greedy. Feed in spring with a general balanced fertiliser such as Growmore, or use one specifically for roses. A feed after the first flush of flowers won't go amiss either.

- **Water, water:** Regular watering after planting to help plants establish is essential. To encourage deep rooting and better drought resistance, one good soak a week is better·than a little every day.

- **Avoiding disease:** Bush roses and some miniatures are more prone to disease than other groups. However there are now many varieties available that are more resistant, particularly to the big three: blackspot, mildew and rust. Choose these for peace of mind and to minimise the workload. Always practise good husbandry too – that is watering and feeding regularly; do this and even disease-prone roses are less likely to succumb to problems.

- **Deadhead:** Remove spent flowers to encourage more to develop, unless you have a species or wild rose such as *Rosa setipoda* or an old rose, like *R. gallica* var. *officinalis*, that is also grown for its beautiful hips in autumn.

Opposite: Barriers can be beautiful! When grown in vulnerable spots such as front gardens and side passageways, thorny climbing roses such as *Rosa* 'Climbing Iceberg' are useful to deter intruders.

Left: Modern bush roses usually work best in large groups, while old or shrub roses – and particularly modern shrub roses (here, the ever-popular *Rosa* Gertrude Jeykll = 'Ausbord') – are the ideal partners for perennials and even grasses in mixed beds and borders.

Groups & uses

Roses are the perfect partners for perennials, and you won't find a cottage garden without one. Today, roses also feature in contemporary designs combined with 'modern' ornamental grasses for example. To identify exactly where they work best in the garden, and which ones meet your idea of maintenance, it helps to understand the different rose groups. Rose classification is confusing and differs around the world, so for expediency I've grouped them simply, as below.

BUSH & SHRUB ROSES

Mounding shrubs whose height and spread are similar to each other, ranging from 80cm (2½ft) to more than 3–4m (10–13ft). This group can be subdivided as follows:

- **Species or wild roses:** The ancestors of all other roses have simple, open-faced flowers in summer. Many such as *R. glauca* have wonderful foliage; some have subtly scented flowers; almost all have attractive hips (if you don't deadhead). Being particularly at home in natural settings, species or wild roses should be placed in wilder parts of the garden or at the back of a deep border – some are big, vigorous plants. They are maintenance-free once established.

- **Modern bush roses:** Traditionally grown in large groups, hybrid teas (single-flowered), floribundas (cluster-flowered) and grandifloras (a blend of the two, common in the USA) repeat-flower on new wood, so need to be pruned back hard each spring and fed copiously too. All need deadheading regularly and generally struggle with competitive plants around them so don't do well in mixed borders. Better to grow them in specimen groups, some perhaps trained into pom-pon shapes called standards, or tree roses in the USA. With older varieties, the big three diseases – blackspot, rust and mildew – are problematic so choose modern disease-resistant ones instead.

- **Old or shrub roses** (aka 'Antique', 'Old English', 'Old Garden' roses): This enormous group, with many of the roses dating back to Roman times, includes Alba, Bourbon, China, Damask, Gallica, Moss, Portland, Provence (centifoila), Sweet Briar and Rugosa types – to name the most common. They are often highly scented, but few flower repeatedly. All are cherished by rose aficionados, and look beautiful at the back of traditional herbaceous borders. Space to spread is necessary, as hard pruning adversely affects flowering and spoils the attractive, sometimes floppy shape. Some (notably Rugosa roses) make great informal hedges.

- **Modern shrub roses** (including 'English' roses aka 'David Austin' roses and 'Heirloom' roses): Bred to have the appearance and scent of old roses, but with better disease resistance, modern shrubroses are ideal for low-maintenance, mixed plantings in small gardens where a long season of interest is important. All flower repeatedly, and require pruning back by only one third, if at all. They're tidy growers too.

PATIO & MINIATURE ROSES

A useful group of dwarf miniature floribundas and multiflowering polyantha roses, along with smaller modern shrubs – in fact anything that flowers freely and isn't too unruly to grow in patio pots. Some miniatures are trained as half-standards with a short clear stem; others even climb too. Most require little pruning but regular feeding is necessary if they are grown in pots.

GROUNDCOVER ROSES (AKA 'LANDSCAPE' ROSES)

A broad group featuring roses that are wider than they are tall and which cover the ground – as the name suggests. Being deciduous, few curtail weeds like evergreen ground cover (see p80). Repeat flowering and disease resistance are common traits.

CLIMBERS

Climbing forms of modern bush, shrub or old roses reach 2–3m (6½–10ft). Most flower repeatedly. Annual pruning is essential to improve flowering and rejuvenate plants that become bare at the base. Climbing roses are ideal for growing up walls, posts, heavy ropes, pergolas and tripods, perhaps partnered with *Clematis* to double the season of interest.

RAMBLERS

Vigorous ramblers typically flower once, in midsummer, and grow to 4m (13ft) or more. Allow them to ramble up big arches and trees. While certainly too thuggish for a small garden, ramblers are very tough, being related to species or wild roses. Pruning is simple – a rolling programme of rejuvenation by cutting out some of the old stems to the base.

Opposite, above: Climbers and ramblers are the biggest, most vigorous roses, so need space to spread, otherwise they can quickly swamp a small space.

Opposite, below: While old roses are generally more susceptible to disease than modern ones, they are still well worth the effort. Here *Rosa* 'Reine Victoria' (a bourbon rose) and *R*. 'Reine des Violettes' (a hybrid perpetual) trained over woven hazel domes make beautiful focal points among a sea of traditional perennials. Both have a strong fragrance and flower repeatedly.

Some of the best… roses

- *Rosa* 'Belle de Crécy' (old rose: Gallica; ✤✤✤ Z3–9)
- *Rosa gallica* var. *officinalis* 'Versicolor' (old rose: Gallica; ✤✤✤ Z3–9)
- *Rosa* Gertrude Jekyll = 'Ausbord' (modern shrub; ✤✤✤ Z5–9)
- *Rosa glauca* (red-leaved rose) (species/wild; ✤✤✤ Z2–8)
- *Rosa* 'Königin von Dänemark' (old rose: Alba; ✤✤✤ Z3–9)
- *Rosa* 'Madame Boll' (old rose: Portland; ✤✤✤ Z5–9)
- *Rosa* 'Madame Isaac Péreire' (old rose: Bourbon; ✤✤✤ Z6–9)
- *Rosa moyesii* (species/wild; ✤✤✤ Z6–9) and cvs
- *Rosa* Munstead Wood = 'Ausbernard' (modern shrub; ✤✤✤ Z5–9)
- *Rosa* 'Rambling Rector' (rambler; ✤✤✤ Z5–9)
- *Rosa rugosa* (Japanese rose) (shrub rose; ✤✤✤ Z2–9) and cvs
- *Rosa* 'William Lobb' (old rose: Moss; ✤✤✤ Z4–9)

Herbaceous perennials

Defined as plants that die back over winter and don't become overly woody, herbaceous perennials are a broad group that brings exciting seasonal interest to any garden whether it's sunny or shady, dry or damp. They were once popular in the long, high-maintenance herbaceous borders of the 'English' summer garden of the late 19th and early 20th century, but tastes have since changed. Small gardens with empty-looking beds over winter are unacceptable to most nowadays, plus we've less time for regular staking, feeding, watering and deadheading. Instead perennials today are grown in mixed borders, or in naturalistic schemes – here 'new' robust varieties are partnered with ornamental grasses, subshrubs and sometimes topiary, to cut down the workload and prolong the season of interest.

Size wise

Tall perennials such as fennel (*Foeniculum*) and cardoon (*Cynara*) bring contrasting flowers and foliage to the back of mixed borders. When partnered with shrubs or tall grasses in naturalistic schemes, they also form the apex of the subtle pyramidal-shaped groups you often see. Waist-high perennials such as bergamot (*Monarda*), Balkan clary (*Salvia nemorosa*) cvs and *Astilbe* – commonly banded into a group called 'mid-range' plants (or middle-of-the-border plants; see p183) – come in the middle. Plants here should flower for as long as possible and also complement, often through contrast, the plants around them, whether it's with their flowers or leaves. Flowers with strong form such as foxglove (*Digitalis*) and mullein (*Verbascum*) are also good accent plants to attract the eye (see p178). Shorter species of herbaceous perennial, notably mounding forms, are front-of-border plants. These provide foreground contrast and help cover any 'bare legs' behind. Evergreen groundcover perennials such as elephant's ears (*Bergenia*) and coral flower (*Heuchera*) are particularly useful here. These have a year-round presence and help to keep weeds down.

Flower power

Perennials are traditionally cherished for one thing: flower power – you'll find flowers in every colour, shape and size imaginable. However plants with attractive foliage, a sculptural shape or autumnal seedheads are highly prized too. Designers choose these to help anchor a composition and extend seasonal interest, especially in small gardens and perennial-heavy, prairie-style schemes that can look bare from winter to early summer. Of course long-flowering perennials and those that respond well to the 'Chelsea chop' (see p169) are also invaluable to lengthen the season of interest.

Above: This layered perennial planting includes a tall purple loosestrife (*Lythrum salicaria* 'Zigeunerblut') and purple top (*Verbena bonariensis*) at the back with a coneflower (*Echinacea purpurea* 'Leuchtstern') nestled just in front.

Opposite, above: While the traditional herbaceous border is time-consuming to maintain, the effort is well worth it – in summer the effects are stunning. Notable cottage perennials here include a cranesbill (*Geranium × magnificum*) in the foreground, partnered with lavender (*Lavandula*), roundheaded leek (*Allium sphaerocephalon*) and foxgloves (*Digitalis purpurea*).

Left: In prairie-style plantings (here, a scheme inspired by the North American tall grass prairies) plants such as coneflower (*Rudbeckia*), gayfeather (*Liatris*) and prairie coneflower (*Ratibida pinnata*) are cherished both for their flowers and their wonderful seedheads.

GROWING SUCCESS

- **Speed of growth:** All perennials reach maturity in only three to four years, so give them space – especially rapid spreaders such as bear's breeches (*Acanthus*) and loosestrife (*Lysimachia*).

- **Tender perennials:** Perennials originating from hotter climates are tender in colder ones. In the UK, central–northern Europe and the northerly USA and Canada, Indian shot plant (*Canna*), marguerites (*Leucanthemum vulgare*), coleus (*Solenostemon*) and other 'patio' perennials can't be grown outside year-round, as they need temperatures higher than -5°C (23°F) to thrive. Either overwinter them under cover or protect *in situ* with straw or fleece – for this reason such plants are best grown in containers, or replaced annually.

- **Lifespan:** Most hardy perennials such as globe thistle (*Echinops*) and cranesbill (*Geranium*) last for years, but favourites including columbine (*Aquilegia*), purple top (*Verbena bonariensis*), coneflower (*Echinacea purpurea*) and Macedonian scabious (*Knautia macedonica*) are short-lived. Fortunately they seed readily so can be easily replaced.

- **Double up:** Don't be afraid to grow perennials – I include ornamental grasses (see pp54–57) and ferns (see pp68–69) here – in large groups of 3 to 5+ to maximise their impact. Single plants, particularly those with subtle characteristics, look lost.

- **Staking:** Many 'modern' tall perennials don't need staking but some tall traditional favourites, especially those that don't become woody at the base as the seasons progress, will. Position supports in spring, so plants discreetly hide them as they grow. For tall clump-formers such as perennial sunflower (*Helianthus*), bamboo canes and hairy string, brushwood sticks or 'link-together' supports will do. Support bushy perennials such as broad-leaved bellflower (*Campanula latifolia*) and blowsy peonies (*Paeonia*) with 'grow-through' grids. Giant peasticks or circular rings are good for those with single stems or large single blooms such as lupins (*Lupinus*).

- **Slugs & snails:** Damage is most common in spring. Copper slug rings, crushed seashells, ferrous sulphate slug pellets (as a safer alternative to those based on metaldehyde) – even beer traps – are worth trialing around susceptible plants such as coneflower and *Delphinium*.

- **Cutting back:** Convention demands an early autumn cutback once the flowers fade for all but evergreen species. But late-summer flowerers with attractive seedheads should be left until spring, unless they collapse in wet winter weather.

- **Feeding:** Grown where they're naturally happiest, perennials won't need feeding once established. Never feed taller types – they'll quickly flop.

- **Division:** Many clump-formers such as fibrous-rooted Michaelmas daisy (*Aster*), cranesbills and stonecrop (*Sedum*) become unproductive with age, and need splitting in autumn or early spring to rejuvenate them (although spring-flowering perennials such as irises are best done after flowering). But it's not necessary for all; those with a carrot-like taproot – including false indigo (*Baptisia australis*), bugbane (*Actaea*) and columbine – or those with multiple stems arising from a single crown – such as oriental poppy (*Papaver orientale*) and pinks (*Dianthus*) – don't respond well. Peonies, anemones and hellebores positively hate it.

Above: Shade-tolerant perennials don't scream for attention like their sun-loving cousins, a subtlety that means gardeners often cherish them more. This woodland scheme features foam flower (*Tiarella cordifolia*), columbine (*Aquilegia*) and a hellebore (*Helleborus × hybridus* Ballard's Group) alongside ferns and snowy woodrush (*Luzula nivea*).

Opposite: Robust 'modern' perennials (many of which are recent introductions) such as this orange-red yarrow (*Achillea* 'Walther Funcke') and lilac-purple Balkan clary (*Salvia nemorosa* 'Amethyst') should never need staking.

Some of the best... herbaceous perennials

SMALL–MEDIUM – H: TO 1M (3FT)

- *Aquilegia vulgaris* (granny's bonnet; ❀❀❀ Z3–8) and cvs
- *Astrantia major* (masterwort; ❀❀❀ Z4–7) and cvs
- *Bergenia cordifolia* (heart-leaf bergenia; ❀❀❀ Z3–8) and cvs
- *Campanula persicifolia* (peach-leaved bellflower; ❀❀❀ Z3–8) and cvs
- *Dicentra* (bleeding heart; ❀❀❀ Z3–9, depending on spp)
- *Geranium pratense* (meadow cranesbill; ❀❀❀ Z4–8)
- *Iris germanica* (❀❀❀ Z3–11) and cvs
- *Monarda* (bergamot; ❀❀–❀❀❀ Z4–10, depending on spp)
- *Pulmonaria saccharata* (Jerusalem sage; ❀❀❀ Z4–8) and cvs
- *Sedum telephium* (orpine; ❀❀❀ Z4–9) and cvs

MEDIUM–LARGE – H: OVER 1M (3FT)

- *Acanthus spinosus* (bear's breeches; ❀❀❀ Z5–9)
- *Agapanthus campanulatus* (African blue lily; ❀❀❀ Z7–15) and cvs
- *Anemone hupehensis* (Japanese anemone; ❀❀❀ Z5–7) and cvs
- *Echinacea purpurea* (coneflower; ❀❀❀ Z3–9) and cvs
- *Eupatorium purpureum* (Joe Pye weed; ❀❀❀ Z3–9) and cvs
- *Helianthus × multiflorus* (perennial sunflower; ❀❀❀ Z5–9) and cvs
- *Macleaya microcarpa* (plume poppy; ❀❀❀ Z4–9) and cvs
- *Symphyotrichum novae-angliae* (New England aster; ❀❀❀ Z4–8) and cvs
- *Thalictrum delavayi* (meadow rue; ❀❀❀ Z4–7) and cvs
- *Veronicastrum virginicum* (culver's root; ❀❀❀ Z4–8) and cvs

Ornamental grasses

Fine, often colourful foliage and graceful feathery flowers make ornamental grasses popular with beginners and experienced gardeners everywhere. Needing little attention once established, most are tough, suffer few pests and diseases and many tolerate drought. Ornamental grasses on offer include short arching evergreens such as Mexican feather grass (*Stipa tenuissima*) and pheasant's tail grass (*Anemanthele lessoniana*) as well as tall, elegant, deciduous plants including silver grass (*Miscanthus*) and switch grass (*Panicum virgatum*). These fade in autumn but the dead stems and leaves remain through winter looking glorious covered in frost.

For convenience, sedges and rushes – both of which contain many evergreen species – are included here, although these typically require damper soil than ornamental grasses. Usefully, many tolerate shade.

Natural thinking

The popularity of ornamental grasses has trebled in the last 15–20 years, coinciding with the rise of naturalistic planting design. Fine-textured flowers and foliage bring airy contrast to broad-leaved herbaceous perennials typically from midsummer to late autumn. Designers also use taller vertical grasses such as *Panicum virgatum* cultivars, giant feather grass (*Stipa gigantea*) and feather reed grass (*Calamagrostis × acutiflora*) cultivars as dynamic focal points that whisper in the wind. Because of their reliable, long-lasting presence grasses also have an important structural role, particularly where plants are intermingled in seemingly haphazard, naturalistic patterns. In this planting style, grasses repeated throughout help bring a welcome sense of order.

All mixed up

While ornamental grasses are commonplace in naturalistic plantings, they're also perfectly at home in the mixed border. Tall species make good backdrops, notably from midsummer onwards, and when brought forward they will help break up a planting into little 'bays' – just like short shrubs and roses (*Rosa*) do – which makes it easier to plan the rest of the planting. Again, those with a sculptural shape are also ideal focal points (see pp176–177). Medium-sized grasses can be tucked among roses, perennials and short shrubs, preferably in large groups. Short grasses – those knee height and below – are useful ground cover in front. But to create a feeling of depth, designers will often sweep them deeper into the border too. As most short grasses grow in fierce little clumps or hair-like tufts, they're the ideal textural foil for bulbs such as tulips (*Tulipa*) when intermingled liberally throughout.

Left, above: Many grasses such as this feather reed grass (*Calamagrostis* × *acutiflora* 'Karl Foerster') have a truly sculptural shape – dead or alive. This designer favourite, planted en masse for impact in this garden, complements the formal rill and crisp stepping stones perfectly.

Left, below: Grasses, including golden oats (*Stipa gigantea*), add informal reliable structure to this naturalistic, late summer planting featuring a yellow coneflower (*Rudbeckia fulgida* var. *sullivantii* 'Anthony Brooks') and orange red hot pokers (*Kniphofia rooperi*).

Below: Grasses are ideal to help both soften and structure mixed borders. Here, feather grass (*Stipa lessingiana*) and silver grass (*Miscanthus sinensis*) partner a white sage (*Salvia* × *sylvestris* 'Schneehügel'), lavender (*Lavandula angustifolia* 'Hidcote'), bronze fennel (*Foeniculum vulgare* 'Giant Bronze'), purple top (*Verbena bonariensis*) and graceful *Gaura lindheimeri*.

Some of the best… ornamental grasses

EVERGREEN GRASSES

- *Anemanthele lessoniana* (pheasant's tail grass; ❀❀ Z8–15) – 1 × 1m (3 × 3ft)
- *Carex testacea* (orange New Zealand sedge; ❀❀ Z8–9) – 1.2 × 0.6m (4 × 2ft)
- *Cortaderia selloana* 'Pumila' (dwarf pampas grass; ❀❀❀ Z7–11) – 1.5 × 1m (5 × 3ft)
- *Deschampsia cespitosa* 'Goldtau' (tufted hair grass; ❀❀❀ Z5–9) – 75 × 75cm (2½ × 2½ft)
- *Festuca glauca* 'Elijah Blue' (blue fescue; ❀❀❀ Z4–8) – 30 × 30cm (1 × 1ft)
- *Helictotrichon sempervirens* (blue oat grass; ❀❀❀ Z4–9) – 1.5 × 1m (5 × 3ft)
- *Luzula nivea* (snowy woodrush; ❀❀❀ Z4–9) – 60 × 50cm (24 × 20in)
- *Sesleria nitida* (nest moor grass; ❀❀❀ Z5–8) – 60 × 40cm (24 × 16in)
- *Stipa gigantea* (golden oats; ❀❀❀ Z8–15) – 2.5 × 1m (8 × 3ft)
- *Stipa tenuissima* (Mexican feather grass; ❀❀❀ Z8–15) – 1 × 0.5m (3 × 1½ft)

LATE SUMMER-INTEREST GRASSES

- *Briza media* (common quaking grass; ❀❀❀ Z4–11) – 80 × 30cm (32 × 12in) (grow as an annual)
- *Calamagrostis* × *acutiflora* 'Karl Foerster' (feather reed grass; ❀❀❀ Z5–9) – 1.8 × 0.6m (6 × 2ft)
- *Calamagrostis brachytricha* (Korean feather reed grass; ❀❀❀ Z5–9) – 1.5 × 1m (5 × 3ft)
- *Chasmanthium latifolium* (sea oats; ❀❀❀ Z5–9) – 1 × 0.5m (3 × 1½ft)
- *Miscanthus sinensis* 'Ferner Osten' (silver grass; ❀❀❀ Z6–9) – 1.5 × 1m (5 × 3ft)
- *Miscanthus sinensis* 'Morning Light' (silver grass; ❀❀❀ Z6–9) – 1.5 × 1m (5 × 3ft)
- *Molinia caerulea* subsp. *arundinacea* 'Transparent' (purple moor grass; ❀❀❀ Z5–9) – 1 × 0.6m (3 × 2ft)
- *Panicum virgatum* 'Rehbraun' (switch grass; ❀❀❀ Z5–9) – 1 × 0.75m (3 × 2½ft)
- *Pennisetum alopecuroides* 'Cassian's Choice' (fountain grass; ❀❀ Z6–9) – 1 × 1m (3 × 3ft)
- *Pennisetum orientale* (oriental fountain grass; ❀❀ Z6–10) – 1 × 1m (3 × 3ft)

GROWING SUCCESS

- **Warm season or cool season?** Grasses are grouped into cool-season and warm-season species. Knowing this helps plan your planting and determines the best time to plant. Cool-season grasses such as fescue (*Festuca*) begin growth in late winter/early spring, when the temperature is still relatively cool, and flower early in the growing season. Many – but not all – are semievergreen over winter. Plant these in autumn for best results. Warm-season grasses, including fountain grass (*Pennisetum*), start into growth later when the weather is warm before flowering in late summer then going truly dormant over winter. Plant these in spring. Because of their late start, warm-season grasses do mean gaps in the spring and early summer border, unless you partner plants with spring perennials to hide them.

- **Growth habit:** Most grasses form tidy clumps, but a few such as blue lyme grass (*Leymus arenarius*) spread using underground rhizomes or stolons and can be invasive. Avoid these in a small garden. Prolific self-seeders such as pendulous sedge (*Carex pendula*) can be invasive too. Fortunately their offspring are easy to control and often welcomed in all but naturalistic plantings (curious as it may seem). Here overly competitive plants will affect the rhythm and balance of the planting, so should be avoided.

- **Cut back:** Only deciduous grasses need cutting back – gather dead foliage and chop off 10–20cm (4–8in) above ground in early spring, or earlier if the stems have collapsed. Evergreens can be left alone. Just comb them through, wearing gloves, every other month to remove dead growth.

- **Shade-lovers:** While they're in the minority, not all grasses need full sun. Bowles's golden sedge (*Carex elata* 'Aurea'), greater woodrush (*Luzula sylvatica*), tufted hair grass (*Deschampsia cespitosa*) and *Hakonechloa macra* all make great ground cover in semishade and they're ideal partners with woodland perennials and ferns.

- **Containers:** Evergreen grasses are perfect for contemporary pots, either grown alone or with colourful evergreen perennials. Unless you have a big container, choose shorter plants such as bronze-leaved New Zealand hair sedge (*Carex comans*) and blue fescue.

Above: Tidy, clump-forming grasses such as oriental fountain grass (*Pennisetum orientale*) should be first choice in small beds and borders. Here they have been used to structure a gravel planting.

Left: Warm-season grasses such as silver grass (*Miscanthus*) burst into growth when the weather is warm enough, reaching their peak from midsummer to autumn. This fabulous modern scheme features both *M.* 'Purpurascens' (front left) and *M. sinensis* 'Ferner Osten' (front right) alongside a dark pink Joe Pye weed (*Eupatorium maculatum* Atropurpureum Group 'Riesenschirm').

Bamboos

These are tough plants and easy to grow, making them popular for gardeners everywhere. With such a distinctive appearance, bamboos are great 'theme' plants – ideal for tropical designs – and being evergreen means they have an important year-round structural or screening role too (see pp76–77). Some bamboos such as pygmy bamboo (*Pleioblastus pygmaeus*) grow to 30cm (12in) tall and make great ground cover, while others such as moso bamboo (*Phyllostachys edulis*) can reach 10m (33ft) in temperate climates and 30m (100ft) or more in warmer ones! All are highly ornamental and come in different forms, from upright *Phyllostachys*, which contrasts well with mounding shrubs, to floppy *Fargesia*, which arches gracefully.

Bamboos are part of the grass family but, unlike those discussed on pp54–57, the stems – known as 'culms' – eventually turn woody.

GROWING SUCCESS

- **Growing conditions:** All bamboos grow well in semishade, although some will tolerate full sun or full shade. Usefully, most survive in poor soil provided it is moist yet free-draining. Hot, arid climates should be avoided, and do be particularly mindful of the minimum temperatures that plants need in order to thrive. In cool-temperate climates 'cold hardy' bamboos are best. Fountain bamboo (*Fargesia nitida*) for example tolerates temperatures to -28°C (-18°F; Zone 5).

- **Clump-formers:** Bamboos can be split into two main groups: clump-formers and runners. Clump-formers such as Chilean bamboo (*Chusquea*) and fountain bamboo (*Fargesia nitida*) grow in tight clumps 1–4m (3–13ft) wide, depending on the species. These are far the best option for a small garden; just don't grow them tight to walls – as the clump swells, it might put pressure on foundations.

- **Running amok:** Running varieties such as broadleaved bamboo (*Sasa palmata*) and *Sasaella* produce underground rhizomes that forage far from the parent plant. How invasive they are depends on the soil and climate. Black bamboo (*Phyllostachys nigra*) for example is relatively well behaved in cool-temperate climates, but can be a nuisance in warmer ones. While sufficient space is preferable, running bamboos can be controlled using raised planters, concrete-walled beds or plastic, root-control barriers inserted vertically into a trench around plants. It is also possible to grow them in pots, but restricting the roots of wide spreaders will see plants tire quickly; clump-formers grow best here.

- **Colourful culms:** Many bamboos, particularly fountain bamboo and cultivars of *Phyllostachys*, produce colourful or attractive 'knobbly' culms. Some gardeners strip off the lower leaves to appreciate them more, although such a manicured look isn't for everyone.

- **Maintenance:** Bamboos need little aftercare, but never let them dry out as they establish. For container-grown plants, regular watering is vital.

Above, left: *Fargesia murielae* 'Bimbo' – a small umbrella bamboo cultivar – only reaches 1m (3ft). It's ideal on this balcony, where taller species with a large 'sail area' might struggle to establish well.

Opposite: Both golden bamboo (*Phyllostachys aurea*) and black bamboo (*P. nigra*) can run in warm, moist or favourable conditions, particularly in warm-temperate or subtropical climates. Plant them in large troughs or containers if it's necessary to keep the roots in check.

Some of the best... bamboos

c = clump-forming
c/s = typically clump-forming in cool-temperate climates (such as the UK), but will run in warm, moist, favourable conditions
s = running/spreading (might be invasive in warm, moist, favourable conditions)

- *Chusquea culeou* (Chilean bamboo; ❀❀ Z8–13) (c)
- *Fargesia murielae* (umbrella bamboo; ❀❀❀ Z5–9) (c)
- *Fargesia nitida* (fountain bamboo; ❀❀❀ Z5–9) and cvs (c)
- *Fargesia robusta* (❀❀❀ Z5–9) and cvs (c)
- *Phyllostachys aurea* (golden bamboo; ❀❀❀ Z7–11) (c/s)
- *Phyllostachys flexuosa* (zigzag bamboo; ❀❀❀ Z6–15) (c/s)
- *Phyllostachys vivax* f. *aureocaulis* (golden Chinese timber bamboo; ❀❀❀ Z7–10) (c/s)
- *Semiarundinaria fastuosa* (narihira bamboo; ❀❀❀ Z6–9) and cvs (c/s)
- *Shibataea kumasaca* (ruscus-leaved bamboo; ❀❀❀ Z6–15) (c/s)
- *Thamnocalamus crassinodus* (❀❀❀ Z8–10) (c)

Above: Not all bulbs, corms and tubers sing in spring; some such as autumn crocus (here, *Colchicum* 'Rosy Dawn') wait until the season is nearly over before they steal the show.

Opposite: Fragrant old pheasant's eye (*Narcissus poeticus* var. *recuruus*) thrives in long grass together with sky-blue forget-me-not (*Myosotis sylvatica*) and cow parsley (*Anthriscus sylvestris*). Could this work at the bottom of your garden?

Bulbs, corms & tubers

These all come in a staggering range of kiss-me-quick colours, need little maintenance and take up virtually no space at all. While botanically different, they're all herbaceous perennials – albeit ones more ephemeral in nature – emerging only when conditions are perfect before dying back underground, often just as quickly. All are used in the same way – to extend the season of interest, especially in early spring when there's little else around. But who could forget fragrant summer lilies and architectural ornamental onions (*Allium*), autumn meadow saffron (*Colchicum autumnale*) and winter *Cyclamen* – there are bulbs, corms and tubers for every season, and because they originate from numerous habitats they can be used almost anywhere.

Clever tricks

Bulbs flower to take advantage of the conditions. Spring ones seize on the moist but warming weather, and flower before the trees overhead have a chance to form a dense leaf canopy. Autumn bulbs time flowering for when the leaves fall. Snowdrops (*Galanthus*), wood anemone (*Anemone nemorosa*), winter aconite (*Eranthis hyemalis* Cilicica Group) and choice dog's-tooth-violet (*Erythronium*) originate under trees, so naturalise them under hedges and trees and next to buildings; they'll carpet the ground like jewels. **Note:** Being usually short in stature, many woodlanders struggle to compete in grass.

Au naturel

Bulbs with subtle characteristics are ideal for naturalising in lawns, mini meadows, gravel, woodland and in informal drifts within mixed borders or prairie-style plantings, where they're used extensively. For a natural look, use only a few varieties and drop handfuls from waist height before planting where they fall. For lawns and grassland, early-flowering species daffodils (*Narcissus poeticus* and *N. papyraceus* are favourites), *Gladiolus communis* subsp. *byzantinus*, spring *Crocus*, *Camassia cusickii* and *C. leichtlinii* subsp. *leichtlinii* are among the best, flowering well before the grass ever needs cutting.

Some of the best... bulbs, corms & tubers

SPRING INTEREST

- *Chionodoxa* (glory of the snow; ✤✤✤ Z3–9)
- *Crocus vernus* (Dutch crocus; ✤✤✤ Z3–8) and cvs
- *Eranthis hyemalis* (winter aconite; ✤✤✤ Z4–9)
- *Erythronium* (dog's-tooth violet; ✤✤✤ Z3–9)
- *Galanthus nivalis* (common snowdrop; ✤✤✤ Z3–8) and cvs
- *Muscari armeniacum* (Armenian grape hyacinth; ✤✤✤ Z4–8) and cvs
- *Narcissus* (daffodil; ✤✤–✤✤✤ Z3–10, depending on spp)
- *Scilla siberica* (Siberian squill; ✤✤✤ Z5–8) and cvs
- *Tulipa* (tulip; ✤✤–✤✤✤ Z4–8, depending on spp)

SUMMER–AUTUMN INTEREST

- *Allium* (ornamental onion; ✤✤–✤✤✤ Z4–11, depending on spp)
- *Camassia* (quamash; ✤✤–✤✤✤ Z4–11, depending on spp)
- *Cardiocrinum giganteum* (giant lily; ✤✤✤ Z7–9)
- *Colchium autumnale* (meadow saffron; ✤✤✤ Z4–9)
- *Dierama pulcherrimum* (angel's fishing rod; ✤✤ Z8–10) and cvs
- *Gladiolus murielae* (Abyssinian gladiolus; ✤✤ Z9–12)
- *Lilium* (lily; ✤✤✤ Z3–9, depending on spp)
- *Nectaroscordum siculum* (Sicilian honey garlic; ✤✤✤ Z6–10) and cvs
- *Nerine bowdenii* (Bowden Cornish lily; ✤✤✤ Z8–10) and cvs

GROWING SUCCESS

- **Massing:** By themselves bulbs have little impact, so mass them in groups proportionate to the location. In a small mixed border, groups of 6–10 bulbs is best. In larger beds individual drifts of 20–40+ are common.

- **Maintenance:** Bulbs grown where they're happiest need no aftercare although tall hybrid lilies (*Lilium*) and giant lily (*Cardiocrinum giganteum*) may need staking; use ring supports or bamboo canes. Bulbs in containers require regular watering and feeding.

- **Division:** Bulbs rarely need dividing. Only those that have stopped flowering (known as going 'blind') will benefit from being lifted and split when necessary. However *Nerine* detests division, and it flowers best when congested.

- **Planting:** Spring bulbs, including daffodils (*Narcissus*), tulips (*Tulipa*), *Crocus*, *Scilla* and hyacinths (*Hyacinthus*), are planted 'dry' in autumn. So too are hardy summer bulbs sich as lilies and ornamental onions (*Allium*), although on heavy soil they're best left until spring. Plant tender summer bulbs such as *Gladiolus* in early spring. Autumn bulbs are planted in early summer. Snowdrops (*Galanthus*) are the notable exception to the 'dry' rule; these establish best when planted after flowering in spring when they're still in leaf ('in the green'). Only large hybrid tulips will need replacing regularly (every 1–2 years), as these deteriorate rapidly wherever they're grown. Alternatively grow species types but these are smaller in size.

- **Depth gauge:** Plant bulbs three times as deep as the bulb's height – four, for tulips, ornamental onions and fritillaries (*Fritillaria*) – and at least the width of each bulb apart. Madonna lily (*Lilium candidum*) and *Nerine* are exceptions – these shouldn't be covered by more than 3cm (1in) of soil.

- **Cultivation:** Most bulbs, corms and tubers prefer a warm sunny site and fertile, free-draining soil. But depending on their origin, some bulbs are fussier than others. Tulips come from the Mediterranean and Middle East, so good drainage really is essential. Sun-loving lilies need rich moist soil and, depending on the species, have particular pH preferences too. Woodland bulbs such as English bluebell (*Hyacinthoides non-scripta*) need a similarly cool, moist position. Snake's head fritillaries (*Fritillaria meleagris*) come from damp meadows; again, plant accordingly. One caveat does apply to all bulbs, corms and tubers: cold, waterlogged soil is out. Heavy soils can be improved with horticultural grit or compost but that's impractical if you're naturalising bulbs over large areas.

- **Cutting back:** Don't! After flowering, let the leaves die back naturally for a minimum of six weeks. Next year's flowers depend on it. Never tie them in knots either. Bear this in mind when naturalising bulbs in lawns, as you won't be able to mow for 2–3 months. Avoid planting close to the house, or keep bulbs in tight drifts, so untidy areas aren't so obvious.

Above: Large 'bedding' tulips such as *Tulipa* 'White Triumphator' (of the lily-flowered Group) don't persist with the same vigour as species tulips and will probably not flower the following year. Unlike almost all other bulbs, they therefore need to be replaced every year.

Opposite: With bulbs such as ornamental onions – here, *Allium hollandicum* 'Purple Sensation' partnered with granny's bonnet (*Aquilegia vulgaris*) – the more there is the merrier. Single plants and small groups have little impact.

Annuals & biennials

Annuals complete their life cycle in one year, while biennials do it all in two, making vegetative growth in the first year before flowering in the second. For brilliant seasonal colour, annuals and biennials are hard to beat. Both do have a high-maintenance reputation, however, but they're a diverse tribe. At one end are tender *Lobelia* and *Petunia*, which in temperate climates die at the first frosts. Tough, frost-tolerant wild flowers such as cornflower (*Centaurea cyanus*) and foxglove (*Digitalis purpurea*) come at the other. What plants you choose depends on how much time you have, where you plan to use them and how promiscuous they are.

Biennial blooms

Like many hardy annuals, biennials can seed freely every year if conditions are right. This makes for a truly dynamic, ever-changing display. Distinctive taller types, or smaller ones generously used en masse, are key theme plants too. Sweet rocket (*Hesperis matronalis*), white-flowered honesty (*Lunaria annua* var. *albiflora*) and Icelandic poppy (*Papaver nudicaule*) are cottage garden classics. No shade planting would be complete without foxgloves. Biennials also feature extensively in prairie-style schemes. Stately rusty foxglove (*Digitalis ferruginea*), biennial clary (*Salvia sclarea*) and cotton thistle (*Onopordum acanthium*) make wonderful focal points partnered with floppy perennials and grasses such as hair grass (*Deschampsia*) for contrast.

Right: Biennials such as tall, white-flowered foxglove (*Digitalis purpurea* f. *albiflora*) are versatile plants and don't just suit more traditional designs, but also modern ones such as this.

Opposite: Half-hardy annuals such as *Petunia*, *Lobelia* and *Pelargonium* need work, so, if low maintenance is important, restrict displays to tubs and baskets where it's easier to make a success of them. Large containers are best, as plants will need less water and feeding.

Half-hardy & hardy annuals

Annuals that don't tolerate frost, cool temperatures and cold drying winds are half-hardy. Loved in the 19th century in particular and used in large formal summer bedding schemes, half-hardy annuals, including African marigolds (*Tagetes*) and busy Lizzies (*Impatiens*), were replaced each autumn with early spring biennials such as wallflowers (*Erysimum*) and sweet Williams (*Dianthus barbatus*). In public parks this tradition remains, but at home most modern gardeners keep bedding displays to pots or baskets, where they're easier to maintain.

Meanwhile hardy annuals tolerate frost. Nowadays the traditional hardy annual border has been replaced by the mini meadow for a more natural look, and this needs less work. However, in smaller gardens, bare patches for long periods are unacceptable. Here, sow seed in mixed borders where the gaps aren't so obvious. Hardy annuals are particularly useful as temporary gap fillers between maturing shrubs and conifers.

Myosotis sylvatica (forget-me-not)

Orlaya grandiflora (white laceflower)

Onopordum acanthium (cotton thistle)

Digitalis ferruginea (rusty foxglove)

Nigella damascena (love-in-a-mist)

Eschscholzia californica
(California poppy)

Matthiola longipetala subsp. *bicornis*
(night-scented stock)

Lunaria annua var. *albiflora*
(white-flowered honesty)

Some of the best... annuals & biennials

- *Agrostemma githago* (corn cockle; ❋❋❋ zone not applicable) and cvs
- *Ammi majus* (bullwort; ❋❋❋ zone not applicable)
- *Digitalis ferruginea* (rusty foxglove; ❋❋❋ Z4–9)
- *Eryngium giganteum* (Miss Willmott's ghost; ❋❋❋ Z4–9) and cvs
- *Eschscholzia californica* (California poppy; ❋❋❋ zone not applicable) and cvs
- *Hesperis matronalis* (sweet rocket; ❋❋❋ Z4–9)
- *Limnanthes douglasii* (poached egg plant; ❋❋❋ zone not applicable)
- *Lunaria annua* (honesty; ❋❋❋ Z3–9) and cvs
- *Matthiola longipetala* subsp. *bicornis* (night-scented stock; ❋❋❋ zone not applicable)
- *Myosotis sylvatica* (forget-me-not; ❋❋❋ Z5–9) and cvs
- *Nigella damascena* (love-in-a-mist; ❋❋❋ zone not applicable) and cvs
- *Onopordum acanthium* (cotton thistle; ❋❋❋ Z6–8)
- *Orlaya grandiflora* (white laceflower; ❋❋❋ zone not applicable)
- *Papaver somniferum* (opium poppy; ❋❋❋ zone not applicable) and cvs
- *Salvia scalarea* (biennial clary; ❋❋❋ Z5–9)
- *Verbascum thapsus* (great mullein; ❋❋❋ Z3–9)

Opposite: Many hardy annuals such as red poppies (*Papaver*) are prolific self-seeders and will find a niche among more competitive perennials and ornamental grasses. Here a ribbon of *P. commutatum* 'Ladybird' complements a buff-peach mullein (*Verbascum* 'Helen Johnson') and purple cow parsley (*Anthriscus sylvestris* 'Ravenswing').

GROWING SUCCESS

- **Be generous:** Grow annuals and biennials in large groups, or allow them to intermingle freely at an appropriate density. By themselves, individual plants make little impact.

- **Self-seeders:** Judicious weeding is sometimes necessary, especially with prolific self-seeders such as red orache (*Atriplex hortensis* var. *rubra*) that might inadvertently affect the rhythm of the composition (see p130). Hoe off seedlings you don't want or transplant them to where you do.

- **Climbing annuals:** Use annuals such as canary creeper (*Tropaeolum peregrinum*) and sweet pea (*Lathyrus odoratus*) varieties to climb new trelliswork, arches and arbours or shade-tolerant shrubs and hedges rapidly. Popular plants including Chilean glory flower (*Eccremocarpus scaber*), purple bell vine (*Rhodochiton atrosanguineus*) and cup and saucer plant (*Cobaea scandens*) are technically perennial but are also grouped here – all originate from tropical climates, so in temperate zones are usually grown as annuals. Sow seed under cover in late winter, as some do take time to get going.

- **Sowing:** Half-hardy annuals are sown under cover and then planted out once there is little danger of frost. Plug plants are available if you don't want to sow your own. Hardy annuals including squirrel tail grass (*Hordeum jubatum*) and love-in-a-mist (*Nigella damascena*) can be sown direct in autumn for an early display, requiring protection only in harsh winters. Others such as night-scented stock (*Matthiola longipetala* subsp. *bicornis*) aren't so tough. Sow under cloches or horticultural fleece, or in pots planted out in spring when the weather warms.

- **Position:** Light, free-draining soil in a sunny position is necessary for most annuals and biennials. A fine surface finish or tilth is necessary too, especially for seeds that are sown where they're to flower. Young seedlings will need protection from birds, slugs and snails. Sow thinly to avoid diseases such as damping off.

- **Maintenance:** Annuals and biennials need work initially but after they're established, simply water well in dry spells and watch for weeds. Deadheading does keep plants flowering for longer, but this is often impractical for anything other than container plants.

Left: Giant tree ferns loom over this dining space, creating a sense of drama. However all tree ferns are slow-growing, and you'll need to wait years for plants to reach a similar size. Instead consider buying specimen plants for instant impact.

Opposite: No marsh/bog garden is complete without a fern or two, particularly the aptly named royal fern (*Osmunda regalis*), which grows to a majestic 2.5m (8ft). Partners here include candelabra primulas (*Primula*) and umbrella plant (*Darmera peltata*).

Ferns
Dating back to the Cretaceous Period, ferns are some of the oldest plants on the planet. From huge tree ferns to tiny maidenhair spleenwort (*Asplenium trichomanes*), they'll grow anywhere that's damp and shady. Although ferns feature no flowers – spreading by spores instead of seeds – they do have textural feathery fronds in every shape and shade of green you can imagine. Some such as shuttlecock fern (*Matteuccia struthiopteris*) and male fern (*Dryopteris filix-mas*) have a distinctive shape too. Use ferns in naturalistic woodland plantings under trees, as feature plants in shady borders, or tuck them in at the feet of hardy palms and bamboos in jungle-like designs.

GROWING SUCCESS

- **Deciduous or evergreen ferns?** The young fronds (called crosiers) of deciduous ferns unfurl theatrically in spring. Evergreens including common polypody (*Polypodium vulgare*) and soft shield fern (*Polystichum setiferum*) look good year-round, and particularly in winter. They tolerate more exposure too.

- **Ideal situation:** Damp shade is preferred. However some ferns – shield fern (*Polystichum*) in particular – don't mind dry conditions, as long as they're not in too sunny a spot.

- **Overwintering:** In temperate climates cold-hardy tree ferns native to Australia, New Zealand and Tasmania are popular theme plants and dramatic focal points. *Dicksonia* and *Cyathea* are the most common. Both are very slow-growing, so for instant impact buy mature specimens. Most are hardy to only -10°C (14°F), so will need protection in harsh winters – stuff straw into the crown and wrap the trunk with horticultural fleece.

- **Soil:** Fertile, moist but free-draining soil is necessary – few ferns like waterlogged soil. Some ferns have a distinct pH preference too.

- **Aftercare:** Ferns need little maintenance. Clear away dead fronds in spring and spread an insulating mulch of leafmould or garden compost around plants in colder climates. That's it.

Some of the best… ferns

**TOP 10 EASY-TO-GROW GARDEN FERNS
TOLERANT OF MOST SOILS**

e = evergreen; se = semievergreen; d = deciduous

- *Asplenium scolopendrium* (hart's tongue fern; ✿✿✿ Z6–8)
  40 × 40cm (16 × 16in) (e)
- *Athyrium filix-femina* (lady fern; ✿✿✿ Z4–9) – 1.2 × 0.75m (4 × 2½ft) (d)
- *Cyrtomium fortunei* (fortune's cyrtomium; ✿✿✿ Z7–10) – 1.5 × 1m
  (5 × 3ft) (e)
- *Dryopteris affinis* 'Cristata' (golden shield fern; ✿✿✿ Z6–8) –
  80 × 80cm (32 × 32in) (e)
- *Dryopteris erythrosora* (broad buckler fern; ✿✿✿ Z5–9) – 60 × 60cm
  (2 × 2ft) (se)
- *Dryopteris filix-mas* (male fern; ✿✿✿ Z4–8) – 1 × 1m (3 × 3ft) (d)
- *Osmunda regalis* (royal fern; ✿✿✿ Z2–10) – 2 × 4m (6½ × 13ft) (d)
- *Polystichum munitum* (sword fern; ✿✿✿ Z3–8) – 1 × 1.2m (3 × 4ft) (e)
- *Polystichum setiferum* 'Herrenhausen' (soft shield fern; ✿✿✿ Z6–9)
  – 50 × 80cm (20 × 32in) (e)
- *Matteuccia struthiopteris* (shuttlecock fern; ✿✿✿ Z2–8) – 1.5m ×
  90cm (5ft × 36in) (d)

Water plants

Water is an integral part of contemporary gardens, and plants often play a key role (see pp236–239). In formal pools a few clumps of architectural yellow flag (*Iris pseudacorus*) will echo the strong geometry and help link the pool to surrounding plantings. With informal pools a more naturalistic planting design is preferable to evoke a sense of place and also encourage wildlife. But before you plan the planting it helps to understand why 'water' plants naturally grow where they do. Essentially it comes down to how much they like getting their feet wet.

Opposite: Marsh plants such as this purple Siberian iris (Iris 'Linda Mary') thrive in moist but well-drained soil. Here they're the perfect vertical contrast to these horizontal decking platforms, which would also work wonderfully suspended above a still pool.

Types of water plants

MARSH/BOG PLANTS

These grow in natural wetlands or the periphery of pools and streams, needing wet, but not permanently waterlogged soil. For heavy clay borders, they're ideal. Appearance-wise, plants fall into two groups: those with thin, sword-like leaves and those with large, broad leaves. Examples include leopard plant (*Ligularia*) and giant cowslip (*Primula florindae*).

MARGINAL PLANTS

Marginals grow at the water's edge; needing their roots submerged in 5–30cm (2–12in) of water, the specific depth dependent on the species. As well as being essential for wildlife, they also form the transition from aquatic plants to surrounding shrubs and trees. In artificial pools, shallow 'shelves' are necessary to grow marginal plants. Examples include flowering rush (*Butomus umbellatus*) and bog arum (*Calla palustris*).

AQUATIC PLANTS

These are essential for water ecosystems and to support aquatic life.

- **Oxgenators:** Permanently submerged, these plants aerate the water and shelter pond dwellers. Examples include frog's lettuce (*Groenlandia densa*) and mare's-tail (*Hippuris vulgaris*).

- **Floating plants:** Growing without their roots in soil, free-floaters provide shade and stop algae. Examples include water soldier (*Stratiotes aloides*) and frog-bit (*Hydrocharis morsus-ranae*).

- **Deep-water emergents:** These root on the bottom of a pond with their flowers and leaves on the water's surface. The necessary depth of water is 0.3–1m (1–3ft). Examples include waterlily (*Nymphaea*).

Above: Waterlilies (Nymphaea) are one of the most popular water plants, even though most grow pretty big. Fortunately, choice miniature cultivars such as N. 'Pygmaea Helvola' spread to only 50cm (20in) – ideal for small pools. Plant in baskets sited under 7.5–10cm (3–4in) of water.

GROWING SUCCESS

- **Rate of growth:** Pond plants grow fast, so allocate sufficient space or pick similar, less vigorous plants. Plant Chinese rhubarb (*Rheum palmatum*) instead of huge *Gunnera manicata*, for example.

- **Wildife?** For a sustainable wildlife pond, aim to cover at least half of the water surface with plants.

- **Dry soil?** A man-made pond set where the soil isn't wet enough for marsh plants needs a suitably boggy area to accommodate them, typically by burying a butyl liner under the soil.

- **Lookalikes:** Perennials and ferns tolerant of drier conditions are useful where the soil is not naturally boggy. Ornamental grasses such as silver grass (*Miscanthus*) suggest reeds, while day lilies (*Hemerocallis*) would also work.

- **Native or non-native?** For a natural look, choose native plants or non-natives with similar characteristics – avoid variegated leaves and huge bicoloured flowers. Natives are less likely to be invasive.

Some of the best… marginal & aquatic plants for small ponds

- *Aponogeton distachyos* (water hawthorn; ❀❀ Z9–10)
- *Butomus umbellatus* (flowering rush; ❀❀❀ Z3–11)
- *Caltha palustris* (marsh marigold; ❀❀❀ Z3–7)
- *Cyperus involucratus* (umbrella grass; ❀ Z13–15)
- *Hydrocharis morsus-ranae* (frog-bit; ❀❀❀ Z6–11)
- *Iris ensata* (Japanese water iris; ❀❀❀ Z3–9) and cvs
- *Juncus effusus* f. *spiralis* (corkscrew rush; ❀❀❀ Z6–9)
- *Lobelia cardinalis* (cardinal flower; ❀❀❀ Z2–8) and cvs
- *Myosotis scorpioides* (water forget-me-not; ❀❀❀ Z5–9) and cvs
- *Orontium aquaticum* (golden club; ❀❀❀ Z6–10)
- *Pontederia cordata* (pickerel weed; ❀❀❀ Z3–11)
- *Ranunculus flammula* (lesser spearwort; ❀❀❀ Z3–9)
- *Schoenoplectus lacustris* subsp. *tabernaemontani* (grey club-rush; ❀❀❀ Z6–9) and cvs
- *Typha minima* (reedmace; ❀❀❀ Z3–11)
- *Zantedeschia aethiopica* (arum lily; ❀❀❀ Z8–10) and cvs

Note: In very small ponds (and those made with a liner), grow pond plants in special pond baskets; this will also help control the growth rate of vigorous species.

3.

Plants with a Purpose

In the last chapter we looked at the various different plant groups, from trees to annuals and everything in between. But before we concentrate on how to combine them all in attractive arrangements for year-round interest, it's important to note that many plants can also have a functional or practical role, from screening nosy neighbours to providing welcome shade and shelter. Some plants also keep weeds at bay, which can help cut maintenance time in half. Usefully, in almost all cases, plants are a more effective and certainly a cheaper solution to man-made 'engineered' alternatives.

At first glance, trees, hedges, larger shrubs and conifers as well as tall bamboos might appear to be the most useful 'plants with purpose', but even humble groundcover perennials and grasses have a practical part to play.

Stabilizing soil

Soil erosion is a problem, particularly on steep slopes. But it's long been recognised that plants can help here. On large landscape projects they're key 'eco-engineering' tools, while in private gardens plants are also introduced to stablize terraces, banks and berms, especially those created artificially. Plants lessen the impact of heavy rain on the soil below and help to reduce surface water run-off, and their roots bind the soil together. Through natural biological and physical processes, plants can regulate moisture levels too, stopping the soil from becoming waterlogged or drying out.

Drop anchor

Grass or wild flowers are certainly an improvement on bare soil, but mixed plantings with trees, shrubs and carpeting herbaceous plants are better. Together they temper heavy rain more effectively than unplanted areas, and their different root systems stabilize the soil at varying depths. The taproots of trees for example anchor the soil deep down. Suckering shrubs such as *Kerria* and grasses have dense roots that provide support nearer the surface. Spreading, shallow-rooting groundcover perennials are particularly useful. Some such as Mrs Robb's bonnet (*Euphorbia amygdaloides* var. *robbiae*) increase using tenacious underground rhizomes. Others including bugle (*Ajuga*) and periwinkle (*Vinca*) produce stems (called stolons) that root when they touch the soil; both form dense mats on the soil surface.

But a quick word about invasives. Spreading plants are invaluable to stablize slopes (and for weed control, see p80) but they can become a nuisance, depending on your location. Consider carefully anything with 'potentially invasive' in the description.

On large steep slopes access is difficult, so avoid plants that need regular maintenance. Drought-tolerant species always establish more readily here too.

Plants useful for stabilizing soil

- *Arctostaphylos uva-ursi* (common bearberry; ❊❊❊ Z2–6) and cvs
- *Ceanothus thyrsiflorus* var. *repens* (blueblossom; ❊❊❊ Z7–11)
- *Cotoneaster horizontalis* (❊❊❊ Z4–7)
- *Epimedium perralderianum* (barrenwort; ❊❊❊ Z5–8)
- *Euonymus fortunei* (spindle; ❊❊❊ Z5–9) and cvs
- *Euphorbia amygdaloides* var. *robbiae* (Mrs Robb's bonnet; ❊❊❊ Z6–9)
- *Hydrangea anomala* subsp. *petiolaris* (climbing hydrangea; ❊❊❊ Z4–9)
- *Hypericum calycinum* (rose of Sharon; ❊❊❊ Z5–9) and cvs
- *Mahonia repens* (creeping-rooted barberry; ❊❊❊ Z5–8) and cvs
- *Rubus tricolor* (Chinese bramble; ❊❊❊ Z7–9)
- *Stephanandra incisa* (❊❊❊ Z3–8) and cvs
- *Taxus baccata* 'Repandens' (yew; ❊❊❊ Z7–8)
- *Vinca major* (greater periwinkle; ❊❊❊ Z7–9) and cvs

Above: Vigorous carpeting purple aubretia (*Aubrieta* 'Hartswood Purple') and snow-in-summer (*Cerastium tomentosum*) help prevent erosion on this steep bank and provide a colourful spectacle in late spring and early summer.

Left: To stablize soil effectively, a mixture of different plants whose roots grow to different depths is best. Also note that with a bank or a slope, plants can be appreciated differently, either by looking down at them from above or by viewing them from below. Consider this when you plan the planting.

Privacy & screening

Taller plants can solve privacy problems. In urban areas where strict regulations exist regarding the height of garden features and boundary walls and fences, they're often the only suitable option. Large semimature specimens are ideal for instant impact, but these aren't cheap. Smaller plants cost less but aren't immediately effective. Whatever you choose means compromises.

Stand tall

With their size in mind, trees are invaluable; one by itself is often enough to screen neighbouring windows for example. Evergreen or coniferous species provide year-round cover, but deciduous trees might work too. Admittedly these do lose their leaves in winter, but privacy then might not be all that important.

If height is necessary, but there's no room even for a conical tree, tall bamboos are useful. Pleached trees (hedges on 'stilts') are popular too, but these are costly and need pruning regularly; plant at least 80cm/32in from boundaries, so that you can get in behind to trim.

For effective privacy and screening, consider leaf size and canopy density. A dense conifer might solve privacy problems, but could it plunge the garden into darkness? Conversely small- or narrow-leaved deciduous trees do let in more light, but reveal more behind them.

Tidy-but-tall evergreen screening solutions

- *Arbutus unedo* (strawberry tree; ❋❋❋ Z8–9) – 9 × 9m (30 × 30ft), tolerates pruning
- *Chusquea culeou* (Chilean bamboo; ❋❋ Z8–13) – 8 × 2.5m (25 × 8ft)
- *Eriobotrya japonica* (loquat; ❋❋ Z8–11) – 6 × 6m (20 × 20ft), tolerates pruning
- *Eucryphia* × *nymansensis* 'Nymansay' (❋❋❋ Z8–9) – 12 × 4m (40 × 13ft)
- *Fargesia murielae* (umbrella bamboo; ❋❋❋ Z5–9) – 4 × 2.5m (13 × 8ft)
- *Ligustrum lucidum* (Chinese privet; ❋❋❋ 8–10) – 10 × 10m (33 × 33ft), tolerates pruning
- *Magnolia grandiflora* (bull bay; ❋❋ Z7–9) – 6–20 × 8–15m (20–60 × 25–50ft), relatively slow growing, tolerates pruning
- *Olea europaea* (olive; ❋❋ Z8–10) – 10 × 10m (33 × 33ft), tolerates pruning
- *Quercus ilex* (holm oak; ❋❋❋ Z4–9) – in pleached/box-head form
- *Trachycarpus fortunei* (Chusan palm; ❋❋ Z8–11) – 12 × 2m (40 × 6½ft)

Opposite, left: In gardens overlooked from above, beams covered with climbers could be a most attractive feature. They don't always need to be huge timbers, like these though; the mere 'suggestion' of privacy using wire braid to support slender, summer-flowering *Clematis* for example is often enough.

Above, left: In gardens overlooked from all angles it's better to work on creating privacy in certain areas using trees and hedges like this rather than try – often in vain – to make the whole garden private.

Above: Avoid plants with colourful variegated leaves, as these might inadvertently draw attention to the spot you're trying to screen; the black bamboos (*Phyllostachys nigra*), here on the left, are ideal.

Left: Dividing up a garden into a series of different zones or rooms is part of every garden designer's toolkit. These golden oats (*Stipa gigantea*) partially screen the seating area behind, making for a more intimate space while encouraging investigation of what's on the other side.

Security

Nowadays security is high on the agenda for many homeowners. Shrubs such as holly (*Ilex*) and firethorn (*Pyracantha*) can create beautiful yet spiky barriers while dense conifer hedges are almost impassable once mature.

First positions

In the front garden create hedges with short shrubs such as *Rosa* 'Fru Dagmar Hastrup' or barberry (*Berberis*) that welcome regular pruning – tall hedges will only screen intruders so are best used in the back garden. But like trees used to screen eyesores (see pp76–77), hedges aren't an instant solution, so for immediate impact it's necessary to buy big plants. If you are prepared to wait, partner young hedges with temporary fencing while they mature.

Side gates and fences are an obvious entry point for burglars. Here train thorny climbers and wall shrubs such as firethorn and climbing roses through trellis affixed on top to make them difficult to climb. Similarly spiky shrubs and 'border' conifers can be used below windows and at the foot of drainpipes.

Medium–large security hedging
– H&S: 1–1.8m (3–6ft)

- *Berberis* × *stenophylla* (barberry; ✲✲✲ Z6–9) and cvs
- *Chamaecyparis lawsoniana* (Lawson's cypress; ✲✲✲ Z5–9) and cvs
- *Crataegus laevigata* (Midland hawthorn; ✲✲✲ Z5–8) and cvs
- *Crataegus monogyna* (common hawthorn; ✲✲✲ Z5–7) and cvs
- *Hippophae rhamnoides* (sea buckthorn; ✲✲✲ Z3–8)
- *Ilex aquifolium* (English holly; ✲✲✲ Z7–9) and cvs
- *Pyracantha coccinea* (firethorn; ✲✲✲ Z6–9) and cvs
- *Thuja plicata* (western red cedar; ✲✲✲ Z6–8) and cvs
- *Zanthoxylum piperitum* (Japan pepper; ✲✲✲ Z3–7)

Small–medium spiky shrubs/hedges
– H&S: 60–1.2m (2–4ft)

- *Berberis thunbergii* (Japanese barberry; ✲✲✲ Z5–8) and cvs
- *Chaenomeles* × *superba* (Japanese quince; ✲✲✲ Z5–9) and cvs
- *Genista hispanica* (Spanish gorse; ✲✲✲ Z7–9)
- *Ribes uva-crispa* (gooseberry; ✲✲✲ Z5–9) and cvs
- *Rosa rugosa* (Japanese rose; ✲✲✲ Z2–9) and cvs
- *Ulex europaeus* (gorse; ✲✲✲ Z6–8) and cvs

Ilex aquifolium 'J C van Tol' (English holly)

Pyracantha 'Orange Glow' (firethorn)

Crataegus monogyna (common hawthorn)

Berberis × *stenophylla* 'Mount Etna' (barberry)

Ulex europaeus 'Flore Pleno' (gorse)

Rosa rugosa 'Alba' (Japanese rose)

Chaenomeles speciosa (Japanese quince)

Ribes uva-crispa 'Invicta' (gooseberry)

Above: Given room, dense planting such as this in a front garden will act as a buffer and absorb traffic noise. Psychologically, hiding the source of nuisance noise always lessens its impact too.

Noise control

Nothing will drown out the sound of a jet engine, but plants can deaden noise from nearby roads or even neighbours. Unlike hard surfaces, which refract sound waves and bounce them around, leaves and branches absorb noise like a sponge.

Sound choice

Dense hedges work best – the thicker the better. Choose evergreens, especially broadleaved species such as cherry laurel (*Prunus laurocerasus*) for year-round control – with their large leaf area they're more effective than conifers with slender needles. Height-wise try to screen the source of nuisance noise – if you can't see it, then it's never so loud.

Thick, mixed planting will also dampen sounds – just avoid gaps. If there's room to make one, a low planted bank will block noise better still.

In urban areas an emphasis on hard landscaping will only exacerbate noise problems. Here include plenty of planting, especially tall grasses and bamboos that rustle in the wind, to dampen down the sound. Clad walls and fences with climbers, or perhaps create 'living walls'. These will stop echoes reverberating around the space.

Weed control

Plants you do want can help stop those you don't. While any plant that closely shadows the soil will suppress weeds, carpeting groundcover plants are most effective. See them as a 'living' mulch, helping to inhibit weeds.

Cover-up

For landscape designers, 'ground cover' means essentially anything from formal lawns and meadows to heathland, which grows over the ground. For gardeners, the term is more commonly used for a diverse range of low-growing perennials, grasses, prostrate shrubs and conifers planted in the foreground of beds and borders and also in areas where grass won't grow – under dense trees for example.

For year-round weed control, evergreen plants are essential – there are lots to choose from. But even more important to consider is how much they'll spread and how quickly. Perennials and grasses that forage far using rhizomes or stolons (see p57) are useful to cover large areas. However they can be invasive, unless you're prepared to chop them back regularly. For small borders, select evergreen clump-formers that simply 'swell' instead. Just plant them closer together than normal,

at 0.3–1m (1–3ft) apart (depending on the species), so that together they cover the soil more quickly.

Although most groundcover plants won't tolerate foot traffic, a select few don't mind being walked on two to three times a day. Favourites include carpeting thyme (*Thymus*) species and lawn chamomile (*Chamaemelum nobile* 'Treneague'). Usefully, neither needs mowing.

Tidy evergreen ground cover

- *Alchemilla mollis* (lady's mantle; ❋❋❋ Z4–7) and cvs
- *Bergenia* (elephant's ears; ❋❋❋ Z4–9, depending on spp)
- *Campanula portenschlagiana* (Dalmation bellflower; ❋❋❋ Z4–7)
- *Duchesnea indica* (mock strawberry; ❋❋❋ Z6–8)
- *Epimedium* × *versicolor* (barrenwort; ❋❋❋ Z5–9)
- *Hakonechloa macra* (❋❋❋ Z7–9) and cvs
- *Liriope muscari* (lilyturf; ❋❋❋ Z6–10) and cvs
- *Mahonia repens* (creeping-rooted barberry; ❋❋❋ Z5–8)
- *Osteospermum jucundum* (❋❋ Z9–11)
- *Pachysandra terminalis* (Japanese spurge; ❋❋❋ Z4–8) and cvs
- *Persicaria affinis* (❋❋❋ Z3–8) and cvs
- *Stachys byzantina* (lambs' tongues; ❋❋❋ Z4–8) and cvs
- *Vinca minor* (lesser periwinkle; ❋❋❋ Z4–9) and cvs
- *Waldsteinia ternata* (❋❋❋ Z3–8)

Alchemilla mollis (lady's mantle)

Hakonechloa macra 'Aureola'

Bergenia 'Silberlicht' (elephant's ears)

Stachys byzantina 'Silver Carpet' (lambs' tongues)

Pachysandra terminalis (Japanese spurge)

Waldsteinia ternata

Persicaria affinis 'Donald Lowndes'

Liriope muscari (lilyturf)

Air cleansing

Plants are nature's air fresheners and many help mask unpleasant seasonal smells, such as smelly bins in summer, and reduce air pollution, which is most acute in urban areas.

Freshen up

Powerfully scented plants such as mock orange (*Philadelphus*) are most effective at deodorising the air. Just note when odours are most obnoxious and choose perfumed plants that flower at the same time. Typically this is in spring and summer when you're out in the garden the most (for more on scent see pp158–161).

Plants 'clean' the air too. By roadsides, plants can trap pollen, pollutants and harmful particulates such as brake dust on their leaves, which are washed into the soil after rain. Trees and native shrubs with a large leaf area are the most successful. Yet all plants are the 'lungs' of our cities, and trees in particular 'breathe in' tons of carbon dioxide (CO_2) during photosynthesis.

'Free scents' to mask seasonal smells

- *Calycanthus floridus* (Carolina allspice; ❋❋❋ Z5–9)
- *Cestrum nocturnum* (night-blooming jasmine; ❋❋❋ Z9–11)
- *Chimonanthus praecox* (wintersweet; ❋❋❋ Z7–9) and cvs
- *Daphne bholua* 'Jacqueline Postill' (Nepalese paper plant; ❋❋❋ borderline Z7–10)
- *Gardenia jasminoides* (cape jasmine; ❋ Z14–15) and cvs
- *Jasminum sambac* (Arabian jasmine; ❋ Z10–11)
- *Lilium* – trumpet or oriental hybrids (lily; ❋❋–❋❋❋ Z2–9, depending on spp)
- *Lonicera fragrantissima* (shrubby honeysuckle; ❋❋❋ Z4–8)
- *Lonicera japonica* (Japanese honeysuckle; ❋❋❋ Z4–10) and cvs
- *Magnolia figo* (banana shrub; ❋ Z12–15)
- *Mirabilis jalapa* (four o'clock flower; ❋❋ Z10–11)
- *Osmanthus fragrans* (sweet tea; ❋ Z8–11)
- *Polianthes tuberosa* (tuberose; ❋ Z7–11)
- *Ptelea trifoliata* (hop tree; ❋❋❋ Z5–9) and cvs

Above: Fragrant lilies such as Easter lily (*Lilium longiflorum*) are a popular favourite for masking unwanted summer smells. Many lilies grow well in large pots so can be moved close to open doors and windows to perfume the home too.

Above: Any windbreak, no matter how big, should be wider than the area needing protection, or else wind will whip around the sides. This fountain grass (*Pennisetum*) hedge is ideal here.

Trees/large shrubs for providing shelter & shade

- *Carpinus betulus** (common hornbeam; ❋❋❋ Z4–8) and cvs
- *Cercis siliquastrum* (Judas tree; ❋❋❋ Z6–9) and cvs
- *Crataegus laevigata** (Midland hawthorn; ❋❋❋ Z5–8) and cvs
- *Genista aetnensis* (Mount Etna broom; ❋❋ Z9–10)
- *Lagerstroemia indica* (crepe myrtle; ❋❋ Z7–9) and cvs
- *Pinus pinea** (stone pine; ❋❋❋ Z9–11)
- *Podocarpus salignus* (willowleaf podocarp; ❋❋❋ Z8–11)
- *Quercus ilex** (holm oak; ❋❋❋ Z4–8)
- *Sorbus aria* (whitebeam; ❋❋❋ Z4–5) and cvs
- *Sorbus aucuparia* (rowan; ❋❋❋ Z4–7) and cvs
- *Thuja plicata* (western red cedar; ❋❋❋ Z6–8) and cvs

* tolerant of full exposure to salt-laden winds

Shelter & shade

Being baked by hot sun is annoying, not to mention dangerous for children, so some shade is necessary. Sitting in a windy garden is uncomfortable too. But it's not just humans that suffer. Strong winds can dislodge plants (tearing their roots), break branches and desiccate young foliage. Therefore in exposed gardens some shade and shelter are particularly important. Wherever you're planning to grow fruit and veg, it's essential.

Breeze barrier

To temper strong winds, solid barriers are a poor choice – the wind will eddy on both sides creating turbulence that few garden plants can cope with. A permeable barrier is better. Hedges, large shrubs and feathered or multistemmed trees are ideal. These slow and diffuse the wind rather than deflecting its full force downwards or up and over the top of the barrier.

Plants used to provide wind protection must be tough and, in coastal locations, salt-tolerant. Broadleaved evergreens are best. Conifers such as Leyland cypress (x *Cuprocyparis leylandii*), Lawson cypress (*Chamaecyparis lawsoniana*) and western red cedar (*Thuja plicata*) make quick-growing hedges too,

but being dense growers these can block rather than filter the wind – just like a solid wall will do.

It helps to look to nature for inspiration and select plants that naturally grow in exposed spots. In large gardens native trees and shrubby species can help blend a garden sympathetically into its surroundings (a deciduous/evergreen mix is preferable on this scale). In small gardens anything goes, providing the plants suit the growing conditions and complement the desired style or theme.

The success of a windbreak is dependent on its height and width. As a guide, a windbreak is most effective to a distance 10 times its height. A standard 2m (6½ft) high hedge will provide excellent protection up to 20m (60ft) away on the leeward side for example.

Made in the shade

Trees and large shrubs are ideal to cast shade and provide protection from the hot midday sun. Deciduous species with small leaves and slender branches create dappled light, making the space underneath suitable for dining. Dense evergreen species, particularly with a low canopy, conjure a more intimate atmosphere. As the tree matures it may become too dark and gloomy below, so lift the crown by trimming off lower branches carefully when the need arises. Tall but floppy bamboo might work well too; just choose clump-formers if space is tight (see p58).

Opposite, above: Plants like pines (*Pinus*), flax (*Phormium*) and half-hardy flax lily (*Dianella*) tolerant strong, salt-laden winds, so are the perfect choice to provide protection on exposed balconies and roof terraces. All are drought-tolerant too.

Opposite, below: Hedges and grasses partner hardscape and a canvas parasol to shelter and shade this modern seating space. Consider how hardscape and plants could complement and work with each other.

Making space with plants

While hedges, larger shrubs, bamboo and trees are commonly introduced to structure ornamental plantings in beds and borders (more on pp172–77), they're also used on a larger scale earlier in the design process to determine the layout and spatial arrangement of shapes on the ground. Designers include them to define different spaces for various functions, control visual experience, manipulate the way we move through a garden, and divide a large space into smaller areas, or create a small, more intimate space within a bigger one.

Spatial design

On this topic I like to use an architectural analogy. Walls and ceilings in the home divide what would otherwise be an open-plan interior into a series of rooms or areas, each one having a particular role and function. Partitioning space in this way outside is just as important for practical and aesthetic purposes. Hedges, shrubs, multistemmed trees, large grasses and bamboos make up the 'walls' in a garden. Trees, arches and arbours covered with climbers form a 'ceiling' where some intimacy, shade or shelter is necessary.

The height and transparency of a 'wall' or 'ceiling' depend on the scale of the space as a whole, the proportion of one 'room' to another, and the role of each area. For example tall yew hedges would effectively divide a big, football-friendly lawn from more adult territory, whereas a low row of lavender simply wouldn't work in such a situation and on this scale it's likely to be out of proportion as well. Similarly in small gardens, tall hedges used to separate one space or 'room' completely from another might make the garden feel more claustrophobic. Instead, low-level plantings or taller ornamental grasses and lacy perennials such as meadow rue (*Thalictrum delavayi*) or purple top (*Verbena bonariensis*) are a better option – these plants have a veil-like quality so you can easily catch glimpses of what's on the other side of them.

Right: The height, width, opacity and density of a planted barrier, baffle or screen will determine whether the space behind is completely private or just subtly separated. Here different-sized hedges and pleached trees do a bit of both jobs.

Effective space makers

- lofty grasses such as *Miscanthus* × *giganteus* (silver banner grass; ✾✾✾ Z8–9)
- medium–large shrubs such as *Viburnum tinus* (laurustinus; ✾✾✾ Z8–10)
- small-garden trees such as *Malus* × *robusta* 'Red Sentinel' (crab apple; ✾✾✾ Z5–8)
- pleached/box-head trees such as *Fagus sylvatica* (common beech; ✾✾✾ Z4–7)
- tall bamboo such as *Fargesia murielae* (umbrella bamboo; ✾✾✾ Z5–9)
- tall formal hedges such as *Taxus baccata* (yew; ✾✾✾ Z7–8)
- tall informal hedges such as *Rosa glauca* (red-leaved rose; ✾✾✾ Z2–8)

Note: Bear your style or theme in mind when choosing. If it's necessary to keep children or pets off an area, then any barrier needs to be at least waist high and, ideally, woody and evergreen too.

4.

Get the Look

For clarity, it always helps to decide on a style or theme. Personal taste and how you plan to use the garden have an influence, but so should the idea of a sense of place – essentially working sympathetically with the garden and its surroundings.

Helpfully most gardens hold clues as to the best approach, especially when parallels are drawn with natural habitats: for example a shady courtyard = urban woodland; a sunny, south-facing slope = Mediterranean gravel garden, perhaps. Location and architecture are part of the picture too. Rural gardens for example should embrace the wider landscape by using similar plant forms and colours to forge links. House and garden should also marry well together, especially in urban and suburban settings.

Many design styles come complete with guiding principles, often referencing history or culture. However designers sometimes combine styles to break the mould – as you'll see in this chapter.

Inspiration: Making a mood board

A mood board sounds like a cliché but it's a tried-and-tested way of capturing a style or theme, and of communicating ideas. If you haven't yet focused on a design direction, creating a mood board will almost always reveal one. What to include is very personal, but there's inspiration aplenty. Use books and websites, tear out pictures from magazines and make collages with them. Flower shows are fantastic, with lots of different designs to see in a relatively small space. Explore the gardens of friends and family, photographing anything that appeals, too.

Adore these colours! (not the black background)

Beautiful arrangement but are my borders big enough?   *Lavender yes, yes, yes!!!*   *Love the vibrancy and intensity of these colours!!*

Tips & tricks

A scrapbook is useful to collate all your ideas, although a giant sheet of paper is better still. It should have enough space to arrange images so that you can pythem together and rearrange them in different configurations if you want. Room to annotate the images, recording what you like – and of course what you don't like – is important too. Use pencil rather than permanent marker, so it can be rubbed out easily as you re-evaluate your choices.

While plant portraits and planting combinations are invaluable when planning a new planting scheme, don't be afraid to include images that capture a particular atmosphere you're trying to evoke, whether you source these as interior furnishings you like, famous artworks with inspiring colours or your holiday snaps. The image itself is not as important as how it inspires you. That said, pictures of entire gardens should ideally be from gardens a similar size to your own, rather than from expansive landscapes, which won't easily translate to your own smaller plot.

Below: With a mood board it doesn't matter what the actual images are, or where they come. If it inspires you, include it!

Touchy feely for kids?

Orange and blue contrast essential

Bright lights after dark a must!

Plants for bees, butterflies and birds essential!

Focus on... formal

Rooted in classical Greek and Italianate architecture and made famous by the Moorish gardens of the Alhambra, Spain, and the Italian Renaissance, formal gardens are easily recognisable – both the layout and design details are usually put together with mathematical precision. In the classic formal garden, a geometric, often-symmetrical design arranged around a central axis is common. So too are long views, bold focal points, reflective pools, a repetitive palette of plants and intricate design details. Generous proportions are also important in the size of both paved and planted areas; this helps to evoke a sense of space and grandeur.

Abstracting the style

While the principles of classic formal gardens endure today, designers also experiment with the blueprint – in fact you'll see key elements appear in many other styles and themes. Modernist designers appreciate the clarity and clear geometry that define the formal garden but reject the rigid symmetrical layout and necessary focal point in favour of more informally arranged asymmetric designs, where highly controlled views and vistas aren't so obvious. Naturalistic planting designers embrace the geometry too, but often look to soften it completely with meadow or prairie-like planting for contrast. Conversely, many formal garden-makers favour exclusively dramatic collections of clipped topiary or stands of tree ferns, partnering them with contemporary materials, sometimes in very curvaceous informal layouts.

AT A GLANCE

- precise geometry that brings order – the key feature of a formal style;
- repetition of key plants or combinations;
- axial organisation of design layout with a focal point positioned at the end or, where there's space, on the cross-section of two axes arranged perpendicular to one another;
- clipped hedges that emphasise design geometry and sometimes define planting space. Low hedges might be introduced to create formal parterres and knot gardens – a tradition popular in the 17th century;
- modest materials palette, repeated throughout.

Left: Clinically precise geometry, generous proportions and a restrained palette of plants are features indicative of formal gardens, whether the layout is symmetrical or asymmetrical or, as in this case, a beautiful combination of the two.

Opposite, above: Formal style influenced this crisp design but doesn't dominate; instead the asymmetric rectangular layout merely defines the space and underpins the relaxed design details and planting perfectly.

Opposite, below: Renowned plantswoman Helen Dillon's symmetrical formal garden is packed with a profusion of plants and shows that formality needn't always be sombre and serious.

Formal gardens: Where this style works best...

Formal gardens sit comfortably with both traditional and modern homes featuring strong architecture, and help to create all-important links between the two. This style works particularly well in gardens defined by rectilinear boundaries – especially those that run parallel to each other – although the proportions of beds and borders need to be carefully considered to suit the size of the space; the classic golden ratio is useful here. Based on the Fibonacci Sequence, the golden section, as it's also known, is a mathematical ratio that can help create pleasing proportions.

Maintenance depends on the severity of the layout and clinical nature of the design details. Formal gardens in the classic tradition featuring extensive collections of hedges and topiary that need regular clipping will take much longer to look after than a formal garden filled with naturalistic, informal, prairie-like or woodland planting.

Left: A central axis with layered borders, where plants are arranged with height in mind from front to back, is common in formal design. Here the central path and necessary visual 'reward' are partnered with two 'backed' borders spilling with frost-tender exotics such as *Echium pininana*.

Key theme plants

- *Buxus sempervirens* (common box; ❋❋❋ Z6–8) and cvs
- *Fagus sylvatica* (common beech; ❋❋❋ Z4–7) and cvs
- *Ilex crenata* (box-leaved holly; ❋❋❋ Z5–7) and cvs
- *Iris* (❋❋–❋❋❋ Z3–10, depending on spp/cvs)
- *Ligustrum delavayanum* (delavay privet; ❋❋❋ Z8–9)
- *Lilium regale* (regal lily; ❋❋❋ Z4–7) and cvs
- *Narcissus* (daffodil; ❋❋–❋❋❋ Z3–9, depending on spp/cvs)
- *Rosa* (rose; ❋❋–❋❋❋ Z2–10, depending on spp)
- *Taxus baccata* (yew; ❋❋❋ Z7–8) and cvs
- *Tulipa* (tulip; ❋❋–❋❋❋ Z3–9, depending on spp/cvs)
- *Wisteria* (❋❋❋ Z5–9, depending on spp)

TIPS FOR SUCCESS

- **Simplicity is essential:** Restrict your plant palette rather than including any- and everything you like.
- **Repetition:** Repeat key plants throughout; this brings necessary order.
- **Year-round performance:** In minimalist formal gardens, plants that perform for long periods are particularly important – evergreen shrubs (often clipped), topiary and grasses being first choice.
- **Be bold:** Avoid tiny groups of individual species; instead arrange plants in larger masses, in proportion to the space.
- **Lighten up:** Use pale flowers to brighten dark evergreens that might otherwise appear oppressive, especially in shade. Colourful spring and autumn bulbs are useful here.
- **Modern contrast:** In crisp, modernist interpretations a strong juxtaposition between vertical and horizontal forms is desirable: for example, fastigiate trees or columnar-shaped grasses contrasting with carpeting groundcover perennials or low, clipped topiary cubes.
- **Formal v. informal:** A formal layout doesn't necessarily require similarly formal planting. Many modern formal gardens feature naturalistic plantings within a crisp symmetric or asymmetric framework for contrast.

Focus on... cottage

Quintessential, romantic cottage gardens are much loved. They're informal, the mood is tranquil, the ambience relaxing. But at their origin, in the 19th century, practicality won out over appearance. Livestock, fruit and vegetables were the primary focus, with flowers chosen for their medicinal or edible qualities tucked in around the edges. However today's cottage garden – a stylised homage to its more productive predecessor – is literally packed with plants of all kinds. Fragrant roses and honeysuckle (*Lonicera*) tumble from archways, and arbours and containers burst with seasonal bedding plants, while colourful perennials spill from large beds and borders, with many allowed to self-sow and colonise cracks where they will.

Features & fittings

Cottage gardens exemplify abundance, but underneath all those plants a clear geometric pattern is common. In larger gardens, formality gives way to informality with winding paths further away from the house. This may not occur however if there's space allocated for fruit and vegetables; then a strict formal framework reappears for practical purposes.

Traditional materials are most appropriate and complement the often-eclectic mix of plants.

They also suggest the humble origins of this style. Terraces are commonly made from reclaimed bricks, weathered clay pavers or cobbles brushed with sand or screened topsoil, so lichen and moss may colonise the cracks. For paths, gravel or bark are similarly rustic choices; these allow plants to self-sow freely too.

For features and focal points, rustic wooden benches, Butler sinks, tin baths, stone statues and millstones add character and charm.

Left: Paths, paving and other hardscaping take a back seat to plants in a cottage garden. *Iris* 'Blue Rhythm', here partnered with pink lupins (*Lupinus*), blue *Delphinium* and purple ornamental onions (*Allium*), are all cottage garden classics.

Opposite, below: Modern cottage-inspired plantings often use fewer colours than traditional ones, repeating them throughout for harmony and to help unify the scheme. Pink *Delphinium* Astolat Group, valerian (*Centranthus lecoqii*) and mullein (*Verbascum* 'Cherry Helen') feature here, partnered with silver perennials and subshrubs including scotch thistle (*Onopordum acanthium*), wormwood (*Artemesia*) and Lambs' tongues (*Stachys byzantina* 'Big Ears').

AT A GLANCE

- intimate and abundant design style;
- dense and diverse plant collection, which typically peaks in summer;
- functional geometric layout, softened by profuse planting;
- complementary traditional or reclaimed materials such as woven hazel, brick paths, weathered natural stone, rusty steel, eclectic agricultural *objets d'art*.

Left: Abundant profuse planting is a key characteristic of both traditional cottage gardens and modern interpretations of them. At first glance the planting here might look as if it's been left to 'go wild', but the skill is to know when to intervene and when not to.

Above: Cottage gardens do need more maintenance than most other garden styles, so always provide somewhere to sit and immerse yourself in the fruits of your labour – it's only gardening after all. Here two heavily fragrant roses – rambling *Rosa* 'Francis E Lester' and climbing *R.* 'Alchymist' – are prizes for such endeavours.

Key theme plants

- *Alchemilla mollis* (lady's mantle; ✼✼✼ Z4–7) and cvs
- *Aquilegia vulgaris* (granny's bonnet; ✼✼✼ Z3–8) and cvs
- *Campanula lactiflora* (milky bellflower; ✼✼✼ Z5–7)
- *Clematis* (✼✼–✼✼✼ Z4–10, depending on spp/cvs)
- *Delphinium* (candle larkspur; ✼✼✼ Z3–8, depending on spp/cvs)
- *Deutzia* (✼✼✼ Z4–8, depending on spp/cvs)
- *Digitalis purpurea* (foxglove; ✼✼✼ Z4–8) and cvs
- *Erysimum cheiri* (wallflower; ✼✼✼ Z3–7) and cvs
- *Lavatera* (mallow; ✼✼–✼✼✼ Z7–15, depending on spp/cvs)
- *Lonicera periclymenum* (common honeysuckle; ✼✼✼ Z5–9) and cvs
- *Paeonia* (peony; ✼✼✼ Z3–8, depending on spp/cvs)
- *Phlox paniculata* (perennial phlox; ✼✼✼ Z4–8) and cvs
- *Rosa* (rose; ✼✼–✼✼✼ Z2–10, depending on spp/cvs)
- *Sidalcea malviflora* (checkerbloom; ✼✼✼ Z5–7) and cvs

Cottage gardens: Where this style works best...

Cottage gardens are suitable for people who love plants and have the time for necessary maintenance. While a traditional country cottage is the obvious partner, bold swathes of plants, rustic 'new' materials or traditional ones used in a modern way also complement more modern architecture.

Some shelter from strong winds is important. Many cottage garden classics such as hollyhocks (*Alcea*) won't survive in exposed spots. If you're planning a cottage garden from scratch, protective hedges or windbreaks should be considered and introduced first, if need be.

Above: Clematis (*Clematis* 'Barbara Dibley' in this image), foxgloves (*Digitalis*), rose campion (*Lychnis coronaria*) and oriental poppies (*Papaver orientale*) are a classic cottage combination. But a beautiful border such as this doesn't happen by accident, even if it might look as though it does.

Below: Deciding on a colour theme in the Gertrude Jekyll tradition is helpful to bring order to what might otherwise look chaotic. In these pink borders yarrow (*Achillea*), burnet (*Sanguisorba*), toadflax (*Linaria*) and loosestrife (*Lythrum*) jostle for star billing.

TIPS FOR SUCCESS

- **Structure first:** Hedges, trees and topiary throughout bring order, provide contrast and can help to differentiate one area or garden space from another. Structure the scheme first before considering colourful combinations of plants.
- **Keep it practical:** Cottage gardens do need work, so ensure the design layout is easy to navigate to make maintenance as easy and painless as possible.
- **The best-made plans:** Cottage garden planting may seem haphazard and unplanned, however it's anything but; the arrangements can be quite complex, so a plan is essential to start with.
- **Colour harmony:** While sometimes 'anything goes' in cottage gardens, a harmonious colour palette brings clarity to the composition. One area could be themed differently from the next by a range of colours; use decorative gates, arches or pergolas covered with fragrant climbers to herald the change perhaps.
- **Big is best:** Generous-sized beds and borders are essential. In a smaller garden the lawn is usually sacrificed to provide plenty of planting space.
- **Year-round interest:** Cottage gardens inevitably look best in spring and summer, but don't forget to include plenty of plants that perform in autumn and winter.
- **All mixed up:** Fruit and vegetables are often integrated into beds and borders. For small gardens choose attractive herbs and cut-and-come-again salads, for example, which are quick to mature and, here, rotation isn't necessary for success. Similarly robust runner beans and potatoes that cope with competition are good too.
- **Wildlife is crucial:** Simple, open-faced, nectar-rich flowers — particularly in early spring and autumn — and berrying shrubs will support birds and insects, which in turn help with pest control.

Focus on... productive

The edible garden has enjoyed a comeback in recent years, but the history of growing fruit and vegetables stretches back a long way. In medieval monasteries, monks created physic gardens, cultivating crops to heal body and mind in carefully organised beds and borders. During the Renaissance the French elevated the vegetable plot into an art form by creating the elaborate formal potager, in which edibles were intermingled with flowers in elegant geometric parterres. Several hundred years later saw the rise of the much-loved, 19th-century, walled kitchen garden, designed to serve the country houses of the rich and powerful. Productive gardens today typically have a formal framework: a geometric, often symmetrical, network of paths and beds (see pp90–93) or gardeners mix herbs and vegetables alongside ornamentals in more informal groupings.

Practical purpose

Whether the design is formal or informal, functionality is key in the productive garden. A simple layout with wide paths surfaced with gravel, brick or inexpensive natural stone paving is preferable – this makes it easy to move freely with heavy wheelbarrows. Decorative obelisks, hazel wigwams and rustic arches support runner beans, peas and gourds. Rectangular raised beds surrounded by oak railway sleepers, old scaffolding boards or treated softwood planks define areas for different crops and also improve drainage; it's also possible to provide the perfect soil for particular crops, regardless of what's underneath. Even delightful, small-scale design details – rhubarb forcers, oak water barrels and weathered terracotta pots for example – are practical at heart.

In the formal productive garden, box (*Buxus*) or lavender (*Lavandula*) hedges are often used to outline and frame beds and borders. However apples, pears and plums trained as traditional fan shapes, espaliers or low 'stepovers' will also provide fruit for the table. All should be braced using post-and-wire supports.

Below: Although this style has traditional roots, 'productive' certainly doesn't always mean 'rustic'. Instead designers constantly reinvent this style by introducing contemporary materials. Today weathered COR-TEN steel, powder-coated alloys, sawn cedar strips, shiny steel braid and even polished concrete feature in modern designs, all to bring the productive garden bang up to date.

AT A GLANCE

- formal geometric, often symmetrical layout with wide paths, sometimes edged in box;
- inexpensive, durable surface materials;
- strictly organised rows of fruit and vegetables, making maintenance easier;
- colourful annuals and perennials positioned to attract beneficial insects and deter pests;
- quirky reclaimed or repurposed *objets d'art*.

Top: Wide and durable paths – here, brick pavers and natural stone – are essential in the productive garden for easy maintenance. Note the unfussy, easy-to-navigate, formal layout too.

Above: In a simple vegetable garden, inspired by the French potager, vegetables are appreciated as much for their looks as their taste. Beautiful low hazel hurdles are used here to make raised beds. However they won't last nearly as long as treated softwood or oak planks.

Key theme plants

(excluding 'traditional' fruit & vegetables)

- *Allium* (ornamental onion; ✳✳–✳✳✳ Z3–10, depending on spp/cvs)
- *Angelica* (✳✳✳ Z4–9, depending on spp)
- *Buxus sempervirens* (common box; ✳✳✳ Z6–8) and cvs
- *Cynara cardunculus* (cardoon; ✳✳✳ Z7–10) and cvs
- *Ficus carica* (common fig; ✳✳✳ Z6–9) and cvs
- *Foeniculum vulgare* (fennel; ✳✳✳ Z4–9) and cvs
- *Lathyrus odoratus* (sweet pea; ✳✳✳ Z9–10) and cvs
- *Laurus nobilis* (bay laurel; ✳✳ Z8–11)
- *Lavandula angustifolia* (lavender; ✳✳✳ Z5–8) and cvs
- *Mentha* (mint; ✳✳✳ Z3–11, depending on spp)
- *Monarda* (bergamot; ✳✳✳ Z4–10, depending on spp/cvs)
- *Myrrhis odorata* (sweet Cicely; ✳✳✳ Z3–7)
- *Nepeta* × *faassenii* (catmint; ✳✳✳ Z4–8) and cvs
- *Origanum vulgare* (wild marjoram; ✳✳✳ Z4–9)
- *Ruta graveolens* (common rue; ✳✳✳ Z5–9) and cvs
- *Salvia officinalis* (sage; ✳✳✳ Z5–8) and cvs

Productive gardens: Where this style works best...

The 'allotment-look' can appear messy and works best at the bottom of the garden, partially screened from view. However formal productive gardens edged in box or low hazel (*Corylus*) hurdles are attractive, and the trend nowadays is to bring such areas closer to the house. They also have strong geometry in common with most houses, thereby creating all-important links.

TIPS FOR SUCCESS

- **Which crops?** Maintenance requirements such as watering and pest and disease controls determine what you can grow. Be realistic; a full-blown kitchen garden sounds idyllic but needs work. Instead perennial herbs such as thyme (*Thymus*) and rosemary (*Rosmarinus*) or soft fruit such as red and white currants can be grown in colourful, low-maintenance, ornamental mixed plantings. Or grow crops in large pots; unlike small containers, these won't need watering and feeding so often, thereby reducing maintenance time. Root vegetables such as potatoes and carrots relish lots of room in particular.
- **Looks count:** Choose attractive crops. When combining them consider their form, colour, texture and scent; steely blue leeks for example contrast well with red-leaved lettuce.
- **Good design:** In winter the productive garden reveals its bare bones, so a strong framework with beds bordered with box (*Buxus*), step-over apples or saw-tooth bricks look good, particularly if the whole garden is themed this way. Include bold, eye-catching focal points too – standard bay laurel (*Laurus noblis*) or roses are common and abstract sculpture suits contemporary designs.
- **Introduce height:** Obelisks and arches punctuate the design and support climbing crops. Use boundary walls and fences too. Sculptural, fan-trained or espaliered fruit trees are useful.
- **Include utilities:** Always allocate space for a compost heap, rainwater storage barrels, a small shed – even a cold frame or greenhouse.
- **Crop rotation:** This is particularly important for beans, brassicas, onions and root crops. Consider this when planning the number of beds. All good books on growing fruit and vegetables will explain crop rotation in detail; look there for help.

Opposite: No room for a dedicated vegetable patch? Arrange plants in the same way you'd organise ornamental beds and borders; many crops are very attractive. Violets (*Viola* 'Bowles's Black'), Swiss chard (*Beta vulgaris* 'Rhubarb Chard'), chives (*Allium schoenoprasum*) and red orache (*Atriplex hortensis* var. *rubra*) feature here.

Left: Plants sown in rows and blocks can be architecturally striking and, of course, it's practical too; crops are much easier to manage this way.

Focus on... urban

Urban gardens reveal elements of many different styles and themes. With those that don't have a fine view, it's not uncommon to find a jungle paradise or a cottage-inspired courtyard right in the centre of the city. But less is always more. Urban gardens are small in size but have to be all things to all people and serve numerous different wants and needs, so a simple, clear layout is best. Designs based on squares or rectangles always fit well and make good use of available space. A touch of formality is usual, helping to forge connections with the urban architecture.

People or plants?

In an urban situation, designers usually approach the planting design in two distinct ways. The first is to sacrifice the space used for rest and relaxation and give it over instead for plants – and sometimes fruit and vegetables. The second strategy is the exact opposite, and the most common, as it's unlikely there will be room for diverse collections, even if a design layout is offset at angles to the boundaries to open up larger areas for planting. Here the plant palette is simplified to maximise usable space with plants chosen not only for colour or scent but also with a structural or functional role in mind – providing privacy for example. Low maintenance is usually important too. Such a 'people come first' approach does restrict options. However with careful planning there's no reason why an urban garden based on the second design approach can't still be beautiful.

Right: In urban gardens, plants usually contribute to the spatial framework of the design. Large ones are also asked to perform additional roles such as providing privacy and screening, whether they're clipped like these 'boxed' holm oaks (*Quercus ilex*) – or not.

AT A GLANCE

- legible, flexible, easy-to-manoeuvre layout;
- bold focal point to reward the eye and 'full-stop' the space;
- modern materials and/or traditional ones introduced in a modern way;
- minimal, bold, often architectural planting, with the repetition of key specimens;
- formal backbone of architectural evergreens, clipped topiary and informal or formal hedges with sometimes little else in the way of planting.

Urban gardens: Where this style works best...

Clean lines, clear design geometry, architectural form and hardworking planting – all characteristics that define the urban 'style' – suit almost any garden where space is tight.

Key theme plants

- *Allium* (ornamental onion; ✱✱–✱✱✱ Z3–10, depending on spp/cvs)
- *Buxus sempervirens* (common box; ✱✱✱ Z6–8) and cvs
- *Carpinus betulus* 'Fastigiata' (fastigiate hornbeam; ✱✱✱ Z4–8)
- *Euphorbia characias* subsp. *wulfenii* (spurge; ✱✱ Z7–10) and cvs
- *Geranium himalayense* (cranesbill; ✱✱✱ Z4–7) and cvs
- *Heuchera* (coral flower; ✱✱✱ Z3–9, depending on spp/cvs)
- *Hosta* (plantain lily; ✱✱✱ Z3–9, depending on spp/cvs)
- *Iris germanica* (✱✱✱ Z3–8) and cvs
- *Magnolia grandiflora* (bull bay; ✱✱ Z7–9) and cvs
- *Miscanthus sinensis* (silver grass; ✱✱✱ Z6–9) and cvs
- *Pittosporum tobira* (Japanese mock orange; ✱ Z9–10) and cvs
- *Quercus ilex* (holm oak; ✱✱✱ Z4–8) and cvs
- *Trachelospermum asiaticum* (✱✱✱ Z7–11)

TIPS FOR SUCCESS

- **Plant performance:** Choose plants that look good for long periods and have more than one role; there just isn't space for one-season wonders.
- **Prioritise:** You simply won't be able to fit in all your favourite plants. Be prepared to make sacrifices.
- **Shape up:** Form and foliage are more important than flowers. Dramatic palms, topiary and pleached trees with attractive leaves or a sculptural shape are invaluable.
- **Be bold:** Dwarf plants and/or tiny groups make a small space feel even smaller, so don't miniaturise the planting even if your garden is small.
- **Space savers:** Tall-but-thin grasses, perennials, bamboos and fastigiate shrubs, repeated en masse for impact, are a good strategy where there are space restrictions. These are sometimes planted in containers (usually in threes or fives) for drama. Clipped topiary is also good for pots. Urban gardens often don't have room for wide beds and borders and can't accommodate deep, layered compositions, especially those featuring larger, mounding shrubs; these soon dwarf narrow borders and affect proportional harmony.
- **Look up:** Boundary walls and fences offer the most scope for planting and can support many different climbers and wall shrubs that won't take up too much ground space.
- **Bulbs are brilliant:** These occupy little space. Select species to emerge in spring, summer and autumn for a dynamic, ever-changing scene.

Left, above: Plants as architecture: an evergreen rosemary (*Rosmarinus*) hedge and three olive (*Olea*) trees help to divide off and partially screen a formal seating space from an informal one on this high-rise terrace.

Left, below: Where space is tight, think vertical. In this relaxed design, clipped medlar (*Mespilus germanica*) trees 'ceiling' a seating space, while a fire bowl in the middle provides the focus, especially at night.

Opposite, above: A simple, Mediterranean-inspired garden where people come first. Floriferous perennials such as blue African lilies (*Agapanthus*) and *Gaura lindheimeri* bring welcome colour. A clipped privet (*Ligustrum*) hedge on the left and olive (*Olea*) trees in raised beds on the right help to screen neighbouring gardens.

Opposite, below: With plants that have a structural or spatial design role, foliage and outline are most important to consider.

Focus on... exotic

The exotic garden, full of bold, dramatic plants, is a design style that's relatively easy to create successfully in all locations, except where there's regular heavy snowfall. An informal organic layout is most common, with reflective pools, gravel and bark paths, decking and eclectic sculpture completing the look. Plants, however, are the principal design tools, chosen not just for colour and scent but also for defining circulation routes, creating pools of space for different functions and teasing views from one space to the next.

Hardy exotics

Thanks to plant hunters there are hundreds of plants from which to evoke that steamy, jungle-like ambience. Hardiness is an important factor to consider. In temperate climates, popular exotics such as ginger lily (*Hedychium*) and Indian shot plant (*Canna*) can't cope with frost. Strong winds desiccate or rip large leaves too – one reason why exotic plantings work so well in warm, wind-still city gardens. For exposed spots, choose hardy plants that look suitably tropical. Flax (*Phormium*), Christmas berry (*Photinia* × *fraseri* 'Red Robin'), elephant's ears (*Bergenia*) and plantain lily (*Hosta*) all have bold colourful leaves and are tough enough to cope with heavy frosts; this reliability makes them ideal structural plants. You can still grow tender species in cool-temperate climates – just bring them under cover or wrap them in horticultural fleece when the temperature drops.

Do note that even in small exotic gardens underpinned by clear geometry, plants are encouraged to soften – even hide – edges and boundaries. Exotic plantings work well in crisp modernist and minimalist designs too. One or two architectural specimens used en masse suit the pared-back approach perfectly.

AT A GLANCE

- relaxed, informal, abundant aesthetic;
- dramatic plants with big and bold-textured leaves;
- dense planting that blurs garden boundaries;
- minimal hardscaping;
- quirky design details often chosen with a specific geographical location in mind.

Left: Tropical half-hardy favourites such as Indian shot plant – here *Canna* 'Orange Punch' and *C.* 'Corsica' (Island Series) – accompanied by a frost-hardy sage (*Salvia* 'Indigo Spires') and *Diascia personata* with a floss flower (*Ageratum houstonianum* 'Blue Bouquet') in front , withstand temperatures only down to 0°C (32°F). Therefore in frost-prone climates they need protection, typically by lifting the rhizomes in autumn for winter storage inside. If frost isn't common but nevertheless possible, leave *in situ* and mulch heavily with compost.

Opposite: Small town gardens are warmer than gardens in the country, so exotics such as loquat (*Eriobotrya japonica*) and silver spear (*Astelia*), which are only frost-hardy, often thrive in urban areas without the need to protect them over winter.

Exotic gardens: Where this style works best…

This style works well in urban gardens, especially sheltered courtyards and basements (see pp208–211) – these are the urban equivalent of a forest or jungle floor. Urban gardens are also warmer than their exposed country cousins, which means some frost-hardy, even tender, species can often be grown without protection.

TIPS FOR SUCCESS

- **Cover up:** Plant densely so you see no soil. Under larger plants grow ferns and tough, exotic-looking perennials to cover every centimetre.
- **Think vertical:** Introduce plenty of height to create a jungle-like canopy. In temperate climates, loquat, Chusan palm and cabbage palm (*Cordyline australis*) are useful – buy big specimens for instant impact. Usefully, all can support annual climbers such as cup and saucer plant (*Cobaea scandens*) if they're grown on the sunniest side of the garden. Taller hardy exotics can also be planted so they shelter tender plants below.
- **Big and bold:** Plants with dramatic, colourful, textured foliage and strong form are essential. Contrast is key here; partner sword-like flax with mounding honey spurge for example.
- **Contrasting colour:** Green is the most common hue in an exotic garden but add splashes of bold colour throughout for interest. Bear's breeches (*Acanthus*), African blue lily and crimson flag lily (*Hesperantha*) are ideal for temperate climates.
- **Multicoloured leaves?** Avoid too many variegated plants, especially in more natural-looking designs. Introduce them sparingly.
- **Clever tricks:** Dark foliage around the perimeter will help the planting recede into the distance, making the whole garden feel bigger than it actually is. Position plants with bright leaves or strong, eye-catching shapes in the foreground.

Opposite: The more plants the merrier in the exotic garden. Always plant to cover every centimetre of soil.

Right, above: In frost-prone areas, tender exotic favourites such as angels' trumpets (*Brugmansia*) should be grown in containers and overwintered in a glasshouse or conservatory, and stood outside only in summer. In small gardens or if space under glass is limited, keep tender plants to a minimum and choose hardy exotics instead, which can stay outside year-round.

Right, below: Foliage in all shapes and sizes is essential to this style. In this warm protected garden, Catalina ironwood (*Lyonothamnus floribundus* subsp. *aspleniifolius*), *Schefflera alpina*, *S. hoi*, *Echium pininana* and Japanese angelica tree (*Aralia elata*) all thrive.

Key theme plants (for temperate climates)

- *Agapanthus campanulatus* (African blue lily; ❋❋❋ Z7–15) and cvs
- *Astelia nervosa* (silver spear; ❋❋❋ Z8–9) and cvs
- *Chamaerops humilis* (dwarf fan palm; ❋ Z12–14)
- *Crocosmia* (montbretia; ❋❋–❋❋❋ Z6–11, depending on spp/cvs)
- *Dicksonia antarctica* (soft tree fern; ❋❋ Z11–15)
- *Eriobotrya japonica* (loquat; ❋❋ Z8–11)
- *Euphorbia mellifera* (honey spurge; ❋❋ Z9–10)
- *Fargesia robusta* (❋❋❋ Z5–9) and cvs
- *Fatsia japonica* (Japanese aralia; ❋❋ Z8–10) and cvs
- *Macleaya* (plume poppy; ❋❋❋ Z4–9, depending on spp)
- *Melianthus major* (honey bush; ❋❋ Z8–11)
- *Musa basjoo* (Japanese banana; ❋❋ Z8–11)
- *Phormium* (flax; ❋❋ Z9–11)
- *Trachycarpus fortunei* (Chusan palm; ❋❋ Z8–11)

Focus on... Japanese

Japanese gardens are fascinating and much loved throughout the world. While the Japanese *karesansui* (rock-and-gravel Zen garden) probably springs to mind, there are however numerous other Japanese styles, including *kaiyū shiki-teien* (stroll garden) and the famous *chaniwa* (tea garden). Each shares similarities, but also features distinct differences, which are important to note if a particular style is for you.

Spiritual foundations

All Japanese styles pay homage to the natural landscape, which is seen as sacred and sometimes reflected 'in miniature'. A deep spirituality also often informs the design too, with religious and cultural beliefs key, particularly in traditional gardens where asymmetry rules. For these reasons, indicative design details such as boulders and rock, gravel, water and key plants like Japanese maples (*Acer palmatum*)

Right: Water, gravel, boulders and rocks, plus contorted trees (here a pine, *Pinus*) and moss, are design details indicative of many Japanese gardens, particularly more traditional designs such as this.

AT A GLANCE

- *kanso* (simplicity) is essential. Over-elaborate design details are out, which helps create calm and contemplative spaces, ideal for rest and relaxation;
- water – whether a still pond, running stream or a 'river' of gravel – is symbolic of the sea and commonplace. When gravel represents water, the rocks are islands, mountains, even boats;
- restrained choice of hardscaping, in particular natural materials, which in more traditional designs partner highly symbolic ornaments such as *chozubachi* (water basins);
- pared-back planting palette where plant form and foliage are as important, often more so, than flowers.

Key theme plants

- *Acer palmatum* (Japanese maple; ❈❈❈ Z5–8, depending on cv)
- *Chaenomeles speciosa* (Japanese quince; ❈❈❈ Z5–9) and cvs
- *Chamaecyparis obtusa* (Hinoki cypress; ❈❈❈ Z4–8) and cvs
- *Cornus kousa* (Chinese dogwood; ❈❈❈ Z5–8) and cvs
- *Fargesia* (❈❈❈ Z5–9, depending on spp/cvs)
- *Ophiopogon japonicus* (lilyturf; ❈❈❈ Z7–10) and cvs
- *Phyllostachys nigra* (black bamboo; ❈❈❈ Z7–11) and cvs
- *Prunus* × *subhirtella* (Higan cherry; ❈❈❈ Z6–8) and cvs
- *Rhododendron indicum* (azalea; ❈❈❈ Z7–10)

are highly symbolic and meticulously placed, with space, proportion and their surroundings in mind. In modern designs, hewn stone, glass, polished concrete and stainless steel might also feature.

The different and complex underlying philosophy behind Japanese gardens and their distinctive appearance mean that the various styles can be tricky to pull off successfully, especially by Westerners. However the principles of proportion, balance, contrast and the clarity of specific design details – including the sculptural way they're used – are lessons to learn and apply everywhere.

TIPS FOR SUCCESS

- **Subtle, controlled contrast is key:** Consciously partner plants with distinctly different forms and textures. Vertical, multistemmed deciduous trees, also chosen for their autumn tints or spring flowers, commonly contrast with flat green ground cover for example. In small gardens, evergreen pines (*Pinus*) – to suggest longevity – are sometimes pruned into contorted shapes and placed singly against neutral backgrounds, so that they stand out.
- **Form & foliage:** In traditional Japanese design, floriferous perennials are rare – these are essentially a Western phenomenon. However in modern designs they're often included in a creative fusion of East meets West; just don't overdo it.
- **Essential evergreens:** Include plenty of green shrubs, clipped into organic, often amorphous forms. Cherish *Camellia*, *Rhododendron* and *Pieris* for their flowers.
- **Go easy on the variegation:** Variegated plants are uncommon in Japanese planting design, so use them sparingly and certainly not as large focal points to attract the eye.
- **Include green ground cover:** Plants such as Japanese spurge (*Pachysandra terminalis*) feature often as ground cover in Japanese gardens and act as a foil for taller ornamentals. In shady spots, moss is widely used.

Japanese gardens: Where this style works best...

Japan, obviously! Elsewhere be inspired by elements that form the various styles; just avoid a pastiche that will stick out like a sore thumb. Use key plants and copy some of the combinations while perhaps avoiding highly symbolic ornamentation.

Focus on... Italianate

Italian formal style is a look that's loved the world over for its simple geometry, grey-green planting and earthy design details such as travertine and terracotta. Scent, trompe l'œil to deceive the eye, idiosyncratic sculpture and splashing water are found in traditional designs and modern interpretations. In the Italian garden there's something to stimulate all the senses.

The bigger picture

Formal Italian gardens are often included under the general banner of Mediterranean gardens, because of their geographical location. However the Mediterranean style also features informal gardens mulched with gravel (see pp122–125). As both these different 'looks' have never been more popular, it's important to differentiate informal Mediterranean or 'gravel' gardens from formal geometric gardens in the Renaissance (and Spanish) tradition.

As mentioned on p90, the Italians were heavyweights in the development of 'formal' garden style, so what applies there also applies here. However, it's the design details, particularly the planting palette, that makes Italianate design so distinctive and worth a separate mention.

Right: Whether they are traditional designs or modern interpretations with an Italianate influence, a formal layout is commonplace, as are simple sculptural evergreens and conifers. Here four (of five) Italian cypress (*Cupressus sempervirens*) stand to attention while clipped burkwood osmanthus (*Osmanthus × burkwoodii*) gives structure to a sea of silvery subshrubs and colourful perennials.

AT A GLANCE

- precise, often rectilinear axial design geometry, a feature shared by all formal gardens, regardless of whether the design is themed with a particular region in mind;
- natural 'earthy' materials such as travertine and oak used sparingly and simply;
- strong structural form – columnar trees or clipped topiary bring vertical interest, perhaps in a regimented pattern, to reinforce design geometry or, more informally, for contrast;
- clipped evergreen trees and shrubs and low evergreen hedges used to separate and define planting from people space;
- shade in hot Mediterranean climates, provided by tidy, perhaps trimmed, umbrella-shaped trees, a pergola or parasol, is key to this style;
- water in rills or still, reflective rectangular pools is very common in formal Italianate gardens.

Above, left: Greens, in every tint and shade, and silver are commonplace, so too are splashes of vibrant colour to lift a scheme, here provided by an African blue lily (*Agapanthus*).

Above, right: A sleek modern roof terrace in London, England, with obvious Italian influences. While a hardy oleander (*Nerium*) provides protection from strong prevailing winds, spiky *Agave americana* 'Mediopicta', lavender (*Lavandula angustifolia*) and *Libertia ixioides* 'Goldfinger' all tolerate some exposure.

TIPS FOR SUCCESS

- **Sun-lovers:** Grey-green or silvery plants such as lavender, which have adapted to hot sun, are essential to evoke this theme. But do note that most will thrive only in a sunny spot with free-draining soil.
- **Contrasting colour:** In Italian gardens perennials are subservient to simple evergreen shrubs and subshrubs. However, punches of vibrant blues, reds, purples and yellows, which come to the fore in hot sun, are useful for contrast, whether they appear in clearly defined areas or are allowed to seed more freely. These will brighten dark evergreens too.
- **Scent-sational:** Spicy, camphor or pine-like scents from shrubs including rosemary, myrtle and oregano are most representative of Italian gardens – the more the merrier.
- **Repeat:** A feature common to all formal gardens – regardless of the theme – is repetition. This makes for a unified and unfussy design.

Italianate gardens: Where this style works best...

Home base might be southern Europe, but other regions like coastal California also have a Mediterranean climate, so this style works well visually there too. Elsewhere, choose symbolic plants and design details rather than going for a full-blown imitation.

Key theme plants

- *Arbutus unedo* (strawberry tree; ✼✼✼ Z8–9) and cvs
- *Buxus microphylla* (small-leaved box; ✼✼✼ Z6–9) and cvs
- *Cupressus sempervirens* (Italian cypress; ✼✼✼ Z7–9) and cvs
- *Euphorbia epithymoides* (spurge; ✼✼✼ Z5–9)
- *Iris* bearded types (✼✼✼ Z3–9, depending on spp/cvs)
- *Laurus nobilis* (bay laurel; ✼✼ Z8–11)
- *Lavandula lanata* (lavender; ✼✼ Z8–9)
- *Myrtus communis* (common myrtle; ✼✼ Z8–9) and cvs
- *Olea europaea* (olive; ✼✼ Z8–10)
- *Origanum vulgare* (wild marjoram; ✼✼✼ Z4–9) and cvs
- *Phillyrea angustifolia* (narrow-leaved mock privet; ✼✼✼ Z7–9)
- *Rosmarinus officinalis* (rosemary; ✼✼ Z8–11) and cvs
- *Salvia officinalis* (common sage; ✼✼✼ Z5–8)

Focus on... naturalistic

Naturalistic planting has never been more popular. With sustainability and a growing appreciation of nature being big design drivers, this trend will continue. The way plants are arranged is the most distinctive characteristic. Swathes of single species are common, as is the intermingling of plants, sometimes in seemingly random matrices, to reflect natural patterns of plants in the wild. But this doesn't mean creating a pastiche. Nor are native plants a necessity. Non-natives needing similar conditions are included, sometimes in formal designs with an urban backdrop, providing the order that helps prevent the composition from looking messy.

Eco thinking

An ecological approach is the other distinguishing factor in naturalistic gardens. Plants are matched to the soil and climatic conditions of the space, on the premise that plants grown where they're naturally happiest (in conditions mirroring those in the wild) should be sustainable and therefore low-maintenance. Dominant spreaders and self-sowers are excluded, particularly in smaller spaces. Instead plants are chosen for their mutual compatibility, the aim being to create plant communities where the gardener's intervention isn't necessary for success.

The concept of combining plants in a natural way isn't new. William Robinson explored the idea in 1870, with German nurseryman Karl Foerster and Danish-American Jens Jensen following soon after. Key exponents today include German gardeners and designers such as Cassian Schmidt, and the Dutchmen Henk Gerristen and Piet Oudolf – originators of the 'new perennial style'. Beth Chatto, Dan Pearson, Keith Wiley, Noel Kingsbury and Sheffield University's Landscape Department in the UK are also worth noting, as is the design practice Oehme Van Sweden in the USA. It would be remiss to ignore their influence and their inspiration.

AT A GLANCE
(characteristics common to all styles)

- careful plant selection considering site characteristics and plant performance, often evoking a particular natural habitat or location such as woodland or prairie;
- relaxed informal associations, the planting design sometimes combined with crisp geometry for contrast and order;
- repetitive palette of plants, arranged in natural-looking patterns;
- large mass of plants arranged in seemingly uninterrupted groups.

Above left: Seed-sown naturalistic plantings inspired by meadows are gaining in popularity, as there is no easier way to create a truly natural-looking effect. The plants are carefully selected for their mutual compatibility, with the unpredictable nature of the scheme – what plant emerges and where – embraced as a key part of the design.

Above right: Right plant, right place and succession are always considered carefully. Royal fern (*Osmunda regalis*), shuttlecock fern (*Matteuccia struthiopteris*), *Rodgersia* and bluebells (*Hyacinthoides*) all thrive in this moist semishaded site. Each plant has also been chosen to complement, not compete with, the others around it.

Left: Most people's ideas of naturalistic planting are prairie-inspired, 'new perennial' schemes such as this. But while this might be the most recognisable, designers also create naturalistic plantings inspired by numerous other habitats – from exposed cliff tops to shady woodland.

Naturalistic: Woodland

Shade is common to almost all gardens but is seen as problematic by many gardeners. However appreciating that dense shade is similar to a forest floor and that semishade is akin to woodland and woodland margins helps to identify appropriate plants. Usefully, it will also determine the most pleasing ways to combine plants in arrangements that appear perfectly at home in their shady setting.

TIPS FOR SUCCESS

- **Degrees of shade:** Few plants will grow in deep shade, yet protection from the midday sun is essential, as many woodlanders are quite delicate. Semi- or dappled shade is best.
- **Damp or dry?** Damp shade is found with heavy clay and peaty soils, while dry shade is common under hedges, buildings and particularly dense trees. However, unless a tree canopy brushes the ground, many plants will still thrive here – just as they do in the wild.
- **Overhead aware:** The density of tree cover is also important to note. The higher it is the better. Consider lifting the crown of trees and removing lower branches to let in more light. The taller the tree the higher you can lift the branches.
- **Soil preparation:** Dig in copious amounts of organic matter prior to planting, to get plants off to a good start; cultivate carefully, to avoid damaging the roots. Mulch annually.
- **Add evergreens:** Most woodland flowers peak in spring – many go dormant in summer once the leaf canopy closes over. In small gardens where gaps for long periods aren't acceptable, evergreen perennials and ferns are useful. Their reliability also makes them important structural plants.

Naturalistic woodland: Where this style works best...

Given partial or dappled shade, a tranquil woodland-like effect can be created in almost any garden. Unlike new-perennial or prairie-like naturalistic plantings (see pp118–121), woodland-inspired schemes work really well on even a tiny scale – under a single tree perhaps or in a tight bed bordering a shady side passageway.

AT A GLANCE

- relaxed, often informal layout. Where the whole garden is woodland themed – not just the planting – bark paths, wooden decking, timber sleepers and log edgings are common;
- to maximise available light, green is the most common leaf colour, so designers carefully consider shape and texture, plus the outline form of plants, and combine for contrast accordingly;
- *Skimmia*, Oregon grape (*Mahonia*), *Viburnum* and other woodland shrubs are bulky, shade-tolerant structural plants, and are used sparingly, while ferns and groundcover perennials make up the majority of the planting.

Key theme plants

- *Actaea simplex* (bugbane; ❋❋❋ Z4–8) and cvs
- *Brunnera macrophylla* (Siberian bugloss; ❋❋❋ Z3–7) and cvs
- *Dicentra* (bleeding heart; ❋❋❋ Z3–9, depending on spp)
- *Digitalis purpurea* (foxglove; ❋❋❋ Z4–8) and cvs
- *Epimedium* (barrenwort; ❋❋❋ Z4–9, depending on spp)
- Ferns (numerous)
- *Geranium phaeum* (dusky cranesbill; ❋❋❋ Z4–8) and cvs
- *Helleborus* (hellebore; ❋❋❋ Z4–9, depending on spp)
- *Lamium orvala* (dead nettle; ❋❋❋ Z4–9)
- *Polygonatum odoratum* (Solomon's seal; ❋❋❋ Z3–8) and cvs
- *Pulmonaria saccharata* (Jerusalem sage; ❋❋❋ Z4–8) and cvs

Left: A naturalistic tapestry-like woodland planting such as this needs as much space as possible for plants. In a shady garden, consider sacrificing a patchy lawn perhaps – grass struggles to grow well in shade anyway.

Naturalistic: New perennial

Also known as 'new wave', 'Dutch wave' and 'prairie' planting, this naturalistic style is probably the most well known, due to high-profile projects such as New York City's High Line and the landscape surrounding the Hauser & Wirth gallery in Somerset, England – both by Piet Oudolf.

As the name suggests, perennials – particularly late-season species such as coneflower (*Rudbeckia*) and bergamot (*Monarda*) – are combined with ornamental grasses to create a composition reminiscent of sweeping American prairies, continental steppes and, to a certain extent, wildflower meadows.

Small space?

Massed new perennial plantings have come under criticism for their lack of winter interest and the huge spaces deemed necessary to appreciate this style. However with subtle tweaks it can work in all but the smallest gardens, if you have moist, free-draining soil and a sunny position.

A strong structural framework is vital. Clipped topiary and sculptural hedging in geometric patterns are often first choice, especially for modernist and minimalist designers. These order the planting, complement architecture of all styles, provide contrast and focus attention in winter and spring when the theme plants – grasses and perennials – are bulking up.

On a smaller scale the plants also need arranging differently. Huge blocks and drifts of single species are traditional in a landscape context; however these aren't feasible in most gardens. Gaps are also obvious. In a garden setting, plants are therefore arranged in smaller groups and often intermingled. Interestingly this creates a composition more akin to the way plants associate in nature.

Below: New-perennial planting and slick contemporary hardscape make for an attractive juxtaposition of formal versus informal – a trend common to all naturalistic planting styles.

Right: A masterclass by Piet Oudolf, in collaboration with architect Peter Zumthor, on how naturalistic, prairie-like planting can work beautifully in a small space, here in a temporary display in the Serpentine Gallery Pavilion in London, England. Note the beautiful juxtaposition between formal modern architecture and informal planting.

Below: Working with just one or two colours is an easy way to unify intermingled mixed plantings. The beech (*Fagus*) hedge at the back (which also features elsewhere in this garden) unifies the scheme on a larger scale too. Note the contrasting flower forms of plants including feather grass (*Stipa calamagrostis*), bistort (*Persicaria amplexicaulis* 'Firedance') and giant hyssop (*Agastache* 'Blackadder').

New perennial gardens: Where this style works best...

The more space the better; in gardens, 'open' borders are necessary. Inevitably this means sacrificing a lawn to either a series of clearly defined beds in more formal layouts or to a sea of plants dissected by snaking paths in informal gardens. If plants are chosen carefully, then maintenance time should be minimal.

TIPS FOR SUCCESS

- **Attractive for ages:** Choose robust perennials with a long flowering season and, ideally, striking seedheads, to prolong the season of interest. Spring and summer bulbs also help here.
- **Repetition is essential:** Don't use too many distinctly different plants.
- **Also focus on form:** Leaf shapes and the forms of flowers (see p136), along with stems and seedheads, are just as important as flower colour.
- **Easy on the shrubs:** A few may be included on the boundaries or as large focal points throughout, but grasses or repetitive groups of a similar, long-lasting perennial are basically what structure the planting.
- **Maintenance-free:** Avoid disease-prone plants and those that need staking or deadheading. Aggressive species aren't suitable either. *Dream Plants for the Natural Garden* by Henk Gerritsen and Piet Oudolf lists numerous appropriate choices.

Key theme plants

- *Achillea millefolium* (yarrow; ✿✿✿ Z3–9) and cvs
- *Calamagrostis × acutiflora* (feather reed grass; ✿✿✿ Z5–9) and cvs
- *Coreopsis verticillata* (tickseed; ✿✿✿ Z4–9) and cvs
- *Deschampsia cespitosa* (tufted hair grass; ✿✿✿ Z5–9) and cvs
- *Echinacea* (coneflower; ✿✿✿ Z3–9, depending on spp)
- *Echinops* (globe thistle; ✿✿✿ Z3–10, depending on spp)
- *Eupatorium maculatum* (Joe Pye weed; ✿✿✿ Z5–11) and cvs
- *Helenium* (Helen's flower; ✿✿✿ Z4–8)
- *Helianthus × multiflorus* (perennial sunflower; ✿✿✿ Z5–9)
- *Kniphofia rooperi* (red hot poker; ✿✿✿ Z6–9)
- *Miscanthus sinensis* (silver grass; ✿✿✿ Z6–9) and cvs
- *Panicum virgatum* (switch grass; ✿✿✿ Z5–9) and cvs
- *Persicaria amplexicaulis* (bistort; ✿✿✿ Z3–8) and cvs
- *Rudbeckia fulgida* (black-eyed Susan; ✿✿✿ Z4–9) and cvs
- *Stipa* (feathergrass; ✿✿✿ Z7–15, depending on spp)
- *Thalictrum aquilegiifolium* (meadow rue; ✿✿✿ Z5–9) and cvs
- *Veronicastrum virginicum* (culver's root; ✿✿✿ Z4–8) and cvs

Top: The rise in popularity of this planting style has meant the introduction of many 'new' perennials such as this coneflower (*Echinacea purpurea* 'Rubinglow'), thereby giving gardeners more choice than ever before.

Above: Tall members of the daisy family such as yellow coneflowers (here, *Rudbeckia fulgida* var. *deamii*) and New England asters (here, purple *Symphyotrichum novae-angliae* 'Septemberrubin') are key plants in prairie-like schemes. Many actually originate from North America, so there's no better way to 'get the prairie look'.

Opposite: In this small town garden, whimsical topiary adds a welcome formal note to the naturalistic perennial planting around it.

Naturalistic: Gravel

Although the formal Italianate garden (see pp112–113) is certainly indicative of Mediterranean 'style' and features similar plants, the informal gravel garden is perhaps what first comes to mind in this genre. It's a relaxed, informal, naturalistic planting style where the division between planting and paths isn't obvious, and it is ideal for gardeners with hot, dry, sunny conditions. Gravel, which acts like organic mulch, is a key component, but the planting inspired by the maquis shrubland of the Mediterranean basin and the Californian chaparral, for example, is the most evocative. Plants with hairy, needle-like, fine or silvery grey leaves feature extensively – each being a natural adaptation to the hot dry conditions prevalent in these climates.

Origins

Beth Chatto has done more than most to popularise this naturalistic style. Her Mediterranean-inspired gravel garden in Essex, England, is world famous, not just for her design but also for her pioneering approach of 'right plant, right place', which today we take for granted. The whole garden is based on ecological principles, that of looking at native habitats for inspiration. But plants aren't just chosen from one geographical location; instead those from similar habitats worldwide are included to broaden the planting possibilities. Ecology aside, plants that come from comparable areas will inevitably share similar visual characteristics. This helps create a unified composition, and is useful for evoking a strong sense of place.

Right: While designers today love to reinvent this style – here, Andy Sturgeon has introduced a modernist layout and contemporary hardscape details – the informal planting indicative of the style rarely changes. In this scheme, the planting softens the crisp layout and design details perfectly.

AT A GLANCE

- relaxed, informal layout with planting areas and paths covered with gravel;
- dense, glaucous green, olive-green and silvery mixed plantings combined in large groups, each arranged in layers with height in mind;
- in hot climates (such as warm-temperate and Mediterranean), trees and pergolas covered in fragrant climbers for casting dappled shade;
- terracotta pots, natural travertine and limestone, small water features, painted tiles and perhaps boulders are the design details of choice, but with contemporary design anything often goes.

Gravel gardens: Where this style works best...

This informal style complements architecture of all designs and, if plants are matched to place, is ideal where low maintenance is desired. A relatively dry climate, free-draining soil and sunny position are essential. In maritime climates, winter wet can cause problems, so choose ultra-reliable plants, some of which might not originate from Mediterranean climates, yet look 'Mediterranean' nevertheless. Use restraint with symbolic design details too, such as glazed amphora-shaped pots; they can look incongruous in the wrong setting.

Right: Beth Chatto's gravel garden features plants from similar climates around the world, all chosen for their ability to thrive in this hot, dry site. As each plant has adapted to similar climatic conditions, it also now shares similar visual characteristics too, which helps to create a unified composition.

TIPS FOR SUCCESS

- **Balance:** Always aim for a healthy ratio of plants to gravel: two-thirds plants to one-third gravel is the minimum. Smaller groups at different densities look best. Repetition is important for unity of design.
- **Continuing interest:** Bright perennials bring most colour, but conifers, shorter small-leaved shrubs, evergreen grasses and ground cover are essential for year-round interest and structure.
- **Eye-catching accents:** Use form and colour to punch up through what can be quite flat planting; taller bulbs including ornamental onions (*Allium*) and Sicilian honey garlic (*Nectaroscordum siculum*) are ideal. For a natural effect, sprinkle these around foreground perennials.
- **Avoid straight lines:** Instead finish plantings in sweeping curves, so that the boundary between paths and planting in informal design layouts is indistinct.
- **Self-sowers:** Embrace plants such as California poppy (*Eschscholzia californica*), although deadhead them early if they become a nuisance.
- **Mulch and path material:** A subtle, natural-looking, preferably local gravel will complement the planting. Size-wise, 10–15mm (⅜–½in) is good and serves well for both mulching and paths.
- **Control weeds:** Use permeable landscape fabric only on paths or small-scale plantings, otherwise it will stop the plants you do want from spreading properly.
- **Dig in:** Always add well-rotted organic matter to help plants establish, especially if the soil is very free-draining and inevitably dries out fast.

Above: Even though bold design geometry (such as that on pp122–123) is commonly used to link house and garden, the informal Mediterranean-inspired gravel garden often does perfectly well without!

Key theme plants

- *Anthemis tinctoria* (oxeye chamomile; ✽✽✽ Z3–8) and cvs
- *Asphodeline lutea* (yellow asphodel; ✽✽✽ Z6–9) and cvs
- *Bupleurum fruticosum* (✽✽✽ borderline Z7–11)
- *Ceanothus* (California lilac; ✽✽–✽✽✽ Z4–11, depending on spp/cvs)
- *Cistus* (rock rose; ✽✽–✽✽✽ Z8–11, depending on spp/cvs)
- *Eryngium planum* (sea holly; ✽✽✽ Z5–9) and cvs
- *Euphorbia characias* subsp. *wulfenii* (spurge; ✽✽ Z7–10) and cvs
- *Genista lydia* (Lydian broom; ✽✽✽ Z6–9)
- *Iris* – bearded types (✽✽✽ Z3–9, depending on spp/cvs)
- *Olearia* (daisy bush; ✽✽–✽✽✽ Z8–15, depending on spp)
- *Perovskia* (✽✽✽ Z6–9)
- *Phlomis italica* (✽✽ Z9–11)
- *Stachys byzantina* (lambs' tongues; ✽✽✽ Z4–8) and cvs
- *Stipa* (feather grass; ✽✽✽ Z7–15; depending on spp)

5.

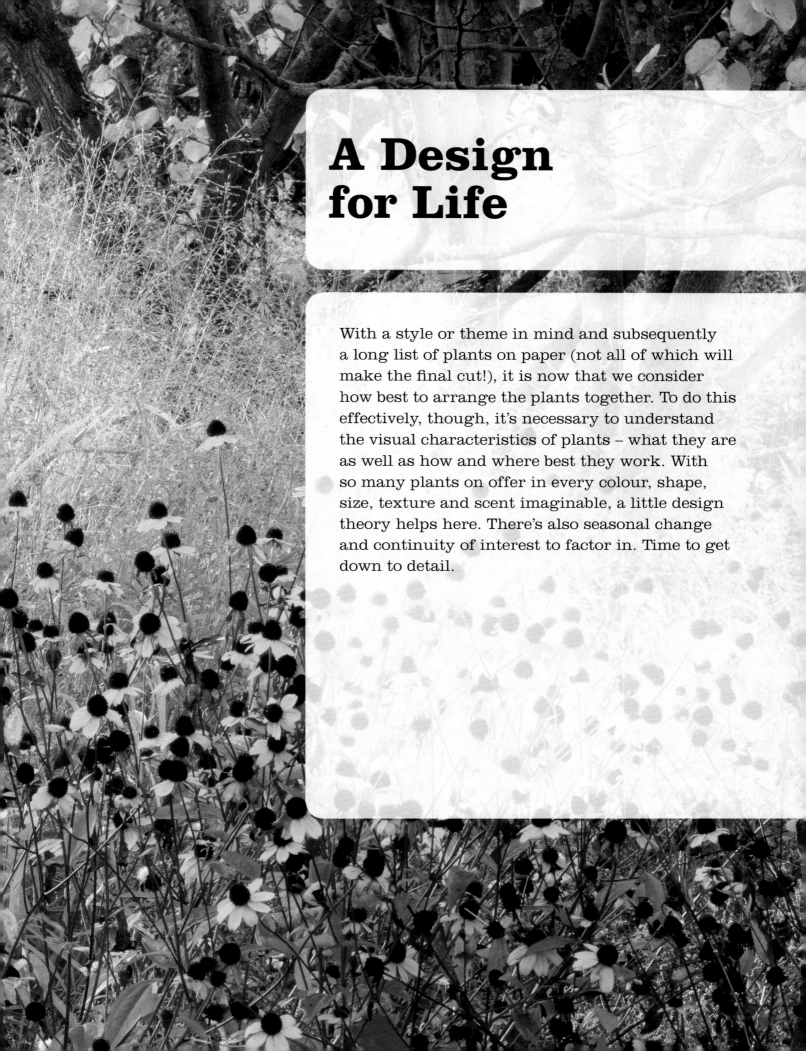

A Design for Life

With a style or theme in mind and subsequently a long list of plants on paper (not all of which will make the final cut!), it is now that we consider how best to arrange the plants together. To do this effectively, though, it's necessary to understand the visual characteristics of plants – what they are as well as how and where best they work. With so many plants on offer in every colour, shape, size, texture and scent imaginable, a little design theory helps here. There's also seasonal change and continuity of interest to factor in. Time to get down to detail.

Top: Keep it simple is a moniker for good design, as demonstrated here. As you can see, simplicity certainly doesn't mean boring.

Above: Even in small gardens, it's possible to include big borders, although inevitably it'll mean sacrificing traditional 'lawn' space. The deeper the border the more layers of plants you can fit in.

Right: This river of stonecrop (*Sedum* Herbstfreude Group 'Herbstfreude') is in perfect proportion with the informal country cottage planting around it. The bigger the border and the garden, the more plants you should use (see p193).

Opposite, above: With similar forms, colours and sympathetic hardscape materials, this roof terrace design borrows from and blends in beautifully with the landscape beyond.

Golden rules of planting design

1. Keep it simple

The temptation is to shove in all your favourites. This almost always results in a bitty, chaotic display, made worse if there's only one of each plant. Instead be bold, reduce the number of species and plant those remaining in larger masses. Less is always more.

2. The wider the border the better

As a guide, a 1.2m (4ft) wide border will accommodate only a wall shrub, plus two strips of smaller perennials in front, or just one if they spread. A 2–2.3m (6½–7½ft) wide bed can fit smaller shrubs and roses, or larger ones if it's wider still. Thin strips are inevitable in small gardens, but they'll take only a climber, a low hedge or a few tidy perennials, so grasp every opportunity to make them bigger,

for example by creating a larger border on one side only rather than having two small strips down each side, while a line of containers on the other side would balance it, yet not eat into people space. Design layouts arranged at angles also open up large pockets for planting. There is always the lawn, of course... could it be sacrificed for plants?

3. Watch scale & proportion

Consider the size of the garden, the buildings and the areas to be planted. Avoid plants that grow too big or arrangements that look too small. Large gardens in particular need large borders and larger plants, or smaller plants arranged in bigger groups. But small spaces require big or, specifically, tall plants too – height is important here. Don't overdo it though or you'll make the garden feel claustrophobic.

4. Unity

Unity can be described as a sense of togetherness. With gardens overlooking a landscape beyond – a country vista for example – similar plants, colours or forms will forge suitable links. Specific site characteristics also determine what works best visually – stick with these and the design won't jar.

5. Repeat, repeat, repeat

Repetition is the easiest way to unify a planting scheme, as plants with similar shapes and colours appeal to the eye and make a connection that brings order to what might be chaos. Reliability is important – evergreen perennials, grasses and topiary are therefore most popular.

6. Rhythm

Repetition gives a planting rhythm, which further helps us make sense of it. Natural, relaxed, flowing rhythms occur when plants are organised in sweeping drifts – the visual equivalent of a soaring violin. Regular rhythms occur when plants are arranged in a distinct pattern. Like the steady bass drum, plants placed in this way add a formal note. Progressive rhythms follow a sequence of steps – a change in height being the most common – imagine the build-up to a rousing guitar solo. The larger the planting the more rhythms might appear in it.

Above, left: Repetition divides 'designed' schemes from those that just happen by accident. Here similar forms, colours and the duplication of particular plants – notably white laceflower (*Orlaya grandiflora*) and box (*Buxus*) balls – make for a unified composition.

Above, right: The full symphony! Irish yew (*Taxus baccata* 'Fastigiata') placed like soldiers on parade bang out a steady structural drumbeat, while drifts of perennials including blue sea holly (*Eryngium × zabelii*) flow melodically around their feet.

7. Harmony & variety

While harmony is important, so too is variety and contrast. Too much of the same thing over a large area – the same colour for example – can be boring, even if it is harmonious. To make a planting more exciting, include plenty of different plants. How much contrast depends on how varied they are. If similar, but not the same, the plant choice is subtle; distinct opposites scream for attention.

8. Focus in

All gardens need at least one focal point to attract the eye. The larger the garden the more focal points it needs. The same applies when designing with plants. Plants with a strong visual energy – distinctive shapes for example – are best. But also include plenty of smaller-scale accents for interest up close.

9. Balancing act

Balance can be described as a state of equilibrium between elements. For example planting huge evergreens on one side of a path and nothing on the other will look lopsided. Given a central axis, balance is easy to achieve; plant each side as a mirror image (known as symmetrical balance). Elsewhere it's a case of finding the 'equivalent' – for example a number of mounding perennials, which together have a similar volume to a columnar shrub nearby, would help balance it. Balance is quite an intuitive thing so when it feels right, it probably is.

Left, above: Different forms and subtly contrasting colours are combined here for a relaxed but refreshing composition. As this design shows, a little goes a long way.

Left, centre: Big focal point plants (see pp176–177) are vital but small-scale accents of form and colour are also important. Here, scarlet *Penstemon* 'Schoenholzeri', together with purple top (*Verbena bonariensis*), attract and direct attention into a pocket of gorgeous naturalistic planting.

Left, below: With a central axis, it is easy to achieve symmetrical or 'formal' balance (as it's also known) – simply mirror one side with the other. The informal planting here is dominated by bullwort (*Ammi majus*), with a sprinkling of purple top (*Verbena bonariensis*).

Form (& habit)

Form (or shape), not colour, is often top priority for many designers when selecting and arranging plants. Form directly relates to the outline of plants, but it is perhaps best described as 'shape in 3-D'. With woody trees and shrubs, it's their outline we consider most; with perennials and grasses, it's the shape of flowers and leaves. Form creates the structure, while colour, texture and scent supply the finish. Why? Form is present for longer – with woody plants that means year round, even if they drop their leaves in winter.

Different plant shapes can be organised into the groups shown on this and the following four pages, each having a different role. Their impact is dependent on size, number and density, and how clearly they can be seen.

Opposite: Plants with different forms (and textures), namely *Rodgersia*, ivy (*Hedera*), grasses and cubed box (*Buxus*), combine beautifully in this simple but very sculptural scheme. Without such contrast, monochromatic plantings such as this could look monotonous.

Rounded, spherical & globular

These are very common shapes and, together with the group below, form the basis for most mixed plantings. However, clipped globular forms are bold and eye-catching. Subsequently they make fine focal points and act as visual 'full stops'. When spaced equidistantly, perhaps in pairs, tightly clipped balls emphasise design geometry and frame views. Rounded trees are used in avenues; solitary specimens become features to catch the eye from afar.

Examples are *Hebe* 'Emerald Gem', whitebeam (*Sorbus aria*), eastern redbud (*Cercis canadensis*), *Hydrangea arborescens* 'Annabelle', clipped box (*Buxus* – see left)

Domed & mounded

Together with naturally rounded forms, dome-shaped plants are very common and 'anchor' most plantings while providing suitable contrast with more dynamic shapes. Use domed or bell-shaped trees to blur the boundaries between garden and landscape, as these are the most common plant shapes found in nature.

Examples are David's viburnum (*Viburnum davidii*), dwarf Japanese mock orange (*Pittosporum tobira* 'Nanum'; see left), common hawthorn (*Crataegus monogyna*)

Conical & pyramidal

Being formal, distinctive and 'weighty', cones and pyramidal shapes combine well with rounded forms while also providing subtle contrast. They give height and draw the eye upwards too. Conifers and many young trees have these shapes.

Examples are sweet gum (*Liquidambar styraciflua*), silver birch (*Betula pendula*), Lawson's cypress (*Chamaecyparis lawsoniana*), fastigiate hornbeam (*Carpinus betulus* 'Fastigiata'; see above)

Columnar & ovoid

Very distinctive columnar trees and shrubs – often with a fastigiate habit – make dramatic focal points; use them carefully. Random groups are visually less powerful than plants used in isolation or spaced equidistant. Fatter oval shapes are less assertive than pencil-like ones.

Examples are Irish yew (*Taxus baccata* 'Fastigiata'), Rocky Mountain juniper (*Juniperus scopulorum* 'Skyrocket'), fastigiate box-leaved holly (*Ilex crenata* Fastigiata Group 'Fastigiata'; see above)

Spiky

This very bold shape is particularly common in hotter climates. For this reason spiky forms work particularly well in formal Mediterranean plantings, gravel gardens or tropical-inspired designs, commonly repeated and partnered with rounded or mounded forms for contrast. Larger spiky plants (such as palms) can be particularly dramatic but, as with striking columnar shapes, don't overdo them.

Examples are Adam's needle (*Yucca filamentosa*), Chusan palm (*Trachycarpus fortunei*), New Zealand flax (*Phormium tenax*), *Agave americana* (see right)

Vase & fan

Broadly vase-shaped plants are graceful partners, so use them freely, whereas narrow vase shapes attract the eye (unless grouped, in which case the individual is lost) so use these sparingly. Trees with this shape are easiest to walk under; two broadly vase-shaped trees opposite each other along a path will also create an informal arch. Many larger, fountain-shaped grasses are included here.

Examples are silver grass (*Miscanthus sinensis* 'Flamingo'), shuttlecock fern (*Matteuccia struthiopteris*; see above), Mexican feather grass (*Stipa tenuissima*)

Square

A few leaves and flowers (including large-flowered tulips) come close, but only clipped hedges, cubes and pleached trees are truly square. As they are striking and very formal, use square shapes to reinforce rectilinear design layouts and provide a tailored presence to billowing perennials and grasses.

Examples are all formal hedges such as yew (*Taxus baccata*; see above), clipped topiary cubes such as box (*Buxus*)

Irregular

Amorphous loosely shaped plants that can't be categorised elsewhere come into this group and, like mounding or rounded forms, have a supporting role. Larger irregular forms such as many pines contrast well with strong architecture.

Examples are smoke bush (*Cotinus coggygria*; see left), stag's horn sumach (*Rhus typhina*), bottlebrush buckeye (*Aesculus parviflora*)

Perennial flower form

The outline form of many herbaceous perennials and grasses isn't that obvious, and it changes dramatically throughout the year. The shape (and texture) of flowers and leaves are therefore just as important. The plantsman Piet Oudolf, with Noel Kingsbury, categorised these cleverly in his book *Designing with Plants*. The groups that he devised, which have been universally adopted, are shown below.

Spires

These perform just like columnar trees and shrubs (see p134), but operate at a lower level. Sparsely spaced single-stemmed perennials like foxgloves can be very theatrical. More delicate multibranched spires have increasing impact when planted in large groups.

Examples are foxglove (*Digitalis parviflora*), culver's root (*Veronicastrum virginicum*; see above)

Buttons & globes

These shapes are visually less arresting than many others but are eye-catching nonetheless, especially in large groups. Perennials with globular flowers contrast well with spires and linear-leaved grasses.

Examples are globe thistle (*Echinops ritro* 'Veitch's Blue'), masterwort (*Astrantia major*; see above)

Plumes

Like the mounded forms (see p133), airy cloud-like plumes help to link strong shapes together and can soften the look. Plant in large groups for impact.

Examples are Chinese meadow rue (*Thalictrum delavayi*; see above), switch grass (*Panicum virgatum*)

Umbels

These are gently rounded or plate-shaped flowers, which, similar to domed shrubs (see p133), have a calming influence on pencil-like forms. They 'ground' the eye and have a very natural look.

Examples are Wallich milk parsley (*Selinum wallichianum*), fennel (*Foeniculum vulgare*; see above), bullwort (*Ammi majus*)

Daisies

Having a supporting role, plants in this big, often colourful, easily identifiable group are often positioned in the fore to mid-ground as, only a few daisy plants grow tall.

Examples are coneflower (*Echinacea purpurea* 'Magnus'), Michaelmas daisy (*Symphyotrichum novi-belgii*; see above)

Screens & curtains

Being light and lacy, it is possible to see through such plants, which are also used to soften strong flower forms if planted densely enough. They are often swept right to the front of the bed for height and to encourage the eye to investigate what's behind.

Examples are purple top (*Verbena bonariensis*; see above)

Above: Famed for its tiered branches, the aptly named wedding cake tree (*Cornus controversa* 'Variegata') steals the show in this cottage garden photographed in early spring. Unlike many other deciduous trees and shrubs, the distinctive habit is still clear after the leaves emerge.

In the habit

Another common horticultural term is 'habit'. This differs from form in that habit refers to the pattern of growth. For example the branches of silver birch (*Betula pendula*) have a pendulous habit (accentuated by leaves that also droop) but the outline form is conical. Likewise, butterfly bush (*Buddleja davidii*) has an arching habit but overall a domed outline.

Plants with weeping, pendulous, horizontal (table-like) or fastigiate habits are most noticeable, particularly in winter. All make great focal points. Plants with twisted habits such as corkscrew hazel (*Corylus avellana* 'Contorta') are also eye-catching, but awkward to combine, especially with strong forms; mounding shrubs are better partners. Mat-forming prostrate shrubs and perennials such as *Hebe pinguifolia* 'Pagei' are commonly used to link layered plantings to the ground. However do mass them at an appropriate scale; one plant by itself has little impact. Not all plants have a distinctive habit that needs considering, though. If it's not obvious, it's not important.

Working with form (& habit)

- **Keep it simple:** Don't mix lots of strong forms together, particularly with structural plants (see pp172–173); most designers will typically work with two to three similar shapes, using something striking as a focal point for contrast.

- **Consider colour & texture:** Different forms and textures with similar colours are more restful than eclectic combinations, which can look chaotic.

- **Design unity:** Mimicking plants with the same form can link the planting together: columnar yew (*Taxus*) in the background, with foxgloves (*Digitalis*) in front, for example.

- **Reward the eye:** Sizeable plants that have dramatic form draw the eye from the distance. Up close, subtle 'accents' of form positioned in the mid-foreground are important to reward the visual journey.

- **Size wise:** Form and habit can be used to manipulate perspective and our perception of size. A stretch of prostrate plants together makes a space feel wider. Verticals pull the eye skyward, which is useful for cramped spaces.

Colour

It is always a joy to work with colour, however complex it is. In gardens we use it to attract attention, make spaces feel bigger (or smaller) and forge links to the wider landscape. Colour can evoke or enhance a particular atmosphere and, depending on how we perceive it – light has a huge influence here – colour also affects our emotions. Red is warm, but can be alarming. Blue is calm, but too much of it appears icy cold. Purple is glamorous, but can be depressing. Green and yellow are the only colours we all interpret in the same way. Most see green as calm and refreshing, and yellow as cheerful and happy.

Colour also reminds us of the changing seasons. Light blue, soft yellow, cream and pastel pinks herald the arrival of spring. Violets, mauves and purple appear in early summer. These make way for deep yellows, oranges and reds in late summer and autumn.

Hot or cold?

Hot/Warm colours

The intense hot hues of reds, oranges and yellows are vibrant, and orange in particular comes packed with energy. All are dominant colours and stand out at a distance, so when placed at the back of a garden, they will have a foreshortening effect, although this is less apparent at dusk when they become muddy and indistinct – darker red/plum-colour foliage goes blurry for example. Being attention-grabbing, hot/warm colours should be used sparingly in smaller gardens; alternatively, introduce pastels and grey tones that aren't so eye-catching.

Cool colours

Greens, blues and violets are calm and relaxing and, being recessive, fade into the distance, which can make a garden feel bigger. Such cool colours show off in shade and falling light levels too – darker blues and violets are the notable exception, both being close to black (see p152).

Yellow–green

Green

Blue–green

Blue

Blue–violet

Violet

Yellow

Yellow–orange

Orange

Red–orange

Red

Red–violet

The colour wheel

Choosing which colours work best in a planting scheme ultimately comes down to personal taste – if pink, tangerine and turquoise sound good to you, go for it. But if you don't want to rely just on personal intuition, the colour wheel will help. Based on the colours of the rainbow, it helps you choose plants with confidence.

There are essentially two ways to use colour in the garden: contrast and harmony. Colours adjacent to each other on the colour wheel are harmonious – blue, green and violet for example. Colours opposite each other complement through dramatic contrast. There are many books written on how to combine colour, but without doubt the easiest way is to choose a tried-and-tested colour combination based on these principles. We'll focus on them on pp140–153.

Primary colours

Red, blue and yellow. All other colours are derived from these hues.

Secondary colours

Green, orange and violet – formed by mixing the primary colours.

Tertiary colours

These are made by mixing a primary colour with a secondary colour adjacent to it: for example orange-red, red-orange, yellow-orange, orange-yellow, green-yellow, yellow-green, blue-green, green-blue, violet-blue, blue-violet, red-violet, violet-red.

Terminology explained

Hue	Another word for colour.
Tint	Any colour plus white. Lots of pale colours and pastels are tints. For example, lilac (purple and white)
Shade	Any colour plus black. Often deep and rich, they can look sombre in shade. For example, navy blue (blue and black)
Tone	Any colour plus grey. For example, gold (yellow and grey)

Factors affecting colour perception

How we perceive colours varies dramatically, and not just because our eyes are all different. Scale plays a big part; the larger the area the more vivid a colour will be (subtle pastel-coloured plants in particular are indistinctive when placed by themselves). Colour intensity (how bright or dull it is) and background colour also have a big impact; light is a key factor here.

Light

We see colour because of pigments, which absorb or reflect different wavelengths of light. Leaves are green because they reflect the green wavelength; daffodils are yellow because they reflect the yellow. Although the proportion of pigments influences how dull or bright a colour will be, it's the intensity and amount of light reflected by a colour that has the bigger impact.

In hot summers or sunny climates near the equator, light levels are intense and pastels in particular bleach out. Here bright colours look best. In temperate climates, autumn light is less intense but relatively warm – one reason why red and orange colours look so good at this time. In winter, however, light is positively grey, which explains why colours we see while on exotic summer holidays abroad don't look as good in our gardens at home at this time.

If light has an impact, so does shade. Darker colours become muddy in shade, whereas at dusk cool combinations look their best, as they reflect more light.

Background

Our perception of colour also depends on the colour behind it. Any colour on a dark background appears lighter, while the same colour on a lighter background appears more intense. But, of course, for colours to stand out, the background has to be different. Bold contrasts are dramatic. Subtle differences are more sophisticated, but can be appreciated only up close,

as they're indistinguishable at a distance. Green is the most common background colour, and mid-greens like apple-green and forest-green are the perfect foil to most colours. Straw colours are good too.

Working with colour

- **Choose a colour scheme for each area:** Your chosen style, the atmosphere you want to create, and your personal taste will have an impact, but so too will the location, as this will limit which plants – and therefore colours – are available at certain times of the year.

- **One colour, or more?** Make a conscious decision as to whether you want one colour year-round by using a succession of plants that share the same colour, or whether you want the scheme to reflect the cyclic pattern of colours dictated by the changing seasons. The latter is more exciting, and no less tricky – making a plant calendar (see pp164–165) will help.

- **Use the colour wheel** but only as a guide. Don't let it overrule personal intuition.

- **Experiment:** Learn from mistakes and cherish happy accidents.

- **Embrace the range of different colours available:** Tints and shades are easier to work with, although the effect might not be as dramatic as you had hoped.

Above: Dramatic contrast isn't always required. Notice how the dusky-pink *Iris* 'Indian Chief' on the left and the deep-blue *Iris* at the back right don't dominate this design, or each other, because of the colours behind them. The viewer here has to decide which is visually most important – a classic characteristic of modernist design, executed here by Christopher Bradley-Hole.

Left: Being the complementary colour, these dark green bay laurels (*Laurus nobilis*) contrast with the red wall. However, while the background colour here never changes, the leaf coloration of deciduous plants in particular does – be mindful of this when planning your planting.

Combining colour

The following common ways to combine colour have been broadly grouped into harmony and contrast. But, do note that most planting schemes contain a bit of both groups.

Harmony

Monochromatic

Monochromatic colour schemes use the different shades, tints and tones of only one colour (with green and/or silver included as standard). The result is a bold sophisticated look, which best suits formal or crisp modernist design. Restricting the options like this makes a monochromatic colour scheme a relatively simple combination to pull off successfully. But always observe your garden's soil type, aspect and orientation, and also note that relying on only one colour means shape and texture become more important than ever. The difficult thing with monochromatic schemes is that many colours are synonymous with particular seasons and seasonal change. Fighting the fact that late summer/autumn is ablaze with hot colours for example is tricky – many other colours (like blue-violet and mauve) aren't around in bulk at this time.

Above: True blue flowers aren't very common so it's rare to find monochromatic schemes founded on blue without foregoing good horticultural practice (i.e. right plant right place). Here the designer has chosen carefully. Blue-purple Balkan clary (*Salvia nemorosa* 'Caradonna'), African blue lily (*Agapanthus africanus*), blue and white *Delphinium* and catmint (*Nepeta sibirica* 'Souvenir d'André Chaudron') will all thrive given fertile, well-drained soil, in sun.

Analogous

Analogous, commonly called 'harmonious', planting schemes consist of colours that are adjacent to each other on the colour wheel, such as red, violet-red and red-violet (see p139). As each colour shares similar pigments – red in this case – it's easy to create a natural-looking planting scheme that's pleasing to the eye over a large area. But don't use each colour at the same density. Choose one colour to dominate, the second to support, a third, even a fourth, as accents to draw the eye. Green and silver, and perhaps black (although not with dark shades) are also included for contrast. White usually appears only with light-coloured combinations. To some, analogous schemes look a little boring, especially on a large scale. Here designers will introduce some complementary colour (see pp144–145) for excitement. For example, in a green, blue-green and green-blue scheme, orange-red might be added to liven things up.

Above: In this hot, harmonious, naturalistic combination of yellow, orange and red, softened by green and straw-coloured grasses, sunny yellow is the dominant colour, with accents of orange, followed by ruby-red, as the supporting cast.

Above: Pretty in pink, and... a little purple. Cottage garden combinations based on pink are always popular, as they are both restful and relaxing. Although pastels do tend to predominate, note the vibrancy and exciting range of tints and tones here from plants including yarrow (*Achillea millefolium* 'Fire King'), perennial phlox (*Phlox paniculata* 'Uspekh') and *Dahlia* 'Peter'.

Above: In monochromatic schemes, different flower shapes and foliage are essential for interest. Here tufted hair grass (*Deschampsia cespitosa*), Mexican feather grass (*Stipa tenuissima*), pale yellow *Scabiosa columbaria* subsp. *ochroleuca* and two yarrows (*Achillea* 'Taygetea' and *A. ptarmica* 'The Pearl') partner a white coneflower (*Echinacea purpurea* 'White Swan').

Below & right: Saturated hues are intense and powerful, whereas adding pastel tints cools a composition, shown here by this red hot poker (*Kniphofia* 'Tawny King') (below) and spherical silver-purple star of Persia (*Allium cristophii*) (right).

Above: Calm mixed plantings using grey-blues, pinks and soft purples – from flowers and/or foliage – are ideal for rest and relaxation. For beginners this is probably the easiest colour combination to pull off successfully. When introduced sparingly, white is an ideal accent; alternatively, choose a complementary partner – primrose-yellow would work well here for example.

Contrast

Complementary

These combinations use colours opposite each other on the colour wheel (see pp138–139), for maximum contrast. Partnerships such as this are lively, sometimes electric (particularly with colours at full intensity or saturation) and always eye-catching, so designers traditionally use them sparingly as focal points. Nowadays, however, many embrace the opportunity to combine colour like this on a larger scale – sometimes with painted walls or bright containers – to bring real drama to a design. Looking at the colour wheel, there are six complementary partnerships. Here I focus on two, one commonly considered, the other not.

Yellow & purple

Yellow and purple are the most attention-grabbing complementary combination, as yellow has the highest visual energy of all the colours. Creating this colour combo using paint or foliage can be overstimulating however, particularly where a restful atmosphere is desired. But with flowers it's a different matter.

Above: An iconic, shocking yet short-lived combination of purple ornamental onions (*Allium hollandicum*) has here been partnered with the golden flowers of Voss's laburnum (*Laburnum × watereri* 'Vossii') by Rosemary Verey. As flowers like these don't last long, you get the best of both worlds – a bolt of excitement for a few weeks or so, without a long-term headache.

Red & green

We look at the soothing power of green on p148–149, but it's often overlooked that green can be consciously used for dramatic contrast with its complementary colour, red. The more red there is the hotter the planting scheme; when the palette is greener any red accents will sparkle like rubies. To some, this blend is a bit boring so they'll introduce red-violet and red-orange with green, or red with blue-green and blue-yellow – the two colours either side on the colour wheel. This is known as a split-complementary combination and, with more choice on offer, it can make designing easier.

Above: Too stark for some but exciting to others, contrasting combinations such as these with little tonal variation to flowers and foliage (or fruit) are an acquired taste, especially with red and green. Different forms and textures for contrast are important, but so too is the plum-purple cherry (*Prunus × cistena*) in the centre. You might say this image belongs in the monochromatic camp, but don't forget there are also leaves, stems and even fruit to consider when working with colour.

Above: For calmer and quieter complementary combinations, partner subtle tints and tones. Here a soft yellow yarrow (*Achillea* 'Taygetea') and frothy bronze fennel (*Foeniculum vulgare* 'Purpureum') feature at the heart of this naturalistic, Mediterranean-style scheme.

Above: Deep blue alkanet (*Anchusa azurea* 'Dropmore'), a cranesbill (*Geranium clarkei* (Purple-flowered Group) 'Kashmir Purple'), orangy *Verbascum* 'Clementine' and golden *Hymenoxys hoopesii* make for vivid contrast in this stylised meadow. Such electric colours together might look gaudy for some but the soft shapes and textures make this association more palatable, having a softening effect.

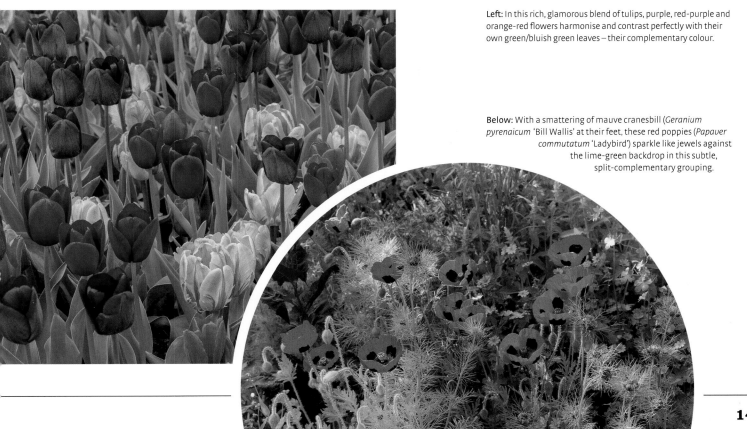

Left: In this rich, glamorous blend of tulips, purple, red-purple and orange-red flowers harmonise and contrast perfectly with their own green/bluish green leaves – their complementary colour.

Below: With a smattering of mauve cranesbill (*Geranium pyrenaicum* 'Bill Wallis' at their feet, these red poppies (*Papaver commutatum* 'Ladybird') sparkle like jewels against the lime-green backdrop in this subtle, split-complementary grouping.

Contrast (continued)

Triadic

A triadic colour scheme uses colours that are spaced equidistant on the colour wheel (see pp138–139) – blue-green, red-violet and yellow-orange for example. With saturated colours you get an explosive, vibrant combination. Using more subtle tints and tones is more acceptable. However, even at its most intense, a triadic scheme is not as dramatic as a complementary one (see pp144–145), where the colours are opposite each other. Colour balance is important; one colour should dominate, and, being a recessive colour, green is the most common (in fact it's rare to find a triadic colour combination that doesn't feature green in one way or another). The other two colours are included for contrast in differing amounts, depending on personal taste. If you dislike the idea of these jumping out too much, then introduce muted tones and tints rather than saturated hues.

Above: Green foliage and yellow flowers are the dominant colours in this triadic scheme, while red and blue flowers used in differing amounts provide the contrast.

Polychromatic

Such a colour scheme combines a mixture of many colours, and their tints, tones and shades. It's an incredibly lively effect, even with pastels. Essentially there aren't any rules with this look but, paradoxically, if you impose a few, it helps avoid the dog's-dinner look. Perhaps use cool colours to form the background, and the other colours as small-scale accents. Alternatively, choose three harmonious colours (see pp142–143) to dominate, intermingling another three to contrast with them. Colours with the same intensity work best too – avoid mixing pastels with saturated hues and their tones and shades. Polychromatic schemes aren't easy to design unless you have a painterly eye for colour combinations. For this reason they work best in naturalistic arrangements, where plants are intermingled with lots of green or straw colours in the background, to link the different colours together.

Above: Green forms the backdrop to a subtle symphony of colour in this informal cottage-style planting. As the tints and tones are of a similar intensity, no one plant dominates or clashes horribly with the others around it. The green foliage also has a unifying effect.

Above: Green, purple and orange – the three secondary colours on the colour wheel – feature here, although deep yellow yarrow (*Achillea* 'Terracotta') has also been included to lift the partnership subtly, harmonising with the orange montbretia (*Crocosmia × crocosmiiflora* 'Emily McKenzie'), yet contrasting with the purple top (*Verbena bonariensis*).

Above: Triadic colour combinations can be soft and relaxing, particularly if you use pastels. Here the mauve and primrose-yellow planting features columbine (*Aquilegia chysantha* 'Yellow Queen') and sweet rocket (*Hesperis*), partnered skilfully with peach-coloured natural stone behind. It's a subtle contrast that doesn't scream for attention.

Left: Mother Nature does it best, and where better to look for inspiration? Blue cornflowers (*Centaurea cyanus*), together with marguerites (*Leucanthemum vulgare*), dominate here. Splashes of yellow, orange and red from plants including field poppies (*Papaver rhoeas*) provide contrasting accents of interest.

Below: A riot of colour using so many different cultivated plants isn't easy to pull off successfully. The green backdrop helps to stop this planting looking chaotic – but only just.

Green

Green is the most important cool colour and warrants special mention, as it forms the background and unifying base to most plantings. It is also nature's great harmoniser. Green helps tone down dominant colours such as bright orange and eases the tension between plants that might otherwise clash. Straw colours (think ornamental grasses) work in a similar way.

There are many different shades, tints and tones of green. Apple-greens are bright and useful to revitalise and rejuvenate the spirits. Softer turquoises and sea-greens have a cooling effect, while yellow-green, olive and avocado are warm. Zingy lime-green and chartreuse draw the eye, especially when partnered with dark blue and silver. Darker greens recede into the distance and are the perfect background colour for bright flowers and pastels alike.

While there are a few green flowers, it's mainly the leaves that we focus on here.

Above: Green flowers aren't commonplace, but in spring the zingy chartreuse-yellow-green flowers of many spurge (here *Euphorbia characias* subsp. *wulfenii*) bring welcome cheer, here contrasting with spherical ornamental onions (*Allium hollandicum* 'Purple Sensation').

Working with green

- **The best backdrop:** In mixed borders, green-leaved shrubs and climbers form the background colour. In a small garden, avoid using too many dark green heavyweights though, as both their colour and size can be oppressive.

- **Texture & form:** Use plenty of different textures and forms for interest with design styles where green is important, for example in Japanese design (see pp110–111), or where it's inevitable, such as in woodland plantings (see pp116–117).

- **Natural links:** In temperate climates, green is the most common colour found in nature. To make your garden feel bigger and blend into the surrounding landscape, introduce as much green as possible.

- **Keep it simple:** Many plants – shrubs in particular – have variegated foliage in green and gold, or green and primrose-yellow. Choose one or two for contrast but don't overdo it, and do not space them too closely, as variegated plants rarely combine well.

- **Complementary contrast:** Green's complementary colour is red (see pp138–139); red flowers really sing against a green backdrop. However, intense pure hues can look uncomfortably stark together, especially over a large area. Often it's best to use tints and tones instead, partnering yellow-greens with red-orange and blue-violet for example.

Left: Green might be the most common colour, particularly in semishade/full shade, however there are numerous tints and hues to choose from. Contrasting forms and textures are vital though if you decide to go it alone with only one colour.

Overleaf: The colours, forms and textures of the hard landscaping and the plants complement yet subtly contrast with each other in this masterful 'green scene' – a country garden with formal undertones. When working with lots of green, or any one colour for that matter, the visual quality of paths, ponds, paving and pergolas becomes more important than ever.

White, black & silver

Although not 'true' colours, white, black and silver affect the way we see and use other colours. They also heavily influence the atmosphere of a garden. White comes from flowers and bark, while silver comes mainly from the leaves. Interestingly, black flowers and foliage aren't actually black – they're dark purple.

White

Green, white and silver are a classic colour combination – particularly in formal geometric design. But being the brightest eye-catching 'colour', white isn't an easy mixer. In strong sun, white flowers often dominate the composition. Introduce pure white sparingly, or choose paler creams. Gloomy shade is the exception perhaps; bright white is sometimes most welcome here.

If you're trying to make a space feel bigger, don't position white flowers by boundaries; here they'll have a foreshortening effect, particularly at dusk. Conversely, if you plan to use the garden at this time, include lots of white flowers, but perhaps in the foreground only.

Black

Although it is restful on the eye, black is another awkward 'colour' to work with. A sunny spot is essential – even glossy-leaved plants look sombre and depressing in shade; if it's really gloomy, black plants appear like a 'hole'. Use black sparingly either to contrast with light greens or darker yellow colours – *Tulipa* 'Queen of Night' with straw-coloured grasses for example – or to boost the impact of hot orange flowers; this technique is common in exotic planting schemes. Don't partner black with pure white – the contrast is too stark; silver or green should be used to smooth the transition.

Silver/silvery grey

Silvery plants help to temper bright colours, or calm garish combinations, just like green does. Silver also brings out the best of most colours, particularly blue – gold-leaved plants are a notable exception to this.

Most silver-leaved plants need a hot sunny spot; this colour is an adaptation that plants use to reflect strong sun. For semishade, silvery cultivars of dead nettle (*Lamium*), lungwort (*Pulmonaria*) and Siberian bugloss (*Brunnera*) are invaluable for contrast and to punch in a little light.

Left: Shiny black or, I should say, dark purple foliage makes for a glamorous addition to exotic schemes, but elsewhere it can appear sombre, especially en masse, so use it carefully. Castor oil plant (*Ricinus communis* 'New Zealand Purple') and bugbane (*Actaea* 'Queen of Sheba') are the 'accents' used here. The jagged plant in the centre is honey flower (*Melianthus comosus*).

Opposite, above: In this Mediterranean-inspired courtyard, bluish grey olives (*Olea europaea*) and silvery grey lavender (*Lavandula*) create a calming, relaxed atmosphere. Silver has the same effect within beds and borders too, where it helps turn down the heat.

Opposite, below: When is white all right? Many designers would say when it's not bright! A copse of silver birch (*Betula pendula*) stand out, but being chalk-white they don't dominate this naturalistic, woodland-inspired design; brilliant white on a similar scale may well scream for attention, however.

Texture

In design terms, texture can be defined as how something feels to the touch, be that silky or coarse, woolly or prickly, sticky or smooth. How the surface of plants and materials looks like they might feel, essentially their 'visual' texture, is also part of the picture.

Rosemary (*Rosmarinus*) might have fine, smooth leaves to the touch, but for me they do look a little prickly, and this can be important in design terms.

Words such as glossy, matt, prickly, leathery, velvety, furry, wrinkled and ridged are useful and commonly employed to describe the texture of plants. However, for convenience, plants are generally classed as having a fine, medium or coarse texture, principally because of their leaf size, shape and surface appearance. With some plants (particularly trees), stems are also important – flowers and fruit less so, unless

they're huge in size, there are many of them, or they persist for ages. Admittedly, texture is the least visually powerful characteristic of plants, compared to colour and form. But, don't ignore it – close up it is the feature that rewards the most.

Opposite: Similar colours but a riot of different, mainly coarse to medium textures make this planting very eye-catching. A coarse–medium–fine progression is most common, although designers often omit the middle for drama!

Bold, coarse texture

Plants that have a clear branch structure or large leaves with serrated edges, spines or thorns are dramatic and draw the eye, even from a distance. Yet lots of different coarse-textured plants together can be overstimulating and will make a small garden feel even smaller; in such a place, site them as eye-catching accents only, so they don't overwhelm.

Rheum palmatum (ornamental rhubarb)

Hosta sieboldiana var. *elegans* (giant blue hosta)

Viburnum rhytidophyllum (wrinkled viburnum)

Phormium tenax (New Zealand flax)

Bergenia 'Morgenröte' (elephant's ears)

Butia capitata (jelly palm)

Crambe maritima (sea kale)

Helleborus argutifolius (holly-leaved hellebore)

Eryngium × *zabelii* 'Forncett Ultra' (sea holly)

Acer griseum (paper-bark maple)

Medium texture

Most plants in this grouping have neither large nor small leaves. The branches and habit aren't overly distinctive either. Medium-textured plants therefore form the backbone of most plantings. They link bold and fine-textured plants together too, softening the contrast between them.

Fagus sylvatica (common beech)

Agastache rugosa (giant hyssop)

× *Heucherella* 'Quicksilver' (coral flower)

Salvia officinalis (common sage)

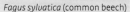

Pittosporum tobira 'Nanum' (dwarf Japanese mock orange)

Elaeagnus 'Quicksilver' (oleaster)

Geranium × *oxonianum* 'Wageningen' (cranesbill)

Penstemon 'Osprey'

Camellia japonica 'Mrs Tingley'

Epimedium × *perralchicum* 'Fröhnleiten' (barrenwort)

Fine texture

Plants with small or very narrow stems and leaves (such as grasses) have a fine texture. Ferns and shrubs with dissected foliage are grouped here too. Unless they're strongly coloured, plants in this group don't scream for attention and tend to recede into the distance. To give the illusion of depth, place bold plants in the foreground with fine-textured plants on the boundaries.

Acer palmatum 'Dissectum' (cut-leaved Japanese maple)

Rosmarinus officinalis var. *angustissimus* 'Benenden Blue' (rosemary)

Taxus baccata (yew)

Panicum virgatum (switch grass)

Dicentra formosa (bleeding heart)

Gaura lindheimeri

Thuja occidentalis (white cedar)

Albizia julibrissin f. *rosea* (silk tree)

Corydalis flexuosa

Dryopteris filix-mas (male fern)

Left: Feathery, fine-textured grasses and perennials combine to stunning effect. It's rare that one texture by itself works so well; here it's also the down to the time of day and the skill of the photographer!

Opposite: This scheme boasts fine-to-medium transition of texture, although the clipped forms are most memorable. Note the gorgeous juxtaposition between frothy and informal on the left and controlled and formal on the right.

Working with texture

- **Base your design on one or two textures:** Plants with the same or similar textures always associate well. A combination of medium- and fine-textured plants is most common. That said, introduce some coarse texture to draw the eye.

- **Contrast:** Some different accents for interest are essential, but never use just one texture en masse – fine-textured plants in particular – as this can look boring, especially with a monochromatic colour scheme.

- **Gradual transition is best:** Coarse through medium to fine textures are easiest on the eye; big jumps from coarse to fine work well for drama, but should be used sparingly.

- **Distance determines our perception of texture:** Jagged sycamore leaves for example look coarse close up, yet finer further away. From a distance, fine textures are unrecognisable, and outline form becomes more important. Colour also has an influence: bright colours enhance texture, while pastels have a softening effect.

- **Hard and soft:** Consider lawns and hard landscaping too: how coarse giant rhubarb (*Gunnera*) for example contrasts with smooth hardwood decking; and wild marjoram (*Origanum vulgare*) harmonises with washed river gravel, the rounded leaves being of a similar shape and size to the gravel.

This page: This scent-sational balcony garden is full of fragrant favourites including French lavender (*Lavandula stoechas* subsp. *stoechas*) and rosemary (*Rosmarinus*). Touchy-feely scents such as these are the perfect choice where strong winds would only whisk free-scented fragrances away.

Scent

Plants with a fabulous fragrance make any garden more appealing (see pp248–249). There are just so many scented plants! Sweet rocket (*Hesperis matronalis*) and butterfly bush (*Buddleja davidii*) are sweetly scented; pinks (*Dianthus*) and chocolate vine (*Akebia quinata*) smell spicy. Other plants such as pineapple broom (*Cytisus battandieri*) have fruity fragrances, while a few – notably regal lily (*Lilium regale*) and common honeysuckle (*Lonicera periclymenum*) – have a heady scent that can make you swoon.

There is also a fragrant plant for every season, sun or shade, so it's possible to achieve scent-continuity throughout the year. Some plants such as the aptly named moonflower (*Ipomoea alba*) save their scent until dusk; choose these if you're out all day. The hotter the weather the more intense the fragrance, as more scent molecules evaporate from flower petals or leaves. To make the most of scented plants, try to avoid placing them in cold corners.

The potency of scented plants does vary, so I have split them into three groups that help determine where they might work best in the garden.

'Touchy-feely' scents

Plants such as cotton lavender (*Santolina*) and rosemary (*Rosmarinus*) have aromatic – often evergreen or ever-grey – foliage, which needs to be crushed or caressed to release the volatile aromatic oils (interestingly what smells nice to us is actually there to repel browsing insects and animals). Position plants at the front of beds and borders or at the edge of paths and paving so you can run your fingers through the foliage as you pass.

Aloysia citrodora (lemon verbena)

Cistus ladanifer (common gum cistus)

Lavandula angustifolia 'Hidcote' (lavender)

Melissa officinalis (lemon balm)

Mentha × piperita (peppermint)

Origanum vulgare 'Aureum' (golden wild marjoram)

Prostanthera cuneata (alpine mint bush)

Rosa rubiginosa (eglantine rose)

Salvia officinalis 'Purpurascens' (purple sage)

Thymus citriodorus (lemon-scented thyme)

'Free scents'

Plants such as the jasmine *Jasminum × stephanense* and late Dutch honeysuckle (*Lonicera periclymenum* 'Serotina') are liberal with strong scent, making them first choice to mask exhaust fumes and other bad smells. However you can have too much of a good thing with such pungent perfume, so don't plant together those that flower at the same time, especially in a small, wind-still garden! Note: some powerfully scented plants cause problems for allergy sufferers.

Chimonanthus praecox (wintersweet)

Daphne bholua 'Jacqueline Postill' (Nepalese paper plant)

Jasminum officinale (common jasmine)

Lilium candidum (Madonna lily)

Lilium regale (regal lily)

Lonicera periclymenum 'Serotina' (late Dutch honeysuckle)

Matthiola longipetala subsp. *bicornis* (night-scented stock)

Philadelphus 'Belle Etoile' (mock orange)

Polianthes tuberosa (tuberose)

Ribes odoratum (buffalo currant)

Left: Most, but not all, honeysuckles (*Lonicera*) have fabulously fragrant flowers. This *Lonicera periclymenum* 'Graham Thomas' will pump sweet perfume over the seating space next to it all summer long.

'Up close and personal' scents

Subtler scents include old roses, perennial phlox (*Phlox paniculata*) and chocolate plant (*Cosmos atrosanguineus*). These are 'up close and personal' scents because you need to get fairly near to catch a delicious whiff (although many are quite powerful at their peak). Position plants within easy reach of the patio, or perhaps on the threshold between one garden 'room' and another, and where the prevailing breeze wafts the scent towards you. A sheltered spot is best.

Abeliophyllum distichum (white forsythia)

Akebia quinata (chocolate vine)

Edgeworthia chrysantha (paper bush)

Dianthus plumarius (pink)

Viola odorata (sweet violet)

Convallaria majalis (lily of the valley)

Hemerocallis lilioasphodelus (lemon day lily)

Rosa Gertrude Jekyll = 'Ausbord' (rose)

Trachelospermum jasminoides (star jasmine)

Viburnum carlesii

Left: A common design trick is to position sweet, subtle fragrances, such as those from roses – here, *Rosa* Eglantyne = 'Ausmak', partnered with dwarf catmint (*Nepeta racemosa* 'Walker's Low'), lambs' tongues (*Stachys byzantina* 'Silver Carpet') and cranesbill (*Geranium nodosum*) – to tempt the nose on a scented journey around the garden.

All change

Driven by the seasons, many plants alter quite dramatically throughout the year. This change is one of the exciting aspects of designing with plants, but it's also quite tricky to deal with. Your chosen design style will have an influence because certain plant groups are indicative of certain styles – so too will the location and when you plan to use the garden. Obviously personal taste also comes into it. But whatever you select, note that in most gardens there simply isn't space for large areas themed with one season in mind. Big gaps aren't acceptable either. So try to aim for continuity of interest throughout the year.

Mixing it up

No one plant group can provide year-round interest by itself. Shrub borders are the most 'reliable' throughout the year, however they can look boring. Conversely, perennial-heavy borders, whether naturalistic (see pp114–115) or traditional in style, are exciting in summer and autumn yet from winter to spring there's little to see. They can lack an obvious structure too. For these reasons the 'mixed border' is most popular, especially around buildings. Here every single plant group mentioned in Chapter 2 can be called on for continuity of interest right through the year.

One size fits all?

Some planting design styles don't embrace all groups because of the location or, with a naturalistic design, some plants might not feature in the natural habitats that inspire the style. With prairie-like plantings for example, mid- to late summer perennials and ornamental grasses are the key plants, whereas woody plants are rare. Inevitably relying on only one or two groups such as this restricts your options, but even in naturalistic perennial-heavy plantings it's possible to prolong seasonal interest without fighting the look. Drifts of simple spring daffodils won't feel out of place. Neither will a couple of sculptural trees with attractive winter bark and/or clipped evergreen topiary, which also help structure the planting. As friend and plantsman Stephen Lacey wisely said in *Real Gardening*, 'See nature as inspiration; don't wear it like a straitjacket.'

Practice makes perfect

Achieving year-round interest takes time. Early efforts will need tweaking once you've noted what works and what doesn't. To begin, study the profiles of plants on your wish list. Visit local gardens at different times of year. Books such as Ian Spence's *RHS Garden Plants & Flowers Through the Year* and *RHS What Plant When* can help. So too does creating planting calendars, as shown on p164.

Left: Deep borders mean more plants. And more plants make it easier to design for year-round interest.

Opposite: Autumn (and winter) is just as important to consider as spring and summer. At this time in temperate climates, acid-greens, blues and purples fade away leaving a glamorous colour palette of reds, oranges and yellows in every tint, tone and shade imaginable.

The plant calendar

When planning a planting scheme, a planting calendar helps enormously – all designers use them. It's easy to make one yourself. Use it to identify successional changes, catch gaps of interest and note emerging colour combinations.

Start by organising plants from your wish list into groups such as trees, shrubs and perennials. Or combine plants according to their likely role in your design – structural plants, focal points and so on.

Plot these down the left-hand side of the calendar. For each plant, note the key time when it looks good and its colour in the appropriate box. Do this by hand or set up a spreadsheet using Microsoft Excel

| Plant type | SPRING | | | SUMME | |
	Early	Mid-	Late	Early	Mid-
PERENNIALS					
Aquilegia atrata					
Aruncus dioicus					
Convallaria majalis					
Iris sibirica 'Dreaming Yellow'					
Matteuccia struthiopteris					
Persicaria amplexicaulis 'Taurus'					
Persicaria bistorta 'Superba'					
Thalictrum delavayi 'Hewitt's Double'					
Gunnera manicata					
GRASSES					
Carex pendula					
Luzula sylvatica 'Aurea'					
Molinia caerulea 'Variegata'					
SHRUBS					
Hebe 'Autumn Glory'					
Hydrangea serrata 'Bluebird'					

(or Numbers for Apple Mac). When such a calendar is created electronically, it is easier to play around with the different combinations.

While flowering period is the most obvious characteristic to record, don't forget to fill in the appropriate box if plants also have beautiful bark in winter, attractive seedheads, brilliant autumn leaves or colourful berries or other fruit. And remember to include evergreen foliage too when it has a season of particular colour interest.

Once you've added a few plants, it's time to evaluate and appraise your selection. Are there any obvious gaps of interest during the year? Collectively might your choices finish too early or peak too late in the season? If you're not happy, tweak your selection, adding in or swapping out plants until you are content.

R		AUTUMN			WINTER		
Late	Early	Mid-	Late	Early	Mid-	Late

Making the most of the mix

Long gaps of interest are undesirable in most gardens. Fortunately there are many strategies to plug them.

- **Avoid thin beds and borders:** The bigger the border the more plants you can include for seasonal interest (see p129).

- **Don't arrange all plants in clumps and blocks:** Intermingle a few so colour gaps aren't so obvious.

- **Match plants to place:** Unhappy plants have a shorter flowering season, plus their flower and foliage quality diminishes.

- **Choose plants that excel in more than one season:** Attractive flowers, sculptural leaves, autumn colour, colourful bark and fruit/seeds – all from the same plant if possible!

- **The whole package:** Leaves and stems are just as important as flowers. Helpfully, many floriferous annuals and perennials such as catmint (*Nepeta*) and columbine (*Aquilegia*) also have attractive leaves.

Below: Learn to love a little decay in autumn and winter. Many fading subshrubs, perennials and grasses have a theatrical quality at this time of year. Jerusalem sage (*Phlomis fruticosa*) in the foreground here now takes centre stage – the spent seedheads often last for ages if the weather stays dry.

Above, left: With random plantings such as this, gaps aren't so obvious. As one plant fades, another soon covers its tracks. Intermingle tall spring perennials and bulbs in particular, rather than place them in large groups.

Above, right: Berries are beautiful and there are few better than the rowan (*Sorbus*) tribe. The berries of Kashmir rowan (*S. cashmiriana*) are white but red-, orange-, pink- and yellow-berried species are also available. Appreciate them before the birds do!

- **For continuity of flower colour,** choose at least one flowering plant per month. Annuals, bulbs, perennials and grasses need repeating in the mid-foreground to unify the scheme throughout the year. Long-flowering plants such as purple top (*Verbena bonariensis*) and giant hyssop (*Agastache* 'Blackadder') will also bridge gaps too.

- **Don't bunch up plants that perform at the same time:** Spread them evenly throughout the composition, partnering spring perennials with summer shrubs, or vice versa. This helps create what designer's call 'successional balance'.

- **Bring on berries and autumn leaves:** For autumn interest, select deciduous trees, shrubs and old roses with fiery tints and/or berries. Rowan (*Sorbus*) trees flame nicely and have attractive berries, as do many ornamental crab apple (*Malus*). Shrubs include scarlet winged spindle (*Euonymus alatus*) and beauty berry (*Callicarpa bodinieri* var. *giraldii* 'Profusion') with iridescent violet berries. Some perennials such as umbrella plant (*Darmera peltata*) and eastern bluestar (*Amsonia tabernaemontana*) have good autumn colour, as do many late season grasses – silver grass (*Miscanthus*), hair grass (*Deschampsia*) and crab grass (*Panicum*) in particular.

- **Cherish seedheads:** Plenty of plants have attractive seedheads that are most welcome late in the growing season. With naturalistic schemes in particular, which might favour perennials, grasses and perhaps hardy annuals exclusively, plants such as globe thistle (*Echinops*) and golden rod (*Solidago*) are essential. Unfortunately the weather does play a big part; in wet winters, plants are prone to collapsing early, whereas if it's dry, the dead stems of even fleshy species such as stonecrop (*Sedum*) will often stand tall well into the new year.

- **Brighten winter with bark:** Many trees and shrubs have brilliantly coloured bark, which shimmers in low winter sunlight. Trees such as Tibetan cherry (*Prunus serrula*) and shrubs such as red-barked dogwood (*Cornus alba*) are ideal. Flowering fragrant winter shrubs such as wintersweet (*Chimonathus praecox*) are invaluable too. Some trees look good in their winter skeletal form – naked juneberry (*Amelanchier*) and sumach (*Rhus*) are living sculpture over winter.

- **Use eye-catching focal points** to see you through barren spells. Topiary is wonderful year-round but comes into its own over winter when it reveals its sculptural quality.

- **Evergreen interest?** Evergreen shrubs are important but if space is tight, choose quirky-leaved ones. Some such as *Mahonia*, holly-leaved sweetspire (*Itea ilicifolia*) and Californian lilac (*Ceanothus* 'Autumnal Blue') also flower in autumn when little else is around. In woodland or shady plantings, evergreen perennials with textured leaves such as elephant's ears (*Bergenia*), lilyturf (*Liriope*) and ferns are also essential for year-round interest.

Above, left: Trees and colourful shrubs with attractive bark should be first choice for all-winter colour. The tree here is the striking Tibetan cherry (*Prunus serrula*), loved for its silky, burgundy-red bark.

Top: In the spring border, bulbs are invaluable. Many will tolerate competition from tidy grasses and perennials, so they can be combined to create two bursts of colour from the same space. Don't forget, there are plenty of summer- and autumn-flowering bulbs too.

Above: Chopping back beautiful perennials such as coneflowers (*Echinacea*) and culver's root (*Veronicastrum*) – both featured in the foreground of this prairie-inspired scheme – early in the season might seem like madness, but it will result in sturdier, more floriferous plants that are less likely to keel over.

- **Climbing high:** Larger mature shrubs, conifers and hedges can support climbing annuals chosen to flower at different times to prolong the period of interest. But consider the size of the host and climber. Canary creeper (*Tropaeolum peregrinum*), purple bell vine (*Rhodochiton atrosanguineus*) and flame nasturtium (*Tropaeolum speciosum*) aren't invasive, so most hosts won't suffer.

- **Bring on the bulbs:** Use bulbs to share space with all but the densest perennials, for accents of colour and form, particularly in early spring and autumn. Take account of height and vigour, reliability and competitiveness.

- **Deadhead regularly:** Removing spent flowers encourages plants to flower for longer – they put their energy into producing more flowers, not setting seed.

- **Prune perennials:** To prolong late summer perennials, cut them back by half in late spring, well before they flower. This technique (sometimes called the 'Chelsea chop') stops plants flopping over and then needing to be staked later on. Cutting back half the plant two to three weeks earlier than the other half will also extend the flowering period. Only perennials with a terminal flower on top of a single stem don't like such rough treatment – therefore leave goatsbeard (*Aruncus*), lupin (*Lupinus*), day lily (*Hemerocallis*), bear's breeches (*Acanthus*) and red hot poker (*Kniphofia*) well alone.

Above: Deciduous clipped beech (*Fagus*) retains its dead leaves all winter long and is a welcome sight when there might be little else around. This phenomenon is known as marcescence. Oaks (*Quercus*) are closely related and can also hold onto withered leaves if clipped.

6.

Putting it All Together

Everything discussed thus far – the characteristics and size of the planting space, maintenance, choosing a style and personal needs such as privacy – will direct your research and help you specify suitable plants for your garden.

With this brief in mind, and an appreciation of colour, form, texture and scent, let's now look at putting the planting together.

First we'll consider the different groups, from structural plants to ornamentals. This will help organise your wish list, edit it to a more manageable size and flag up any gaps. Then we'll discuss the different ways to put everything together.

It is important to mention that it doesn't matter if you don't yet have a long list of plants to grow together. Having an idea of how you'd like them to look and perform is just as important. Many designers don't actually worry about specific plant names until drawing out a design on paper.

Structural plants

The bones of a border

Structural plants create the stage on which the decorative ornamentals perform – they're the backbone that holds everything down and they both establish and organise the composition. They do have differing roles; some might be used as a background foil, others as focal points (see pp176–177). When drawing up a design for a garden, structural plants should always be considered (and plotted) first, especially larger plants such as trees and hedges, which are important to the structural framework and spatial design of the whole garden, not just to ornamental beds and borders. Larger structural plants will also have other more practical roles (see Chapter 3).

Structural plants should be tough, reliable and last for as long as possible. Shrubs (especially evergreens), conifers and bamboo all fit the bill. Clipped topiary is also good, so too are trees and hedges. In prairie- or meadow-inspired schemes, repetitive groups of subshrubs such as *Perovskia* and ornamental grasses help structure the planting. In shade, evergreen ferns play an important part.

What goes where?

The large-scale space-makers aside, most subtle structural plants that have a supporting role appear at the back of garden borders or in the middle of island beds. Woody shrubs – particularly evergreens – and conifers are most common here. However some structure down in front is also desirable. Depending on the design style or theme, squat shrubs such as Japanese mock orange (*Pittosporum tobira* 'Nanum'), cool-season grasses including Mexican feather grass (*Stipa tenuissima*) and short evergreen perennials such as lambs' tongues (*Stachys byzantina*) are ideal for this role, especially if they're repeated. Plants with strong form might also be used to draw the eye (see p176).

With wider, open borders, larger structural plants – fastigiate yew (*Taxus*) or small multistemmed trees for example – should again be positioned first. Usually they're arranged in a precise pattern, although not necessarily over the whole area. The next layer of structural plants – usually grasses and/or subshrubs such as southernwood (*Artemisia abrotanum*) – should then be arranged in bulk underneath.

Spread out

Whatever the style or theme and whichever combination you choose, try to spread structural plants evenly, rather than grouping them in one spot. Otherwise in winter, when they're most obvious, the display will look seriously lopsided.

Placing structural plants throughout also helpfully divides up a large area into a series of little rooms, which makes the actual design and plotting process much more manageable (see pp200–203).

Above: Much-loved box (*Buxus*) balls, together with lavender (*Lavandula*) and clipped columns of variegated Italian buckthorn (*Rhamnus alaternus* 'Argenteovariegata'), are the structural plants in this autumnal garden – in this image their role is unmistakable. Evergreen elephant's ears (*Bergenia*) provide textural contrast in the foreground and, repeated thus, also function as a structural plant.

Left: In naturalistic plantings, reliable grasses and/or repetitive groups of the same, long-lasting perennial are vital to structure the scheme. Note the seemingly innocuous green clump in the bottom right corner and then how this grass is randomly repeated into the distance – repetition brings order.

Key theme plants

Distinctive plants packed with personality help reinforce or evoke a particular style or theme. Because size or 'presence' is important, many theme plants will therefore commonly have a structural role too. Romantic roses for example shout cottage garden (see pp94–97). Clipped yew (*Taxus*) or box (*Buxus*) are synonymous with crisp formal gardens (see pp90–93).

Plants are also 'powerful signatures of place' (to quote a favourite saying from plantsman and designer Dan Pearson). Deciduous berrying shrubs and evergreen ferns, for example, evoke semishady woodland (see pp116–117). Likewise no seaside planting would be complete without coarse grasses and conifers.

Dramatic key plants such as spiky *Agave* can be used as bold focal points (see pp176–177). Those with more modest leaves and flowers (such as evergreen *Camellia* in a woodland-inspired planting) serve well as a background foil to colourful plants around them. Here their subtle appearance is appropriate to the setting; key theme plants don't have to be showy.

Size isn't everything either. Smaller plants – low-level ferns or clumping grasses for example – are also invaluable theme plants if you use enough of them to make their collective presence obvious.

As key plants inevitably have more than one role, from enclosing a space to drawing the eye, they can be plotted on a garden plan at any time. But as they set the trend for everything else, it does help to identify and place them early on in the design process.

Left, above: To evoke an oriental aesthetic, Japanese maples (*Acer palmatum*) are ideal. But think carefully if you plan to use plants with such personality elsewhere. Could they clash with or contradict your chosen style?

Left, below: Clipped yew (*Taxus baccata*) hedges, cubes and quirky topiary are distinctive theme plants used to structure formal gardens. Here they provide a welcome neutral foil to the frothy perennial planting in front – a contrast that boosts the effectiveness of both.

Left, above: No cottage garden I know of is complete without a rose... or five! Scented old roses such as *Rosa × odorata* 'Mutabilis' here are most evocative of this much-loved design style, although many modern shrub roses have been bred to share similar characteristics (without the thuggish tendencies).

Left, centre: Larger-than-life tree ferns – here, *Cyathea australis*, partnered with a dwarf fan palm (*Chamaerops humilis* var. *argentea*), *Rhododendron bureavii* and cabbage palm (*Cordyline indivisa*) – remind us of exotic locations. Should you choose this tropical style, an easy way to 'get the look' is by including them.

Left, below: While size does help, not all theme plants need to be big and bold. The purple top (*Verbena bonariensis*) and squirrel tail grass (*Hordeum jubatum*) in the foreground don't have a structural role – unlike many theme plants. However they certainly evoke an informal gravel garden reminiscent of southern California or the Iberian peninsula (see p122) and therefore are key to this planting style.

Focal points

Sometimes called feature or specimen plants, focal-point plants are key theme ones used principally to attract attention and draw the eye, just like a sculpture or fountain.

In fact designers often introduce eye-catching focal points such as palms and *Yucca* (perhaps in pots) as primary focal points or to emphasise the position of key features such as a still pool or a statue. Alternatively, they'll place them in the foreground as an intermediate focal point – a pause before the main 'event' behind. Larger focal-point plants serve the whole garden design too; they don't just help to structure ornamental beds and borders.

Below: For a plant used as a focal point to be truly successful it must be distinctly different in shape, colour or arrangement from its immediate surroundings, particularly the background. On this balcony, the spiky *Yucca* is set off perfectly by the shrubby olive screen (*Olea europaea* 'Cipressino') and clean architecture.

Stand out

For a focal point to catch the eye it needs to have bright or bold flowers or leaves, or better still a strong shape (see pp132–135). Columnar conifers, spiky shrubs, dramatic grasses such as golden oats (*Stipa gigantea*) are ideal. However they don't have to be evergreen – long-lasting sculptural perennials such as cardoon (*Cynara cardunculus*) also work well. Ultimately the final choice depends on the style or theme (see Chapter 3) and the location; banana palms for example might look odd backed by a rural English landscape.

The success of a focal point also depends on the plants around it – no bright-variegated foliage for example – otherwise this will only distract and cause confusion. Consider and plot supporting partner plants on paper at the same time so you don't forget them (see pp202–203).

Number count

The number of focal points depends on garden size and layout but avoid using too many, as they'll vie for your attention – in a small garden, there might be just one or two. However do introduce them at different heights (and therefore in different layers – see pp182–183). One palm or three smaller pencil junipers (*Juniperus scopulorum* 'Skyrocket' or *J. communis* 'Compressa') could draw interest from the patio, if a short distance away. But each planting area should also have reliable focal points, albeit smaller ones. This will both punctuate and draw the eye into the planting. Plants such as Adam's needle (*Yucca filamentosa*) and the ubiquitous box (*Buxus*) ball are ideal in the foreground.

Left, above: Repeating focal-point plants will both increase their power and presence, and help unify the planting. But don't mix dramatically different plants of the same size, or use them at the same scale, as this will cause confusion. These three clipped Indian bean trees (*Catalpa bignonioides*) share harmony of form and colour, which means they don't jostle uncomfortably for attention.

Left, below: A spherical box (*Buxus*) ball in the foreground is the visual 'pause' before the main event behind – towering but not too tall golden oats (*Stipa gigantea*). Here this grass is positioned to entice you down the beautifully planted path. To gauge the size of a proposed focal point, try cutting out a life-sized template or stack cardboard boxes on top of each other to help picture how it will look *in situ* when mature.

Ornamentals

Accents

Striking perennials, smaller grasses, hardy annuals and larger bulbs, commonly used to attract attention on a small scale, can all be classed as 'accent' plants. These should complement, but not clash with, the focal points (see p176). Think of it like this: focal points grab the eye from further away and direct it to an area; accent plants are the main reward up close. Many classic accents such as foxglove (*Digitalis*) and African lily (*Agapanthus*) are also invaluable theme plants, but only those that flower for a particularly long time – some *Verbascum chaixii* cultivars for example – have any sort of structural role, and then typically only if they're regularly repeated.

Flower & form

Flower form (see p136) followed by colour (see p138) are most important. Spherical ornamental onions (*Allium*) and large lilies (*Lilium*) are ideal accents, so too are slender perennials including mullein (*Verbascum*), lupin (*Lupinus*) and foxtail lily (*Eremurus*). Less dramatic multistemmed perennials such as coneflower (*Echinacea*) and Siberian iris (*Iris sibirica*) also work well. But accents only have power in numbers so they need planting in groups of 5–10+ for impact. Like focal points, the effectiveness of an accent does depend on the plants they're partnered with, so look at these at the same time. Fluffy grasses, mounding geraniums and low-growing subshrubs such as wormwood (*Artemisia*) are good and, in particular, hide the often-straggly lower stems of slender accents, especially bulbs.

Succession

As most accents are perennials or bulbs, not many last longer than a few months, so also consider planting in succession. If you can, choose at least one plant per season for continuity of accent, form and colour. Repeating them throughout the design will further help unify the planting at that particular time or season.

Opposite: White foxtail lilies (*Eremurus* 'Joanna'), towering above dark purple *Iris chrysographes*, are the accents here. At this size, these plants might qualify for focal-point 'status', but because they last for only a short time, it's best not to construct your planting around something so visually short-lived.

Below: These purple *Iris* are distinctive because of the quaking grass (*Briza*) and masterwort (*Astrantia*) beneath them. Both complement through contrasting form and colour. As accent plants depend on their partners, plan these at the same time.

Fillers

The word 'filler' is admittedly an ugly way to describe a huge collection of plants where you'll have the most fun creating exciting colour and texture combinations. Yet it is an appropriate one used by many designers. Plants here support rather than structure a planting, and they plug the gaps around the structural plants (see p172), key theme plants (see p174), focal points (see p176) and perhaps the accents (and their necessary partners) (see p178).

What goes where?

Colourful deciduous shrubs, roses, tall perennials and ornamental grasses are the bulky infill between weighty structural shrubs. Here plants should be chosen to flower at distinct times, either to enhance the display in front or to bridge a gap in interest and pull the eye deep into the planting.

In the foreground, most fillers are herbaceous perennials, which celebrated designer John Brookes fittingly calls the 'pretties'. Here flower colour is definitely the name of the game, although with ferns and grasses the foliage is particularly important. Different plants should be grouped together to harmonise or contrast with those around them. Try to strike a balance between the two however; a showier plant works best next to a more neutral one, and vice versa. Likewise, spread seasonal interest – position a spring-flowering perennial next to a summer shrub, an evergreen next to a deciduous plant for example – to avoid large gaps.

Temporary fillers

Annuals, biennials and short-lived perennials such as *Penstemon*, perennial flax (*Linum perenne*) and coneflower (*Echinacea purpurea*) are used to provide seasonal interest, particularly in summer, but they can also help to fill in space around woody plants as they mature. At the back of borders, tall, short-lived perennials such as purple top (*Verbena bonariensis*) and dittany (*Dictamnus albus*) are particularly useful between larger, slow-growing shrubs and conifers. Both will die off well before they become a nuisance (although both self-seed readily, so hopefully will find a niche somewhere).

Bulbs are wonderful temporary fillers too, particularly in early spring, providing interest when perennials are slowly emerging from their winter sleep.

Above, opposite: Drifts of feathery Mexican feather grass (*Stipa tenuissima*) and a spiky *Agave americana* structure this seaside garden planting. The rest – including red valerian (*Centranthus ruber*) and *Santolina rosmarinifolia* – is a mixture of accents and fillers.

Above, centre: The grasses throughout establish this planting, while shade-tolerant perennials and ferns including stinking hellebore (*Helleborus foetidus* Wester Flisk Group), shield fern (*Polystichum*) and masterwort (*Astrantia*) fill in the gaps. The lime-green umbels of archangel (*Angelica archangelica*) loom overhead.

Right: Under a stand of Himalayan white birch (*Betula utilis* var. *jacquemontii*), perennials including foam flower (*Tiarella cordifolia*), a white dusky cranesbill (*Geranium phaeum* 'Album') and saxifrage (*Saxifraga umbrosa*) bring colour and texture to this partially shady border. Beautiful as they are, none of these plants has a major structural role because they simply aren't visually powerful enough or distinct, nor do they perform for more than a few months.

Arranging plants

Layers of height

Having identified the role of different plants in the composition itself, let's now look at arranging them on the ground. The most common way is in layers according to their ultimate height when mature.

The actual number of layers firstly depends on the planting space – thin borders will accommodate only one or two (such as some tall slender perennials partnered with ground cover in front), whereas deep borders can often house bulky shrubs at the back too. The design style also has an influence. Designers often consciously omit various layers for dramatic contrast – by jumping from sizeable specimens directly to low perennials underneath for example. An essential consideration is the position from where you plan to view the planting – layers should be angled with this in mind. With borders backed by walls or fences for example, plants are traditionally graded from tall at the back to shorter ones in front. In island beds and open borders, the idea is to walk through or around the plants. Here layers are arranged in triangles or pyramids that can be viewed from all sides (see pp184–185). One key thing to note is that when planning the planting, try to pull one layer subtly into another – and vice versa – to create a more natural look, rather than simply arrange the layers like a staircase.

Designers often categorise the layers as the background, mid-ground, foreground and ground-layer, or subtle variations thereof. But, with borders backed by boundaries in particular, words such as 'back, 'middle' and 'front-of-the border' are perhaps more helpful to consider. In naturalistic open, border arrangements, 'top', 'middle' and 'bottom' are useful distinctions commonly used, as here the gradation in the height is much more subtle. Adopt whatever terms work best for you.

Right, above: In all but formal borders arranged around a central axis – see p92 for a prime example – designers typically won't layer a planting scheme as if it were a series of steps. Instead most will sweep lower layers towards the back of a border to pull the eye into the planting. Similarly, taller plants are often brought forward at various points to encourage investigation of what's on the other side.

Right, below: Even at this scale, the layers in this naturalistic woodland planting are obvious. Importantly, the ferns and ground cover tolerate the shade cast by the purple cow parsley (*Anthriscus sylvestris* 'Ravenswing').

The background 'foil'

In a large garden with wide borders, small trees, big shrubs, conifers or large bamboos act as the background foil. Plants here also define different garden 'rooms' and may be used for privacy and screening. In a small garden or a thin border, you may not have space to include many plants this big. However do consider that boundary hedges or trees in surrounding gardens and the wider landscape all perform a background role. So will walls or fences – whether or not they're clad with climbers. Don't forget to think about these too.

Back-of-the-border or mid-ground plants

The main structural heavyweights for deep borders – comprising medium-sized shrubs (around 2–4m/ 6½–13ft tall), conifers and/or larger ornamental grasses such as silver grass (*Miscanthus*) – come in here. Depending on the style, tall perennials, roses and/or floriferous deciduous shrubs fill the gaps in between.

In this layer, evergreens are important for year-round stability – aim to have at least 50 percent of the area planted with them.

Middle-of-the-border or foreground plants

In the main, small roses, most perennials and tall hardy annuals and biennials are mid-border plants. So too are small evergreen grasses and shrubs, which, as mentioned on p172, help structure this layer.

To create a feeling of depth in long linear borders, sweep plants in this layer towards the back of the border. Or draw taller lacy plants such as purple top (*Verbena bonariensis*) to the front to partially obscure the plants behind; this will make the arrangement more interesting.

Front-of-the-border or ground-layer

Prostrate shrubs, half-hardy annuals, spring bulbs, hummocky grasses and/or dwarf perennials cover the ground at your feet.

Repetition is common here to unify the composition. Perhaps pick one or two plants and use them in different-sized groupings throughout. Long-lasting perennials such as *Geranium* Rozanne = 'Gerwat' are ideal. So too are evergreens such as elephant's ears (*Bergenia*), which also smothers weeds.

In large borders, spreading plants are best; in smaller ones, choose those with a more compact shape.

Triangles & pyramids

When arranging plants with layers of height in mind, a technique favoured by many planting designers (Beth Chatto being a prime example) is to plant in triangles. Tall plants – typically shrubs or columnar conifers – form the centre, graduating to smaller plants around the outside, creating a pyramidal-like outline.

Planting in triangles and pyramids is an obvious approach for island beds that are surrounded by grass, paths or paving and designed to be viewed from all sides. However you can also pick out pyramids in open borders where little hillocks of height undulate across the area, the taller perennials and grasses forming each 'peak'. This technique is also popular in borders backed by walls or fences, where the height is arranged in formal layers, from back to front. Here pyramidal arrangements of plants, particularly in the foreground, help stop the composition behaving like a regimented flight of steps.

In narrow borders where there is little room to layer front to back, you should favour planting in triangles or pyramids, essentially layering from side to side instead.

The height, position and number of plants determine whether the pyramid is symmetrically or asymmetrically balanced, and whether it looks subtle – like a mound – or is erect and eye-catching; consider this when drawing out your design.

Left: In mixed plantings, tall shrubs, conifers or roses – here trained over woven hazel domes – form the apex to plants arranged in pyramids with height in mind. With thin borders, which are long but shallow (such as the one at the back here), layering in triangles from side to side if there's limited room to layer from front to back will help create a more interesting, three-dimensional design.

Clumps & blocks

In small gardens and mixed plantings, planting in clumps or blocks is the most common way of organising plants within layers of height. Plants are arranged in distinct groups taking into account the size, shape and colour of their neighbours. The result is a fairly formal look. The size of the clump depends on the scale of the area to be planted and how much impact you want each plant to have. But, as a guide most gardens feature clumps or blocks containing 3–12 plants, depending on whether they're large shrubs or small groundcover perennials for example (see p192).

Above, left: Planting in clumps is most obvious when the plants are distinctly different. In this little vignette, most plants share similarities in terms of form or texture, so the way they've been arranged isn't so obvious. Of course the little ribbon of brook thistle (*Cirsium riuulare* 'Atropurpureum') weaving through the centre also helps here too.

Above: Clumps of white peonies (*Paeonia lactiflora* 'Jan van Leeuwen'), *Rodgersia podophylla* 'Rotlaub', asarabacca (*Asarum europaeum*) and *Hakonechloa macra* feature here alongside drifts of white masterwort (*Astrantia*). In the modernist tradition, these clumps might have clearly identifiable 'square edges', which in turn make them into true 'blocks'. However most designers will shun this, for fear of it looking too severe.

The shape of each block is usually fairly 'blobby' but in modernist and minimalist design, severe rectilinear blocks (of 9–30+ plants) are often used to reinforce bold design geometry. Here they usually form the base for eye-catching perennials mingled throughout for contrast.

In the traditional sense, blocks and clumps aren't naturalistic; planting in drifts (see pp188–189) and intermingling (see pp190–191) are the techniques preferred in massed perennial and meadow-like plantings. However you will find 'blocks' of plants in nature, usually made by dense, clump-forming species such as Joe Pye weed (*Eupatorium purpureum*). If you fancy a slice of naturalistic planting, in place of a lawn perhaps, plan to 'mingle' most plants (see p190), but don't forget to 'clump' a few as well.

Drifts

Planting in drifts is a popular method of arranging plants. It simply means organising them – notably perennials, ferns and grasses – in distinct, interlocking, often tear-drop shapes of different sizes, to create a more informal arrangement. This concept was pioneered by Gertrude Jekyll in the early 20th century, and in part also by William Robinson, who, fed up with plants set in formal blocks in the Victorian tradition, wanted a more relaxed look. When planting, it helps to think of each drift in the Jeykll tradition, that is, as a painterly brush stroke, designed to harmonise or contrast with its neighbours.

The size of the drift depends on the size of the area. In a large garden this might mean each drift features 9–20+ plants. In a small garden it might be 3–12 plants, depending on their vigour, size at maturity and the impact you'd like particular plants to make. Do note that small drifts can look quite 'blocky' (meaning formal), so the bigger they are the better, especially if you want a more natural-looking arrangement.

On a larger scale, drift planting with a restricted palette of plants can look monotonous. To avoid this, it is important to use plants of different heights. Adding accents with contrasting forms or splitting up large drifts into smaller ones, for a patchwork quilt-like effect, is popular nowadays too – the number of plants doesn't change, just the volume of them in each group.

Right: Drifts of yellow lupins (*Lupinus* 'Chandelier') and nettle-leaved mullein (*Verbascum chaixii* 'Album') have been arranged in large meandering drifts of different sizes, for interest. It is always important to consider the size of each drift carefully. If too small, the plants will lack presence, while if a drift is too big, the planting might look monotonous.

Above: Seas of dwarf catmint (*Nepeta racemosa* 'Walker's Low') provide a suitable foil for the flowing painterly drifts of perennials, including purple *Iris* 'Dusky Challenger', chocolate *Iris* 'Provençal' and orangey *Iris* 'Cable Car'. They knit the whole composition together.

Left: A river of purple coneflower (*Echinacea purpurea*) bordered by blue Russian sage (*Perouskia* 'Blue Spire') and giant coneflower (*Rudbeckia maxima*) helps lead the eye along this gravel path. Note how the same plant appears in another drift of a smaller size through a curtain of straw-coloured feather reed grass (*Calamagrostis × acutiflora* 'Karl Foerster') – a repetition that encourages visual harmony.

Intermingling & random planting

A modern and naturalistic way of combining plants, particularly perennials, tall biennials and grasses, is to intermingle them, apparently at random. On a small scale, one or two plants might be sprinkled through others, like glacé cherries over a cake. On a large scale, designers aim to reflect the dynamic and rhythmic patterns of plants found in nature. Here small groups and singletons interweave with larger groups of plants in a seemingly random matrix – picture a wildflower meadow and you'll get the idea.

Over a large area, intermingling or random planting isn't easy. This technique requires a keen understanding of ecological compatibility, maintenance routines, growth cycles and flowering times. So, if your experience is limited, keep both your ambition and ideas simple for best results.

In borders?

Extensive intermingled plantings (especially with plants of a similar height) usually look out of place and untidy in a garden border backed by a wall, fence or hedge. Here most designers will arrange the majority of planting in blocks and drifts, mixing one or two accent plants (see p178) throughout the foreground, perhaps a taller one further back, as though they've self-seeded.

Slender perennials and bulbs are ideal – so too are short-lived species such as oriental poppies (*Papaver orientale* cultivars), which die off and leave big gaps if they're arranged any other way.

A 'mini meadow'

The fastest way to create an intermingled planting in the 'flower' meadow-like tradition (meaning no grass) is quite simply to sow one (there are many seed suppliers online). However this strategy isn't for everyone, particularly those with small urban gardens where 'people space' comes first and there just isn't room. Instead a common approach is to choose only four or five small-flowered ornamentals, each of a slightly differing height and form, and apportion them to one or two rectilinear island beds (replacing part of an unloved lawn, perhaps?). Imposing a strong geometry such as this gives a lovely contrast and also makes an intermingled arrangement look intentional, rather than an untidy accident. At this scale it's also much easier to match and partner compatible plants too. For impact, ideally choose long-flowering species where at least half are in flower at any one time.

Do avoid vigorous or invasive plants and those with dense leafy stems that might shade others. Floppy plants such as peonies (*Paeonia*), which are prone to collapsing on plants underneath, should also be avoided.

Most intermingled plantings peak in summer, so for spring consider underplanting with bulbs to extend the season of interest, especially if the planting is in a prime spot. Low formal hedges to border the area, or strong focal points (see pp176–177) of clipped topiary, are ideal for autumn and winter. Perennials with attractive seedheads are also invaluable. See p166–169 for more on how to make the most of the mix.

Above: Purple coneflowers (*Echinacea pallida*), Carthusian pinks (*Dianthus carthusianorum*) and beardlip penstemons (*Penstemon barbatus*) flourish in this sown, dry-steppe-style planting by James Hitchmough at RHS Garden Wisley, England. Without doubt, the easiest and most effective way to create a naturalistic intermingled planting is to sow the scheme from seed, then sit back and embrace the unpredictable nature of what plant pops up where.

Left: A sprinkling of blue poppies (*Meconopsis baileyi*) throughout this woodland planting makes for a delightful contrast. Short-lived plants such as these always work well when intermingled randomly. When they die off, gaps aren't so obvious.

Massing

Before we look at plotting a planting design on paper, it's important to emphasise that plants need to be grouped or 'massed' at a proportion that is suitable for both the size of the garden and the area to be planted. This applies regardless of whether you arrange plants in distinct blocks or winding drifts or whether you decide to intermingle them instead.

The bigger the area and the bigger the garden, the higher the number of the same plant you should use. Odd numbers look more natural too (although that's not essential, especially with large groups of more than seven).

As well as the size of the space, the role of particular plants in the design has influence too. Theme plants that are central to a particular style (see p174) must appear at a percentage high enough for them to do the required job: for example one tree fern (*Dicksonia*) doesn't make a jungle but five might.

Size, shape and distinctiveness are also key when massing plants. Slender single-stemmed perennials such as columbine (*Aquilegia*) and rusty foxglove (*Digitalis ferruginea*) appear lost and lonely by themselves (in all but the smallest borders) but are dramatic and eye-catching in larger numbers. Also note that small plants used to unify and structure a planting must be sufficiently numerous that they're clearly visible, otherwise they won't be able to perform this role.

Right, above: The larger the garden the more of the same plant you should use, especially with subtler, edge-of-woodland species such as fringe cups (*Tellima grandiflora*) and cranesbill (*Geranium* 'Philippe Vapelle') – just two of those featured here. Plants such as these have power only in numbers.

Right, below: Large masses of the same plant in a small space strike a fine line between boring and dramatic. Designers today therefore often break large masses into smaller, different-sized drifts and blocks, or randomly mingle them for interest as here – a lesson certainly learnt from nature.

Overleaf: Big garden + large beds and borders + commanding architecture = large masses of plants. These blocks of feather reed grass (*Calamagrostis × acutiflora* 'Karl Foerster'), lavender (*Lavandula angustifolia* 'Folgate'), Russian sage (*Perouskia*) and orpine (*Sedum* 'Matrona') are in perfect proportion with their surroundings and with each other.

How many to plant (for a garden)?

Note: The numbers quoted below pertain to the number of plants needed to make an impact, whether they are placed side by side or in relatively close proximity.

* (unless it's a hedge)

TYPE OF PLANT	EXAMPLES	NO.
Evergreen shrubs, conifers and bamboo (2m/6½ft+)	*Viburnum tinus* 'Eve Price' (laurustinus), *Osmanthus* × *burkwoodii*	1–3*
Deciduous shrubs and larger roses (2m/6½ft+)	*Philadelphus* 'Virginal' (mock orange), *Rosa glauca* (red-leaved rose)	1–3*
Medium-sized roses, shrubs (deciduous and evergreen) and conifers (75cm–1.5m/2½–5ft)	*Sarcococca hookeriana* var. *hookeriana* (sweet box), *Rosa* Munstead Wood = 'Ausbernard'	1–5*
Short/groundcover shrubs and conifers (25–75cm/10–30in)	*Lavandula angustifolia* 'Hidcote' (English lavender), *Salvia officinalis* 'Purpurascens' (purple sage)	3–7*
Vigorous alpines, small perennials and grasses	*Thymus pseudolanuginosus* (woolly thyme), *Viola odorata* (sweet violet), *Pulsatilla vulgaris* (pasque flower)	3–15
Small-sized perennials, ferns and tussocky grasses	*Centranthus lecoqii* (valerian), *Polypodium vulgare* (common polypody), *Festuca glauca* 'Elijah Blue' (blue fescue)	3–9
Medium-sized perennials, ferns and grasses	*Gillenia trifoliata* (bowman's root), *Stipa tenuissima* (Mexican feather grass)	3–9
Large (or spreading) perennials, grasses and ferns	*Foeniculum vulgare* 'Giant Bronze' (bronze fennel), *Osmunda regalis* (royal fern), *Miscanthus sinensis* 'Kleine Fontäne' (silver grass)	1–5
Small–medium hardy annuals and biennials	*Nigella damascena* 'Miss Jeykll' (love-in-a-mist), *Papaver nudicaule* (Iceland poppy)	5–15
Medium–large annuals and biennials	*Lunaria annua* var. *albiflora* (white-flowered honesty), *Hesperis matronalis* (dame's violet)	3–10
Small–medium bulbs and biennials	*Narcissus poeticus* var. *recurvus* (old pheasant's eye), *Tulipa* 'Apeldoorn' (bulb), *Crocus speciosus* (large autumn crocus)	10–30
Medium–large single-stemmed perennials, biennials and bulbs	*Verbascum bombyciferum* 'Arctic Snow', *Lilium regale* (regal lily), *Allium hollandicum* 'Purple Sensation' (ornamental onion) *Digitalis purpurea* f. *albiflora* (foxglove)	5–12

Organising the wish list

By now you may well have a long list of possible plants but inevitably there won't be space to fit them all. In fact it's always surprising just how few you will end up using.

First break down the list considering the role of each plant (screening, focal point, accent and so on). Then record the height and spread of each one and group them into the layer in which they belong (see pp182–183). If you've created a planting calendar (see pp164–165), you can do all this there. Revisit your requirements next, using the checklist (see right). If any plants don't work well, remove them. Likewise, if too many plants fall into the same group or the same layer, cut out the weakest, based on your preference.

How many is too many? This is a tricky question to answer, without looking over your shoulder. But if you consider the importance of repetition, massing plants at a suitable scale (see p193), as well as the size of each plant compared to the area to be planted, you'll get a good idea. Check out the amount of plants used in the sample plans in Chapter 7 too.

Some analysis now may also identify gaps. Find a plant to fit, or note the characteristics of plants you still require, naming them later as the planting design develops on paper.

Below: Always factor in views from the home when considering which plants might make the final wish list, especially expensive specimens such as topiary that you may well buy big for instant impact. It's likely you'll spend as much time enjoying the garden from inside as you will when outdoors.

Questions to consider

- **Soil type & climate:** Will plants grow well (see pp10–17)?

- **Users:** Have you considered everyone, including pets (see p22)?

- **Maintenance:** Do you have enough time to look after what you've chosen (see pp24–25)?

- **Plant groups (such as trees, shrubs):** Are those you've selected appropriate, considering the style and theme (see Chapter 4)?

- **Style, theme &/or design 'vision':** What are the key theme plants (see pp174–175)? Do they work by themselves or do they need to be grouped?

- **Roles/categories:** Are the plants selected for different roles – especially practical ones – up to the task (see Chapter 3)? Allocate roles to existing plants you want to keep too, if you haven't already done so.

- **Seasonal interest:** A peak is inevitable but does your collection perform too early or too late? Is there a glut or a big gap? A planting calendar is invaluable here (see pp164–165).

- **Size:** Are plants too tall, too wide or possibly too vigorous (see Chapters 2 and 3)?

- **Repetition:** Which plants will unify the planting? How will they be spaced and what rhythms might appear (see p130)?

- **Colour palette:** Do plants complement, contrast or clash with your chosen colour scheme (see pp138–153)?

- **Shape & texture:** Are they too different or too similar (see pp132–135 and 154–157)?

- **Scent:** Is there enough, considering the times of day you use the garden (see pp158–161)?

Opposite, above: Although many plants are pretty forgiving of less-than-ideal conditions, always make sure that everything on your wish list is suitable for your garden's soil type and aspect. Check carefully and delete any plants that don't conform before you inadvertently plot them on paper.

Opposite, below: A lack of privacy will seriously affect how you use the garden. Always question whether plants intended to provide privacy are fit for purpose and likely to grow to a sufficient size. If you have a pleached tree or another special shape in mind, check it's available at the size you require to do the job.

7.

The Best-Made Plans

It's time to bring together the theory we've looked at thus far, and put it into practice. This chapter features 15 planting designs for 15 different styles, common scenarios and contexts, from shady woodland to protected courtyards.

Use them as you want. Perhaps copy one design completely if the size and growing conditions are the same as in your own garden. Or use them as inspiration, adapting or tweaking them to suit your garden space or personal taste. You will find that some intentionally share similarities in terms of soil type, aspect or style. If so, plants from one design can be incorporated into another. I've also tried to feature a variety of plants in each plan, focusing on species or combinations that always work well or look good together, although everyone, including me, has their favourites!

Planning & plotting

All planting schemes should start out on paper, where mistakes don't matter. A sketch in which you can see the different plant heights and shapes is a helpful first step. Designers often make simple elevation drawings, but sketching on tracing paper over photos of the area to be planted is also useful. Alternatively, create a collage or superimpose a design you like over the photos, if the size and environmental characteristics of the area being replanted are similar. I sometimes find it useful to make a crude model out of balls of paper and bits of foam to gauge how plant shapes and sizes might work together. The time spent visualising the display as though you were standing in front of it will encourage you to consider more carefully the result you're trying to achieve.

Measure up and draw down

After visualising the scheme in 3-D as it were, you'll need to make an actual plan, which eventually you can use to quantify the numbers of plants you'll require, and to cost the scheme. However quantities and the exact final position of each individual plant aren't important at this point. Instead concentrate on the design itself, notably which plants partner each other and at what size and proportion, using your sketches and list of requirements as a guide (we'll worry about practical matters such as spacings, sizes and quantities in Chapter 8).

For this process to be the most useful, measure the area to be planted and draw it to scale; 1:50 is good for most displays. Use a large sheet so there's plenty of room to make additional notes. For most people, graph paper is better than plain – the faint grid lines are useful when quickly comparing the proportion of one group to another as the scheme develops. Four squares on paper to 1 sq m (1 sq yd) works well. Alternatively, draw and use your own grid.

Opposite: When drawing out your design on paper in plan view, it's important to keep referencing the actual area to be planted – whether it's a small garden, or a large one like this – as you go along. This will help ensure that the size of plant 'masses' you plot are in proportion to the size of the space.

Real life

You may find it easier to plan your planting *in situ*, using handfuls of dry sand and some large labels, than create a scale drawing. Differently sized cardboard boxes, upturned plastic pots and bamboo-cane wigwams may help you to visualise the different heights.

Plotting the plants

To mark the plants, work at the same scale, introducing blobs or circles for trees, shrubs and other woody plants. Draw perennials, ferns and grasses as interlocking blobs, sausages and/or elongated tear-drop shapes; they are more likely to appear like this on the ground. For bulbs, simply ring the area where they're to go, with a broken line.

Always consider the height and spread of each plant, as it's these factors that determine which plants you use and what combinations will fit the space available. With trees and larger shrubs, this is especially important. A tree is for life, and you don't want it causing problems later on because it's grown too big. By plotting trees and larger shrubs at their eventual size (at 15–20 years or more) on paper, you also gain a helpful *aide-mémoire* to discourage you from planting big plants around or directly underneath them.

However, slow-growing trees and larger shrubs do take a long time to reach maturity and, consequently, for your scheme to look like you imagined it. For this reason, some designers plot these plants at 7–10 years' height and spread rather than at their mature size, factoring in the probability of a little redesign of the planting at this point in time. Nursery people, plant encyclopedias and the website of your national horticultural association/society (www.rhs.org.uk, for example) can help with size and spread here.

Whether you plot larger trees and shrubs at maturity or at their size after 7–10 years, do note that initially the planting underneath will be temporary – most likely perennials, ferns and grasses – unless you've chosen a specimen plant in a lawn. These medium-term filler plants (see pp180–181) can be removed and replanted as conditions underneath change, from sun to shade, as the plant above matures.

On pp202–203 there is a useful plotting sequence that considers what we've looked at in Chapter 6.

The plotting process

Most designers follow a logical linear sequence such as this when drawing up a planting scheme for a new bed or border. Always remember to label each plant clearly as you go.

1. **Existing plants & climbers:** First add any plants worth keeping. For shrubs that have been pruned hard to rejuvenate them, leave at least 60–120cm (2–4ft) around the outside, depending on how vigorous they are, so they have a space to grow into. Afterwards add climbers and wall shrubs, if appropriate. Set these 2–3m (6½–10ft) apart, depending on their size, vigour and role. For example evergreen climbers needed to screen an ugly boundary should be spaced closer together than those chosen for colour and scent.

2. **Backbone:** Now plot the main structural plants (see pp172–173) and those that theme the display (see pp174–175). Put tall ones towards the back of the bed, and shorter ones in the foreground. Positioning one plant or plant group every 5–6m (16–20ft) is a good starting point. Usefully, this divides the area into a series of little rooms or 'bays', which individually are less daunting to design than if you were tackling the whole border all at once. Deciduous shrubs, roses and tall grasses, which might have a more subtle structural role or merely fill gaps at the back of the border, can be plotted now too (alternatively, wait until step 5).

3. **Focal points:** Plants whose role it is to draw the eye come next (see pp176–177). Position tall ones first, then smaller ones in front, if required. How big and dramatic they are, plus how long they last, will determine whether these plants are placed by themselves or in small groups.

4. **Accents:** Position these with height in mind, to complement the focal points. As accents (see p178) and focal points depend on the plants around them, also identify these now. If you plan to intermingle a few accents, you may find it easier to arrange everything first and do it at the end of step 6.

5. **Filler time:** Start next to one structural plant or group and work outwards with four or five different species to fill in the gaps (see pp180–181). For contrast and interest, consider varying the size of each group. Remember the flowering time too; spread plants evenly that perform in the same season.

6. **And repeat:** Once you're happy with the first one, work on another, similar-sized arrangement alongside. Alternatively, choose another structural plant and work outwards from it in the same way as before. Remember, repetition is important to unify the design. Lastly, add any short-lived perennials or bedding plants to fill temporary gaps, followed by bulbs if required.

Making changes

After planning the scheme on paper, critique the outcome and make changes as appropriate. To do this, lay tracing paper over the first draft, especially if you have to tweak things underneath.

Check that seasonal interest is distributed evenly throughout – perhaps shade all plants that perform in the same season the same colour. Also note the position of structural plants and appraise the combinations, considering colour, form and texture (some sketches might help here). Examine whether the size of each block/drift/group is right too. It won't hurt to revisit your brief again either (see p22); have you done what you set out to do?

Right: The minimal-maintenance design on pp206–207 is used here to illustrate the plotting process. This same process was also used for all the other schemes in this chapter.

The plotting process 'on plan'

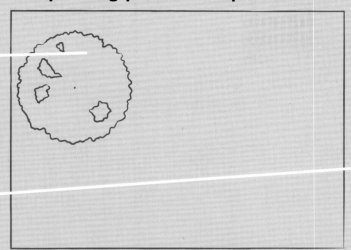

1 Existing plants & climbers: A healthy juneberry (*Amelanchier × grandiflora* 'Ballerina') is the starting point.

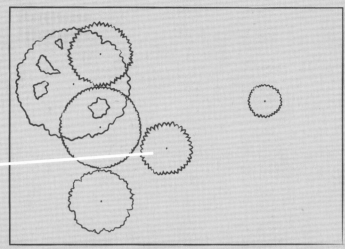

2 Backbone: Arranged with height in mind against a fence on the left; shrubs, including David viburnum (*Viburnum davidii*), establish the composition.

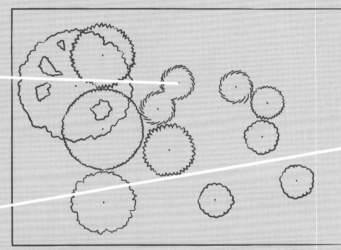

3 Focal points: Three tall maiden grass (*Miscanthus sinensis* 'Gracillimus') accompany three squat dwarf mountain pines (*Pinus mugo* Pumilio Group) in front.

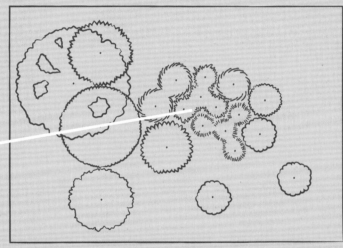

4 Accents: An African blue lily (*Agapanthus* 'Loch Hope'), partnered with New Zealand satin flower (*Libertia grandiflora*), are the main accents of choice here.

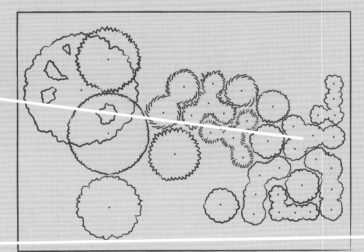

5 Filler time: A floriferous stonecrop (*Sedum* Herbstfreude Group 'Herbstfreude') forms part of this first small group of five species.

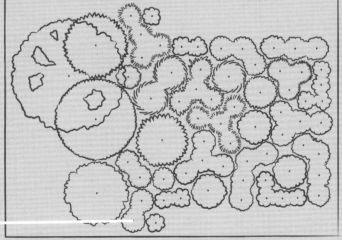

6 And repeat: Cranesbill (*Geranium* 'Johnson's Blue') completes the last group, then bulbs are sprinkled in the foreground. (For all other plants see pp206–207.)

Minimal maintenance

Mention the words 'low maintenance' and dreary displays of shrubs, heathers and conifers bordering supermarket car parks probably spring to mind. But low maintenance needn't mean boring. Some of the most exciting modern planting designs require little more than 10 minutes' work a week to keep them looking good – and often less (see p25). If you choose plants wisely and observe good gardening practice (principally 'right plant, right place'), your low-maintenance garden can be a visual delight, even with heathers and conifers!

Tricks of the trade

- **Low-maintenance selection:** Shrubs (especially evergreens), tidy 'border' conifers (not unruly hedging types), ferns, ornamental grasses and tough groundcover perennials (which help to smother weeds) should be first choice. For large, open borders, try a mini meadow (see p190). All need little attention once established.

- **Avoid demanding plants:** These include bush roses, lots of topiary, annuals and biennials (except tidy and reliable self-seeders) and tall perennials, which require staking. Seasonal bedding displays are out too, unless restricted to large pots that don't need much work.

- **Inbred resistance:** Opt for plants that have pest and disease resistance built in. Many new perennial phlox (*Phlox paniculata*) for example are resistant to mildew, unlike their older counterparts. Likewise, plantain lilies (*Hosta*) such as *H.* 'Sum and Substance' and *H.* 'Dorset Blue' (Tardiana Group) offer some resistance against slugs and snails.

- **The right roses:** Select disease-resistant roses. Wild shrub roses such as white Scotch rose (*Rosa spinosissima*) or pink-flowering, red-leaved rose (*R. glauca*) need far less maintenance than more demanding floribundas and hybrid teas (see pp48–49).

Pittosporum tenuifolium 'Silver Queen' (kohuhu)

Miscanthus sinensis 'Gracillimus' (maiden grass)

Narcissus 'Trevithian' (jonquil)

Agapanthus 'Loch Hope'
(African blue lily)

Pinus mugo Pumilio Group
(dwarf mountain pine)

Rosa rugosa 'Alba'
(white Japanese rose)

Stachys byzantina 'Silver Carpet'
(lambs' tongues)

Viburnum davidii
(David viburnum)

This minimal-maintenance design is intended to be used between a terrace and the lawn in a typical suburban garden. The shrubs and perennials on the left-hand side have been chosen to cope with light shade cast by neighbouring trees. The rest of the bed is in full sun. The plants, backed by a wall or fence, are layered, from tall shrubs on the left to evergreen groundcover perennials on the right – perhaps bordering a path.

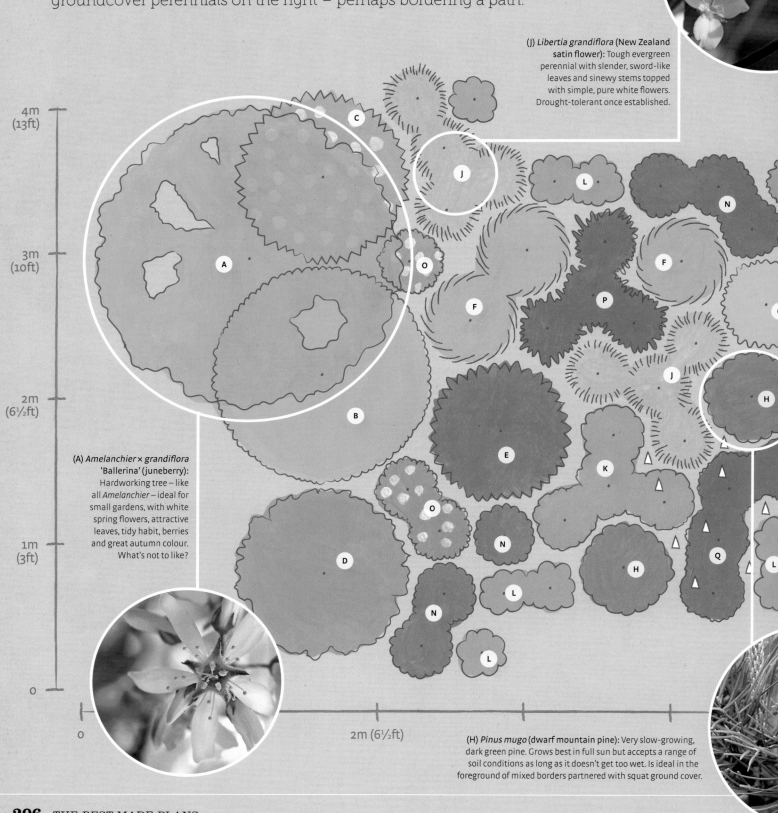

(J) *Libertia grandiflora* (New Zealand satin flower): Tough evergreen perennial with slender, sword-like leaves and sinewy stems topped with simple, pure white flowers. Drought-tolerant once established.

(A) *Amelanchier × grandiflora* 'Ballerina' (juneberry): Hardworking tree – like all *Amelanchier* – ideal for small gardens, with white spring flowers, attractive leaves, tidy habit, berries and great autumn colour. What's not to like?

(H) *Pinus mugo* (dwarf mountain pine): Very slow-growing, dark green pine. Grows best in full sun but accepts a range of soil conditions as long as it doesn't get too wet. Is ideal in the foreground of mixed borders partnered with squat ground cover.

4m (13ft)

3m (10ft)

2m (6½ft)

1m (3ft)

0

0

2m (6½ft)

The fine detail

Aspect: Semishade (by trees or buildings) to full sun.

Soil type: Moist but free-draining.

pH: Slightly acid to neutral.

Peak period of interest: Spring to autumn.

Flower colour: White and yellow in spring; blue, white and green in summer; white and coppery red in autumn.

Foliage colour & texture: Green (in various tints and shades) and silver with burgundy-red/yellow/orange-red autumnal tints. Medium to fine.

Maintenance: Very low to low. In spring, cut back the maiden grass to 15–20cm (6–8in), and also prune the perennials if dead foliage and flowers haven't already flopped over.

Other notes: Japanese rose (C) and sweetspire (D) have scented flowers, and the lavender (I) produces fragrant foliage. For smaller plots, a Japanese rose might be too vigorous; choose a smaller shrub rose instead.

Design decisions

Year-round interest is an important consideration when positioning plants. Tidy evergreens such as a subtly variegated kohuhu (B), dwarf mountain pine (H) along with a long-lasting variegated maiden grass (F) structure the planting and look good in winter. The pine and maiden grass are also important focal points. For spring, elephant's ears (L), spurge (G) and jonquils (triangles) bring welcome colour. In summer, plants such as New Zealand satin flower (J) and a tough white Japanese rose (C) take on this role. Autumn sees a white Japanese anemone (O) and stonecrop (K) flower, while juneberry (A) and summer-flowering sweetspire (D) produce good autumnal leaf tints, as does the rose, which also rewards with large, orange-red hips over winter.

A *Amelanchier × grandiflora* 'Ballerina' (juneberry; ❀❀❀ Z3–7) H&S: 4–8 × 4–8m (13–25 × 13–25ft)

B *Pittosporum tenuifolium* 'Silver Queen' (kohuhu; ❀❀ Z9–11) H&S: 3 × 2m (10 × 6½ft)

C *Rosa rugosa* 'Alba' (white Japanese rose; ❀❀❀ Z2–9) H&S: 1–2.5 × 1–2.5m (3–8 × 3–8ft)

D *Itea virginica* 'Henry's Garnet' (sweetspire; ❀❀❀ Z6–9) H&S: 1.5 × 2m (5 × 6½ft)

E *Viburnum davidii* (David viburnum; ❀❀❀ Z7–9) H&S: 1–1.5 × 1–1.5m (3–5 × 3–5ft)

F *Miscanthus sinensis* 'Gracillimus' (maiden grass; ❀❀❀ Z6–9) H&S: 1.5m × 75cm (5ft × 30in)

G *Euphorbia characias* subsp. *wulfenii* (spurge; ❀❀ Z7–10) H&S: 1.2 × 1.2m (4 × 4ft)

H *Pinus mugo* Pumilio Group (dwarf mountain pine; ❀❀❀ Z3–7) H&S: 2.5 × 4m (8 × 13ft)

I *Lavandula × intermedia* 'Grosso' (lavender; ❀❀❀ Z5–8) H&S: 80 × 80cm (32 × 32in)

J *Libertia grandiflora* (New Zealand satin flower; ❀❀❀ Z8–11) H&S: 90 × 60cm (36 × 24in)

6m (20ft)

K *Sedum* Herbstfreude Group 'Herbstfreude' (stonecrop; ❀❀❀ Z3–10) H&S: 60 × 50cm (24 × 20in)

L *Bergenia* 'Bressingham White' (elephant's ears; ❀❀❀ Z3–8) H&S: 40 × 55cm (16 × 22in)

M *Stachys byzantina* 'Silver Carpet' (Lambs' tongues; ❀❀❀ Z4–8) H&S: 45 × 60cm (18 × 24in)

N *Geranium* 'Johnson's Blue' (cranesbill; ❀❀❀ Z4–8) H&S: 40 × 60cm (16 × 24in)

O *Anemone × hybrida* 'Honorine Jobert' (Japanese anemone; ❀❀❀ Z3–8) H&S: 1.2m × 80cm (4ft × 32in)

P *Agapanthus* 'Loch Hope' (Blue African lily; ❀❀❀ Z7–11) H&S: 1.2m × 40cm (4ft × 16in)

Q *Campanula portenschlagiana* (Dalmatian bellflower; ❀❀❀ Z4–7) H&S: 30 × 40cm (12 × 16in)

Narcissus 'Trevithian' (jonquil; ❀❀❀ Z3–9) H&S: 45 × 20cm (18 × 8in)

Urban exotic

Exotic planting celebrates dramatic form, foliage and brilliantly coloured flowers (see p106). It is a style ideally suited to urban gardens (see p109), and perfectly illustrates the maxim that small spaces need a bold approach. Urban gardens are warmer than their country cousins and are usually more sheltered too. In temperate climates this means it's possible to grow exciting, frost-tender bananas (*Musa* and *Ensete*) and ginger lilies (*Hedychium*), given only a little protection or, if you're lucky, no protection at all.

Tricks of the trade

- **A sense of place:** To suggest a particular region, choose natives (if they'll cope with the conditions) or plants that originate from colder climates but still look exotic. Grasses, cardoon (*Cynara*), *Agave americana* (in fact anything that looks remotely cactus-like) suggest the arid landscape of southern California and Mexico for example. For a slice of subtropical South Africa, grow pineapple lily (*Eucomis*), montbretia (*Crocosmia*), day lilies (*Hemerocallis*) and African blue lilies (*Agapanthus*). The *Encyclopedia of Exotic Plants for Temperate Climates* by exotic gardening guru Will Giles lists them all.

- **Up close and personal:** In temperate climates don't be afraid to space tender plants closer than normal. These might grow huge in tropical climates but they never reach these proportions elsewhere unless you have a really hot, humid spot.

- **Tall but thin:** Lofty plants such as bamboo, tree ferns, bananas (*Ensete* and *Musa*), palms and loquat (*Eriobotrya*) should be first choice. These make good use of space but don't take up much room on the ground; unlike fat shrubs, it's possible to plant underneath them too.

- **Think about foliage:** Avoid too much dark purple and plum-coloured foliage in small spaces. At a distance, they can look like holes, especially at dusk. Use variegated plants sparingly too, as an accent only.

Canna 'Orange Punch' (Indian shot plant)

Lobelia tupa
(devil's tobacco)

Lilium regale 'Album'
(regal lily)

Verbena bonariensis
(purple top)

Dahlia 'Nuit d'Eté'

Crocosmia × crocosmiiflora
'Zeal Tan' (montbretia),
Penstemon 'Blackbird and
Verbena rigida f. lilacina 'Polaris'
(hardy garden verbena)

This exotic scheme is for a sunny urban courtyard or basement, sheltered by walls and buildings on all sides. The planting borders a deck or paved terrace and is orientated at an angle to the surrounding boundaries to open up deeper pockets for planting – a common design ploy in urban gardens.

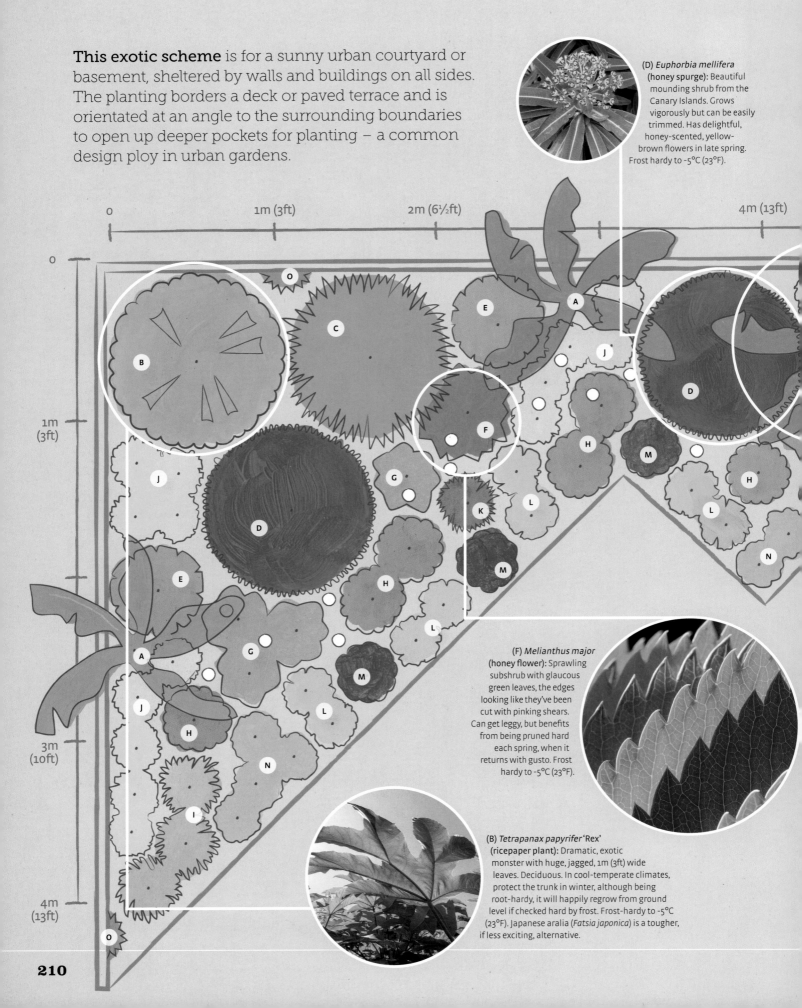

(D) *Euphorbia mellifera* (honey spurge): Beautiful mounding shrub from the Canary Islands. Grows vigorously but can be easily trimmed. Has delightful, honey-scented, yellow-brown flowers in late spring. Frost hardy to -5°C (23°F).

(F) *Melianthus major* (honey flower): Sprawling subshrub with glaucous green leaves, the edges looking like they've been cut with pinking shears. Can get leggy, but benefits from being pruned hard each spring, when it returns with gusto. Frost hardy to -5°C (23°F).

(B) *Tetrapanax papyrifer* 'Rex' (ricepaper plant): Dramatic, exotic monster with huge, jagged, 1m (3ft) wide leaves. Deciduous. In cool-temperate climates, protect the trunk in winter, although being root-hardy, it will happily regrow from ground level if checked hard by frost. Frost-hardy to -5°C (23°F). Japanese aralia (*Fatsia japonica*) is a tougher, if less exciting, alternative.

The fine detail

Aspect: Full sun. A warm, protected microclimate is essential; most plants are frost-tender.

Soil type: Rich, moist but free-draining.

pH: Acid, neutral or alkaline.

Peak period of interest: Mid- to late summer.

Flower colour: Burnt orange, mauve, burgundy-red, blue, silver-blue.

Foliage colour & texture: Green (in various tints and shades). Medium to very coarse.

Maintenance: Medium (if it's a sheltered sunny spot, otherwise winter protection is necessary for most plants). During the growing season, water regularly and deadhead to encourage flowering. Japanese banana (A) in particular requires lots of water – and a high-nitrogen liquid feed. Given free-draining soil, Indian shot plant (G) tubers and *Dahlia* (H) rhizomes can be left in the ground, protected by a thick mulch. If not, they'll need to be lifted and stored under cover over winter.

Other notes: Spring-flowering honey spurge (D), regal lily (white circles) – for early summer – and midsummer-flowering star jasmine (O) are highly scented.

(A) *Musa basjoo* (Japanese banana): Tough, fast-growing species for temperate climates. Known to tolerate temperatures down to -15°C (5°F). Needs protection in cold spots. Unfortunately the fruits are inedible.

Design decisions

While hardy lookalikes are useful in cool-temperate climates, many frost-tender plants have been included here because the sheltered microclimate offers the opportunity to grow them. Although this might mean more maintenance, it shouldn't be too arduous on this scale. Japanese bananas (A) form a canopy and, together with two honey spurge (D), a sword-like mountain flax (C) and a monstrous ricepaper plant (B), structure the planting. Exotic-looking *Dahlia* (H), Indian shot plant (G) and African blue lily (I) bring splashes of vibrant colour underneath and thrive alongside cottage garden classics that are at home in such a setting, including a *Penstemon* (L), cranesbill (M) and hardy garden verbena (N).

 Musa basjoo (Japanese banana; ❊❊ Z8–11) H&S: 2–5 × 2–5m (6½–16 × 6½–16ft)

 Tetrapanax papyrifer 'Rex' (ricepaper plant; ❊❊ Z6–11) H&S: 2–4 × 2–4m (6½–13 × 6½–13ft)

 Phormium cookianum (mountain flax; ❊❊ Z9–11) H&S: 2–2.5 × 2–2.5m (6½–8 × 6½–8ft)

 Euphorbia mellifera (honey spurge; ❊❊ Z9–10) H&S: 1.8 × 1.8m (6 × 6ft)

 Lobelia tupa (devil's tobacco; ❊❊ Z8–10) H&S: 1.8m × 75cm (6ft × 30in)

 Melianthus major (honey flower; ❊ Z8–11) H&S: 1–3 × 1–3m (3–10 × 3–10ft)

 Canna 'Orange Punch' (Indian shot plant; ❊ Z8–11) H&S: 1.2m × 60cm (4 × 2ft)

 Dahlia 'Nuit d'Eté' (❊ Z9–11) H&S: 1.2m × 50cm (4ft × 20in)

 Agapanthus campanulatus (African blue lily; ❊❊ Z7–15) H&S: 1m × 45cm (40 × 18in)

 Verbena bonariensis (purple top; ❊❊ Z7–11) H&S: 1.8m × 45cm (6 × 1½ft)

 Crocosmia × crocosmiiflora 'Zeal Tan' (montbretia; ❊❊❊ Z6–9) H&S: 50 × 10cm (20 × 4in)

 Penstemon 'Blackbird' (❊❊❊ Z7–10) H&S: 75 × 40cm (30 × 16in)

 Geranium himalayense 'Gravetye' (cranesbill; ❊❊❊ Z4–7) H&S: 40 × 50cm (16 × 20in)

 Verbena rigida f. *lilacina* 'Polaris' (hardy garden verbena; ❊❊ Z8–15) H&S: 45 × 45cm (18 × 18in)

 Trachelospermum jasminoides (star jasmine; ❊❊ Z9–10) H&S: 4 × 8m (13 × 25ft)

 Lilium regale 'Album' (regal lily; ❊❊❊ Z4–7) H&S: 1.2m × 25cm (4ft × 10in)

Jungle fever

The scope and range of 'exotic' plantings is huge (see pp106–109). The ever-popular jungle planting favours green leaves in every tint, shade, shape and size you can imagine. Height is important too in jungle planting – and lots of it. Imagine pushing your way through a steamy Amazonian rainforest, monkeys swinging through the trees above (!) and you'll get the idea. Like its colourful brethren (see pp208–211), the exotic jungle look works well in any sheltered spot. Some shade cast by trees or surrounding buildings is helpful too.

Tricks of the trade

- **Spread overhead:** Create a canopy first using tidy evergreen trees/large shrubs such as bull bay (*Magnolia grandiflora*), mimosa (*Acacia dealbata*), *Eucryphia* × *nymansensis* and even small snow gum (*Eucalyptus pauciflora* subsp. *niphophila*). Clump-forming bamboos are also very useful. Then fill in the understorey starting with tree ferns, shrubs, tall herbaceous perennials and ferns, then ground cover. Unless there are big gaps in the canopy, plants underneath should be shade-tolerant.

- **Protect & serve:** All exotic plantings need shelter, so, in windy temperate climates, plant a hedge or windbreak to provide protection and wait until it gets to a suitable size before introducing more vulnerable plants (or buy big plants to start with). For hot, dry climates, some tree cover is essential.

- **Foliage or flowers?** While foliage and form are most important, include a few flowering shrubs and perennials to reflect the changing seasons; a ratio of around 70:30 works well. In cool-temperate spots, use hardy plants that mimic the tropical look.

- **Keep it simple:** Don't include too many different plants. Although rainforests are incredibly diverse, many species aren't distinctly different because each has adapted in a similar way to the shady, humid climate.

Dicksonia antarctica
(soft tree fern)

Darmera peltata
(umbrella plant)

Iris confusa
(bamboo iris)

Acanthus spinosus
(bear's breeches)

Astelia 'Silver Shadow'
(silver spear)

Asarum europaeum
(asarabacca)

Brunnera macrophylla
'Jack Frost' (Siberian
bugloss)

Hosta 'Krossa Regal'
(plantain lily)

This jungle-like planting for cool-temperate areas, packed with form and foliage, is intended for the bottom of a partially shady suburban garden, surrounded by neighbouring buildings that provide protection from strong winds. In larger gardens it could form one of any number of garden 'rooms'. It's also suitable for basements and urban courtyards.

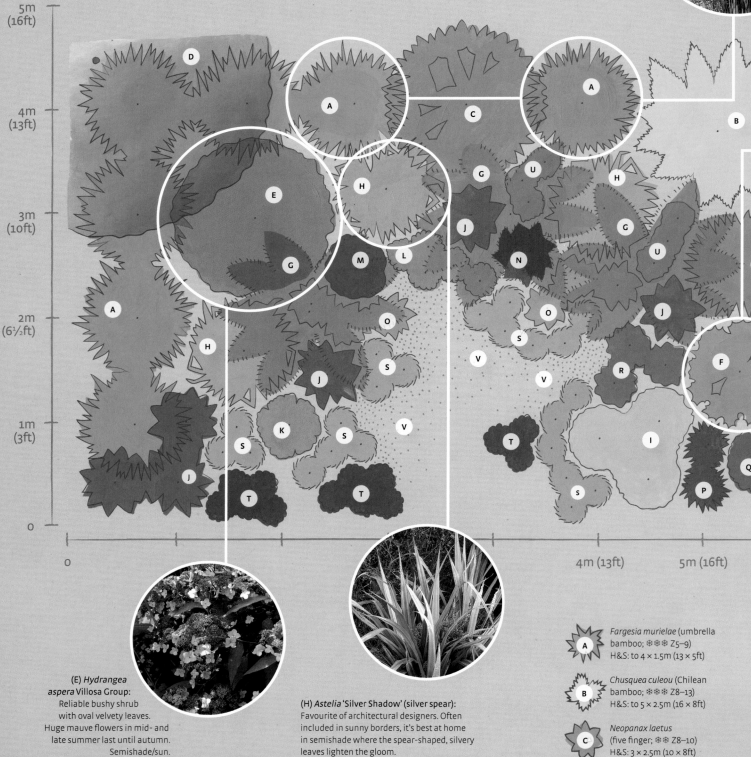

(A) *Fargesia murielae* (umbrella bamboo): Tough, graceful, clump-forming bamboo with arching, yellow-green canes and bright green leaves. Ideal for semishade under trees, although moisture-retentive soil is essential (all bamboos hate drying out).

(E) *Hydrangea aspera* Villosa Group: Reliable bushy shrub with oval velvety leaves. Huge mauve flowers in mid- and late summer last until autumn. Semishade/sun.

(H) *Astelia* 'Silver Shadow' (silver spear): Favourite of architectural designers. Often included in sunny borders, it's best at home in semishade where the spear-shaped, silvery leaves lighten the gloom.

(A) *Fargesia murielae* (umbrella bamboo; ❋❋❋ Z5–9) H&S: to 4 × 1.5m (13 × 5ft)

(B) *Chusquea culeou* (Chilean bamboo; ❋❋❋ Z8–13) H&S: to 5 × 2.5m (16 × 8ft)

(C) *Neopanax laetus* (five finger; ❋❋ Z8–10) H&S: 3 × 2.5m (10 × 8ft)

The fine detail

Aspect: Light/semishade. A garden protected from strong winds is essential.

Soil type: Fertile, moist and damp but not waterlogged.

pH: Acid to neutral to alkaline.

Peak period of interest: Year-round, although the flowering peak occurs in midsummer.

Flower colour: Mauve, buff pink, cream, blue, white, purple.

Foliage colour & texture: Green (in various tints and shades) and silver. Fine to medium to coarse.

Maintenance: Low. While the bamboos (A, B) will provide some protection, five finger (C), silver spear (H), soft tree ferns (G), dwarf Japanese mock orange (I) and Chilean hard fern (J) will need protection in areas where the temperature regularly drops below -5°C (23°F). The foxglove tree (F) will need pollarding every other year.

Other notes: Soft tree ferns are slow-growing, so perhaps buy large specimens, as these are important theme plants. Big bamboos would also be an advantage.

(F) *Paulownia tomentosa* **(foxglove tree):** A medium-sized tree with fragrant, lilac, foxglove-like flowers. Cutting back vigorous young trees to 60–90cm (2–2¾ft) every other year (a process called pollarding) encourages huge leaves – ideal for jungle designs.

Design decisions

Soft tree ferns (G) and shiny silver spear (H) share the spotlight alongside two clump-forming bamboos: umbrella bamboo (A) and Chilean bamboo (B). These provide privacy and protection and also hide garden boundaries, perversely making small spaces feel much bigger. Shade-tolerant perennials and ground cover complement these jungle heavyweights, each being selected primarily for foliage, although many also have attractive flowers. The most dramatic include the meaty common astilboides (M), umbrella plant (K), bear's breeches (N) and a big, blue-green plantain lily (R). Green and silver-green ground cover carpet the soil at their feet.

Eucalyptus pauciflora subsp. *niphophila* (snow gum; ❋❋❋ Z9–11)
H&S: 6 × 4m (20 × 13ft)

Hydrangea aspera Villosa Group (❋❋❋ Z6–9)
H&S: 2.5 × 2.5m (8 × 8ft)

Paulownia tomentosa (foxglove tree; ❋❋❋ Z5–8)
H&S (when pollarded):
3 × 2.5m (10 × 8ft)

Dicksonia antarctica (soft tree fern; ❋❋ Z12–15)
H&S: 4 × 3m (13 × 10ft)

Astelia 'Silver Shadow' (silver spear; ❋❋ Z8–9)
H&S: 1.2 × 1.65m (4 × 5½ft)

Pittosporum tobira 'Nanum' (dwarf Japanese mock orange; ❋ Z9–10)
H&S: 60 × 60cm (2 × 2ft)

Blechnum chilense (Chilean hard fern; ❋❋❋ Z10–11)
H&S: 1.2 × 1m (4 × 3ft)

Darmera peltata (umbrella plant; ❋❋❋ Z5–9)
H&S: 1.5 × 80cm (5ft × 32in)

Brunnera macrophylla 'Jack Frost' (Siberian bugloss; ❋❋❋ Z3–7)
H&S: 45 × 60cm (18 × 24in)

Astilboides tabularis (common astilboides; ❋❋❋ Z5–7)
H&S: 1.2 × 1.2m (4 × 4ft)

Acanthus spinosus (bear's breeches; ❋❋❋ Z5–9)
H&S: 1.2m × 80cm (4ft × 32in)

Athyrium filix-femina (lady fern; ❋❋❋ Z4–9)
H&S: 80 × 60cm (32 × 24in)

Iris confusa (bamboo iris; ❋❋ Z4–10)
H&S: 1 × 0.6m (3 × 2ft)

Macleaya microcarpa 'Kelway's Coral Plume' (plume poppy; ❋❋❋ Z4–9)
H&S: 2 × 1.5m (6½ × 5ft)

Hosta 'Krossa Regal' (plantain lily; ❋❋❋ Z3–9b)
H&S: 70 × 70cm (28 × 28in)

Hakonechloa macra (❋❋❋ Z5–9)
H&S: 40 × 40cm (16 × 16in)

Asarum europaeum (asarabacca; ❋❋❋ Z4–8)
H&S: 8 × 30cm (3½ × 12in)

Pachysandra terminalis (Japanese spurge; ❋❋❋ Z4–8)
H&S: 20 × 60cm (8 × 24in)

Soleirolia soleirolii (mind your own business; ❋❋❋ Z10–15)
H&S: 5cm × indefinite (2in)

Shady ladies

Shady spots tend to be forgotten and are sometimes seen as troublesome. However they have huge potential to be wonderful parts of the garden and often have a special atmosphere all of their own. Don't feel short-changed when it comes to the planting in particular, as there are hundreds of plants to choose from. Many of the most beautiful plants famed for their gorgeous foliage or delicate flowers shun the sun.

Anemone × hybrida
'Königin Charlotte'
(Japanese anemone)

Tricks of the trade

- **Note the difference:** All shade isn't the same and plants will have distinct preferences. With this in mind, choose accordingly:

  – light shade: beds and borders that are open to the sky but screened by direct sunlight, perhaps by buildings;

  – semishade: beds and borders that receive 2–3 hours of direct sunlight, typically in early morning or evening. East-facing boundaries and gardens can be included here;

  – moderate shade/dappled shade: areas below deciduous trees or beds receiving only 1–2 hours of direct, or more likely, reflected light. North-facing sites and woodland are included here;

  – deep shade: common under dense deciduous trees, large shrubs and conifer hedges. Some basement gardens can be included here.

- **Green scene:** Focus on plants with attractive form and foliage, not just their flowers. It's likely these will make up most of the planting mix. Plants with variegated leaves are useful accents, but use them sparingly, especially in natural woodland-inspired designs (see pp116–117). Avoid too much dark green foliage too – this can appear gloomy.

- **Flower power:** White, pale yellow, pale orange, lilac and pink show up well in shade; choose these first.

Convallaria majalis
(lily of the valley)

Magnolia 'Susan'

Viburnum × burkwoodii
(burkwood viburnum)

Luzula nivea (snowy woodrush),
Rodgersia podophylla
'Braunlab' and *Brunnera
macrophylla* 'Betty Bowring'
(Siberian bugloss)

Matteuccia struthiopteris
(shuttlecock fern) and *Persicaria
bistorta* 'Superba' (bistort)

This delicate, feminine, edge-of-woodland-inspired planting is for a neglected corner of a small garden, perhaps next to a log store or garden shed on the right-hand side. White, rose-pink and soft pink flowers prevail, all chosen to stand out in low light. Lime-green and grass-green perennials and ferns provide a suitable low-level foil, as well as textural contrast.

(D) *Viburnum × burkwoodii* (burkwood viburnum): Evergreen shrub treasured for its highly fragrant, white or pale pink, spring flowers. Tough too, tolerating sun or shade and all soils (except those that waterlog easily).

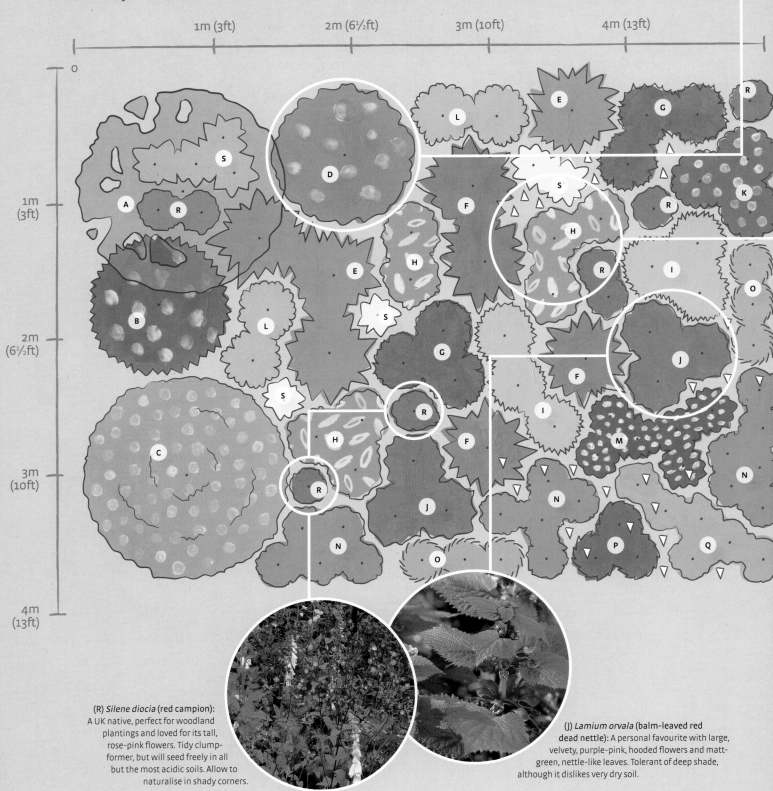

(R) *Silene diocia* (red campion): A UK native, perfect for woodland plantings and loved for its tall, rose-pink flowers. Tidy clump-former, but will seed freely in all but the most acidic soils. Allow to naturalise in shady corners.

(J) *Lamium orvala* (balm-leaved red dead nettle): A personal favourite with large, velvety, purple-pink, hooded flowers and matt-green, nettle-like leaves. Tolerant of deep shade, although it dislikes very dry soil.

The fine detail

Aspect: Light shade/semishade.

Soil type: Moist.

pH: Acid to neutral.

Peak period of interest: Late spring to summer.

Flower colour: Purple, pink, soft pink and white.

Foliage colour & texture: Green (in various tints and shades) and dark bronze. Fine to medium to coarse.

Maintenance: Low. Remove spent foliage and flowers from perennials and ferns in spring. Thin out seedlings from the red campion (R) and foxglove (S) if they start to swamp other plants.

Other notes: Both the burkwood viburnum (D) and lily of the valley (inverted triangles) have a wonderfully sweet scent. Include the *Magnolia* 'Susan' (A) and Japanese snowball bush (C), only if there's enough space – pruning ruins their shape.

(H) *Gillenia trifoliata* (bowman's root): Elegant plant with reddish stems topped by open sprays of starry white flowers, which open in spring and last well into summer. Tidy, clump-forming habit.

Design decisions

For me, no semishady spot in spring is complete without at least one *Viburnum*. Therefore, alongside a small white camellia (B) and a *Magnolia* 'Susan' (A), I've included two: Japanese snowball bush (C), for its fine form, and burkwood viburnum (D), for its sweet scent. In front, the evergreen soft shield fern (E) and aptly named shuttlecock fern (F) help structure a collection of classic spring and early summer perennials such as white Siberian bugloss (M). The shuttlecock fern is an important foreground focal point, so too are a *Rodgersia* (G) and bistort (I) – both included to prolong the season of interest from spring well into summer. Japanese anemone (L) provides blush-pink flowers in late summer and autumn.

 Magnolia 'Susan' (✳✳✳ Z4–9) H&S: to 4 × 4m (13 × 13ft)

 Camellia 'Cornish Snow' (✳✳✳ Z6–9) H&S: 2 × 1.5m (6½ × 5ft)

 Viburnum plicatum f. *tomentosum* 'Mariesii' (Japanese snowball bush; ✳✳✳ Z4–8) H&S: 3.5 × 3.5m (11 × 11ft)

 Viburnum × burkwoodii (burkwood viburnum; ✳✳✳ Z5–8) H&S: 2.5 × 2.5m (8 × 8ft)

 Polystichum setiferum (soft shield fern; ✳✳✳ Z6–9) H&S: 1.2m × 90cm (4ft × 36in)

 Matteuccia struthiopteris (shuttlecock fern; ✳✳✳ Z2–8) H&S: 1.5m × 90cm (5ft × 36in)

 Rodgersia podophylla 'Braunlab' (✳✳✳ Z5–8) H&S: 70 × 75cm (28 × 30in)

 Gillenia trifoliata (bowman's root; ✳✳✳ Z5–9b) H&S: 1 × 0.6m (3 × 2ft)

 Persicaria bistorta 'Superba' (bistort; ✳✳✳ Z4–8) H&S: 80 × 80cm (32 × 32in)

 Lamium orvala (balm-leaved red dead nettle; ✳✳✳ Z4–8) H&S: 60 × 30cm (24 × 12in)

 Geranium phaeum 'Album' (cranesbill; ✳✳✳ Z4–8) H&S: 70 × 45cm (28 × 18in)

 Anemone × hybrida 'Königin Charlotte' (Japanese anemone; ✳✳✳ Z3–8) H&S: 1.5 × 0.6m (5 × 2ft)

 Brunnera macrophylla 'Betty Bowring' (Siberian bugloss; ✳✳✳ Z3–7) H&S: 45 × 55cm (18 × 22in)

 Astrantia major 'Ruby Wedding' (masterwort; ✳✳✳ Z4–7) H&S: 60 × 40cm (24 × 16in)

 Luzula nivea (snowy woodrush; ✳✳✳ Z4–9) H&S: 60 × 40cm (24 × 16in)

 Omphalodes cappadocica 'Cherry Ingram' (Cappadocian navelwort; ✳✳✳ Z6–8) H&S: 30 × 40cm (12 × 16in)

 Lamium maculatum 'Beacon Silver' (spotted dead nettle; ✳✳✳ Z4–8) H&S: 20 × 50cm (8 × 20in)

 Silene dioica (red campion; ✳✳✳ Z6–9) H&S: 80 × 45cm (32 × 18in)

 Digitalis purpurea f. *albiflora* (foxglove; ✳✳✳ Z6–9) H&S: 1.5m × 45cm (5ft × 18in)

 Convallaria majalis (lily of the valley; ✳✳✳ Z2–7) H&S: 25 × 30cm (10 × 12in)

 Leucojum aestivum (summer snowflake; ✳✳✳ Z3–9) H&S: 50 × 10cm (20 × 4in)

Dry shade

Under trees or hedges, or tight against buildings, life in the shadows can be hard – here the soil can be perpetually dry and dusty. Fortunately there are plenty of tough customers that thrive, rather than merely survive, in dry shade. Admittedly, most flower early in the season – before the leaf canopy overhead closes in – but if you choose plenty of evergreens it's possible to prolong the period of interest into summer.

Tricks of the trade

- **Soil conditioner:** A healthy dose of garden compost or leafmould lightly forked into the soil before planting helps plants establish, but don't dig deeply and damage the roots, especially around trees. Regularly mulch with compost or leafmould too; earthworms will pull it in and help condition the soil.

- **Tough nuts:** Bombproof evergreens for dry shade include Mrs Robb's bonnet (*Euphorbia amygdaloides* var. *robbiae*), evergreen barrenwort (*Epimedium*) and periwinkle (*Vinca*). Use these in large groups if all else fails. A little boring perhaps? But better than bare soil, definitely! Note: only English ivy (*Hedera helix*) will grow directly under dense trees with a low canopy (such as conifers); it's too dark and dry there for much else. Under trees with a high canopy, English bluebells (*Hyacinthoides non-scripta*), lily of the valley (*Convallaria majalis*) and hardy cyclamen (such as *Cyclamen coum*) grow well tight up against tree trunks, if you delicately dig in compost to aid moisture retention.

- **Cultural care:** Nurture plants regularly during their first spring and summer, watering regularly. Plants tolerant of dry shade still need help to get going.

- **Good start:** Small plants are more likely to establish well. If possible, avoid those grown in peat-based composts, as they dry out quickly. Planting in autumn is best; plants have more time to establish before they're shaded overhead the following spring.

Digitalis purpurea f. *albiflora* (foxglove)

Iris foetidissima
(stinking iris)

Polystichum setiferum
Divisilobum Group
(soft shield fern)

Bergenia 'Silberlicht' (elephant's
ears) and *Anemone nemorosa*
(wood anemone)

Tellima grandiflora
(fringe cups)

Ajuga reptans 'Catlin's Giant'
(bugle)

In this woodland-style planting, shadowed by tall deciduous trees, all selected plants are tolerant of dry shade to varying degrees, which is reflected in their position. Plants closest to the tree trunk tolerate the darkest and driest conditions, while those plants bordering the path in front require a little more light, and often a bit more moisture.

(N) *Geranium phaeum* 'Lily Lovell' (dusky cranesbill): Versatile cranesbill for sun or shade, with gorgeous, violet-purple flowers in spring and early summer. All soils.

(B) *Sarcococca hookeriana* var. *digyna* (sweet box): Tough evergreen shrub loved for its tiny, fragrant, creamy white flowers in winter, followed by black berries. Tolerates dry shade once established.

4m (13ft)

3m (10ft)

2m (6½ft)

1m (3ft)

0

0

2m (6½ft)

3m (10ft)

4m (13ft)

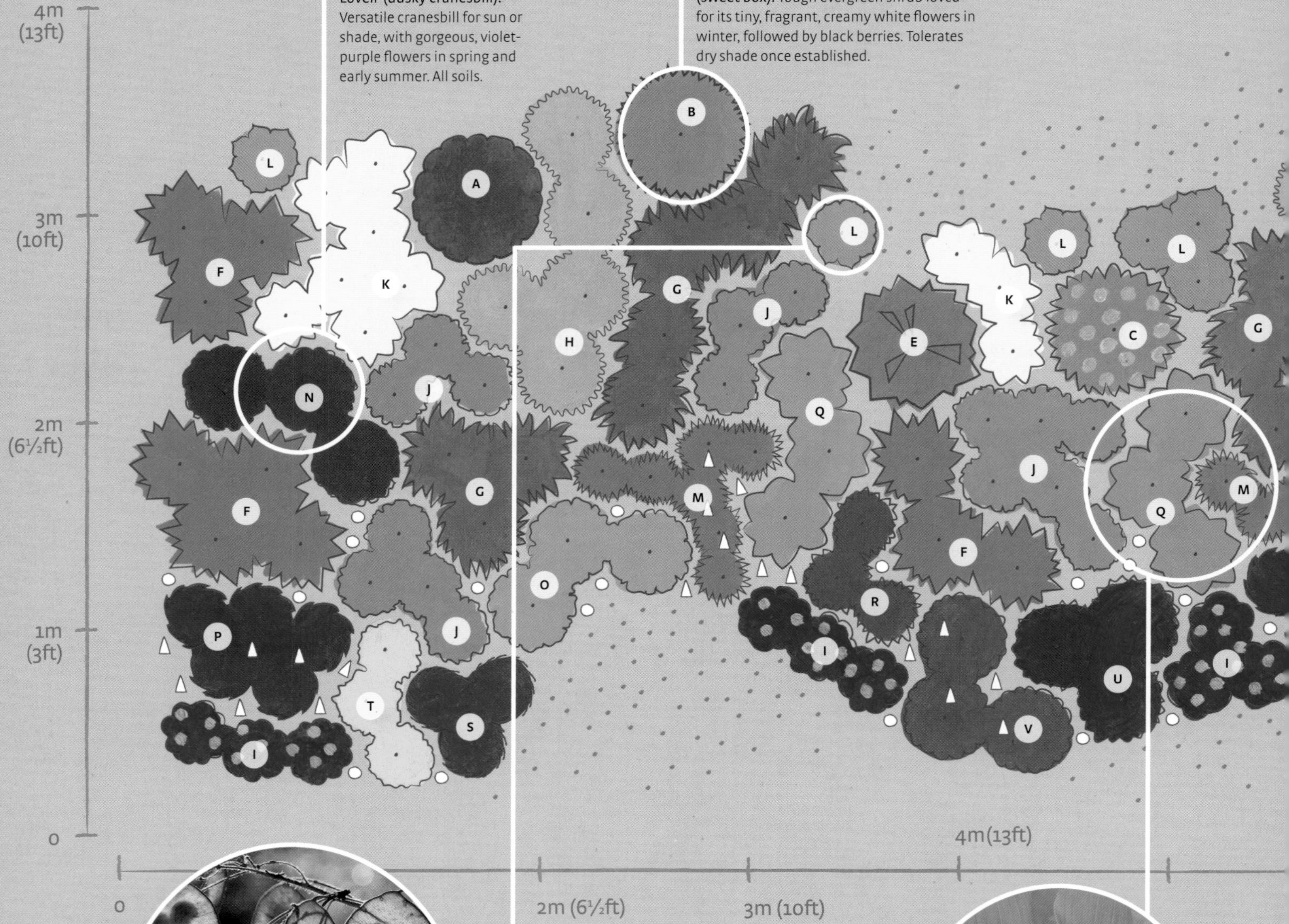

(L) *Lunaria annua* (honesty): Lovely, late spring/early summer-flowering, woodland biennial. White to lilac summer flowers are followed by long-lasting, flat, translucent seedheads. Self-seeds readily in dappled light. Ideal for wild gardens.

(Q) *Polygonatum* × *hybridum* (Solomon's seal): Woodland favourite with gently arching stems that bear nodding, tubular, creamy white flowers in late spring. Prefers naturally moist soil, but copes with dry shade once established. Dig in plenty of organic matter to get it off to a good start.

The fine detail

Aspect: Deep to dappled shade.

Soil type: All plants are tolerant of dry shade once established.

pH: Acid to neutral to alkaline.

Peak period of interest: Early to late spring.

Flower colour: Yellow, white, green and blue in early spring with splashes of lilac and purple appearing in late spring and early summer.

Foliage colour & texture: Green (in various tints and shades) and purple. Coarse to medium to fine.

Maintenance: Very low to low. Tidy spent perennials after flowering. Thin out foxglove (K) or honesty (L) seedlings when required. Spread a thick layer of mulch around plants in spring, after weeding thoroughly.

Other notes: Sweet box (B) is scented in spring. Curiously, the leaves of the stinking iris (M), when crushed, smell of fetid roast beef. Don't let this put you off, however – its flowers and seedheads are stunning.

Design decisions

Four evergreen shrubs – spurge laurel (A), sweet box (B), *Skimmia* (C) and Oregon grape (D) – divide up this space into little bays and, together with groups of golden shield fern (F) and soft shield fern (G), structure the planting. Floriferous perennials such as Mrs Robb's bonnet (H), cranesbill (O), blue lungwort (P), fringe cups (J), hybrid Lenten rose (R), Siberian bugloss (U) and two tall accents – a white foxglove (K) and honesty (L) – are encouraged to self-seed where they want, to fill in the gaps. No woodland planting would be complete without spring bulbs, so daffodils (triangles) and wood anemone (white circles) have also been 'sprinkled' across the front.

Acanthus mollis (bear's breeches; ❋❋❋ Z7–11)
H&S: 1.35 × 1m (4½ × 3ft)

Dryopteris affinis 'Cristata' (golden shield fern; ❋❋❋ Z7–11)
H&S: 90 × 90cm (36 × 36in)

Polystichum setiferum Divisilobum Group (soft shield fern; ❋❋❋ Z6–9)
H&S: 70 × 60cm (28 × 24in)

Euphorbia amygdaloides var. *robbiae* (Mrs Robb's bonnet; ❋❋❋ Z6–9)
H&S: 60 × 60cm (2 × 2ft)

Bergenia 'Silberlicht' (elephant's ears; ❋❋❋ Z3–8)
H&S: 40 × 50cm (16 × 20in)

Tellima grandiflora (fringe cups; ❋❋❋ Z4–8)
H&S: 70 × 30cm (28 × 12in)

Digitalis purpurea f. *albiflora* (foxglove; ❋❋❋ Z4–8)
H&S: 1.5m × 45cm (5ft × 18in)

Lunaria annua (honesty; ❋❋❋ Z3–9)
H&S: 90 × 30cm (36 × 12in)

Iris foetidissima (stinking iris; ❋❋❋ Z4–9)
H&S: 80 × 40cm (32 × 16in)

Geranium phaeum 'Lily Lovell' (dusky cranesbill; ❋❋❋ Z4–8)
H&S: 70 × 45cm (28 × 18in)

Geranium macrorrhizum 'Bevan's Variety' (cranesbill; ❋❋❋ Z4–8)
H&S: 50 × 60cm (20 × 24in)

Pulmonaria 'Blue Ensign' (lungwort; ❋❋❋ Z5–8)
H&S: 30 × 40cm (12 × 16in)

Polygonatum × *hybridum* (Solomon's seal; ❋❋❋ Z6–9)
H&S: 1.2 × 0.3m (4 × 1ft)

Helleborus × *hybridus* (hybrid Lenten rose; ❋❋❋ Z6–9)
H&S: 40 × 40cm (16 × 16in)

Liriope muscari (lilyturf; ❋❋❋ Z6–10)
H&S: 30 × 45cm (12 × 18in)

Epimedium × *perralchicum* (barrenwort; ❋❋❋ Z5–8)
H&S: 40 × 60cm (16 × 24in)

Brunnera macrophylla (Siberian bugloss; ❋❋❋ Z3–7)
H&S: 45 × 55cm (18 × 22in)

Ajuga reptans 'Catlin's Giant' (bugle; ❋❋❋ Z3–9)
H&S: 20 × 60cm (8 × 24in)

Narcissus 'Tete-à-tête' (daffodil; ❋❋❋ Z3–9)
H&S: 15 × 5cm (6 × 2in)

Anemone nemorosa (wood anemone; ❋❋❋ Z4–8)
H&S: 20 × 30cm (8 × 12in)

Daphne laureola (spurge laurel; ❋❋❋ Z7–8)
H&S: 1.2 × 1.5m (4 × 5ft)

Sarcococca hookeriana var. *digyna* (sweet box; ❋❋❋ Z6–9)
H&S: 1.5 × 1.5m (5 × 5ft)

Skimmia × *confusa* 'Kew Green' (❋❋❋ Z6–9)
H&S: 1.5 × 1.2m (5 × 4ft)

Mahonia aquifolium 'Apollo' (Oregon grape; ❋❋❋ Z6–9)
H&S: 90cm × 1.2m (36in × 4ft)

6m (20ft)   7m (23ft)

Bella Italia

The Mediterranean garden is ideal for any location that has a similar climate: warm or hot summers; relatively dry winters (ideally without seriously hard frosts) (see p113); and – very important – free-draining soil. Given these conditions, and the choice of possible plants, this makes for exciting gardening. There's no better inspiration if you're struggling with a hot, south-facing slope or a thin sandy soil that dries out too fast. And the Mediterranean ambience creates the perfect setting for alfresco entertaining on a hot summer's day, surrounded by sweet scents in the warm air.

Tricks of the trade

- **Natural look:** Plants with silvery, hairy, needle-like or thick waxy leaves have naturally adapted to strong sun; choose these wherever possible. Silvery plants are particularly useful – nothing else better suggests the native flora of Mediterranean climates such as those of southern Italy and California.

- **Colour contrast:** For flowers, go for vibrant blues, yellows, oranges and violet-purples, tempered by silver, dark green or olive-green foliage. At northerly latitudes, the brighter the colour the better – the light is much flatter here.

- **Tight clip:** Topiary and clipped hedges are a key design detail in formal Mediterranean gardens, especially those inspired by Italianate style (see pp112–113) or the Moorish gardens of the Alhambra. Box (*Buxus*) is the all-time favourite. However, in wet regions, box blight might be a problem. Delavay osmanthus (*Osmanthus delavayi*) and narrow-leaved mock privet (*Phillyrea angustifolia*) are just as tough as box but are immune to this troublesome fungal disease.

- **Shadow play:** Although a hot, sunny spot is essential, don't forget to create some shade. Grapevines (*Vitis vinifera* and *V. labrusca* cultivars), *Wisteria*, passion flower (*Passiflora*) or fragrant common jasmine (*Jasminum officinale*) draped over a rustic wooden bower look beautiful. Modern designs might utilise sawn oak or steel braid, or perhaps even table-shaped pleached trees, instead.

Ozothamnus rosmarinifolius
'Silver Jubilee'

Eryngium giganteum
(Miss Willmott's ghost)

Verbascum bombyciferum
(giant mullein)

Oenothera biennis
(evening primrose)

Orlaya grandiflora
(white laceflower)

Calendula officinalis
(pot marigold)

Artemisia absinthium
(wormwood)

Agapanthus campanulatus
(African blue lily)

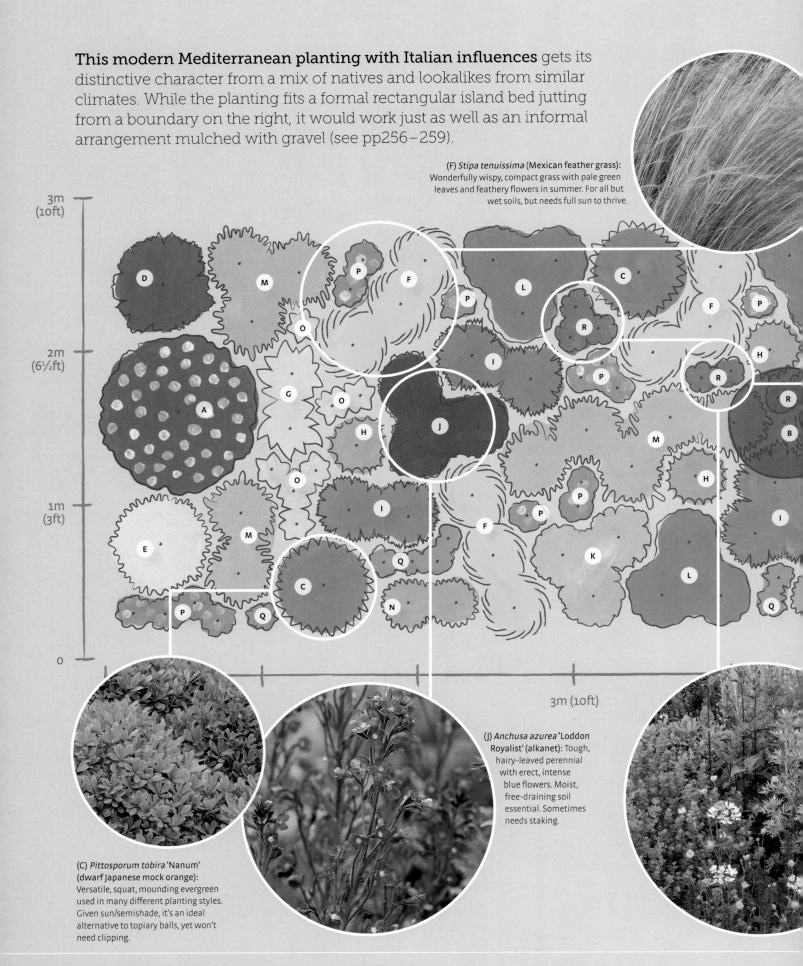

This modern Mediterranean planting with Italian influences gets its distinctive character from a mix of natives and lookalikes from similar climates. While the planting fits a formal rectangular island bed jutting from a boundary on the right, it would work just as well as an informal arrangement mulched with gravel (see pp256–259).

(F) *Stipa tenuissima* (Mexican feather grass): Wonderfully wispy, compact grass with pale green leaves and feathery flowers in summer. For all but wet soils, but needs full sun to thrive.

3m (10ft)

2m (6½ft)

1m (3ft)

0

3m (10ft)

(J) *Anchusa azurea* 'Loddon Royalist' (alkanet): Tough, hairy-leaved perennial with erect, intense blue flowers. Moist, free-draining soil essential. Sometimes needs staking.

(C) *Pittosporum tobira* 'Nanum' (dwarf Japanese mock orange): Versatile, squat, mounding evergreen used in many different planting styles. Given sun/semishade, it's an ideal alternative to topiary balls, yet won't need clipping.

The fine detail

Aspect: Full sun and a sheltered spot are necessary.

Soil type: Dry or free-draining but moist.

pH: Acid to neutral to alkaline.

Peak period of interest: Early to late summer.

Flower colour: Indigo-blue, white, yellow and purple in early summer, turning blue, white, yellow and orange from midsummer to autumn.

Foliage colour & texture: Silver, yellow-green/blonde and green (in various tints and shades). Medium to fine to very fine.

Maintenance: Low to medium. Clip bay laurel (B) in summer to maintain its globular shape, and trim *Ozothamnus* (I) to control its size, when required. Giant mullein (G), Miss Willmott's ghost (H), white laceflower (P), pot marigold (Q) and red orache (R) are annuals or biennials so, unless they self-seed naturally, direct sow in spring then thin out and plant where you want them to flower. Tidy perennials when necessary.

Other notes: Red orache, rosemary (D) and bay laurel can all be used in cooking.

Design decisions

A scented myrtle (A) is the fulcrum here with a spine of tall blue perennials – namely alkanet (J) and African blue lily (M) – drifting to a tall, sentry-like standard bay laurel ball (B) at the other end – the main focal point. Lower down I've resisted the temptation to edge the bed in box (*Buxus*). Instead silver and pine-green shrubs and subshrubs such as wormwood (K) and *Ozothamnus* (I), along with dwarf Japanese mock orange (C) and fine-textured Mexican feather grass (F), provide an informal structural note. Colourful perennials, annuals and biennials – including the spires of giant mullein (G) – fill in the gaps. Evening primrose (O) has been included for its powerful fragrance at dusk. Sometimes it can be a little thuggish, so thin out seedlings diligently.

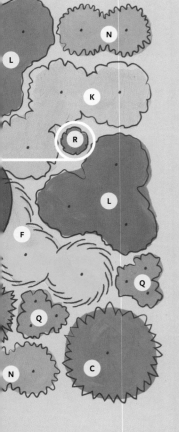

5m (16ft)

(R) *Atriplex hortensis* var. *rubra* (red orache): Hardy annual with purple flowers and blood-red seedheads. Tastes as good as it looks. Self-seeds easily in all but the driest soils. In moist soils it might need staking.

 A *Myrtus communis* (common myrtle; ❀❀ Z8–9)
H&S: 2.5 × 2.5m (8 × 8ft)

 B *Laurus nobilis* (bay laurel; ❀❀ Z8–11)
H&S (standard ball): 1.8 × 0.6m (6 × 2ft)

 C *Pittosporum tobira* 'Nanum' (dwarf Japanese mock orange; ❀ Z9–10)
H&S: 60 × 60cm (24 × 24in)

 D *Rosmarinus officinalis* 'Tuscan Blue' (rosemary; ❀❀ Z8–11)
H&S: 1.35 × 1.1m (4½ × 3½ft)

 E *Euphorbia palustris* (spurge; ❀❀❀ Z7–9)
H&S: 1 × 1m (3 × 3ft)

 F *Stipa tenuissima* (Mexican feather grass; ❀❀❀ Z7–11)
H&S: 60 × 30cm (2 × 1ft)

 G *Verbascum bombyciferum* (giant mullein; ❀❀❀ Z5–9)
H&S: 1.65m × 40cm (5½ft × 16in)

 H *Eryngium giganteum* (Miss Willmott's ghost; ❀❀❀ Z4–9)
H&S: 90 × 30cm (36 × 12in)

 I *Ozothamnus rosmarinifolius* 'Silver Jubilee' (❀❀ Z8–9)
H&S: 1.5 × 1m (5 × 3ft)

 J *Anchusa azurea* 'Loddon Royalist' (alkanet; ❀❀❀ Z3–8)
H&S: 90 × 40cm (36 × 16in)

 K *Artemisia absinthium* (wormwood; ❀❀❀ Z4–8)
H&S: 70 × 50cm (28 × 20in)

 L *Salvia × sylvestris* 'Mainacht' (wood sage; ❀❀❀ Z5–9)
H&S: 75 × 45cm (30 × 18in)

 M *Agapanthus campanulatus* (African blue lily; ❀ Z7–15)
H&S: 1m × 45cm (3ft × 18in)

 N *Euphorbia epithymoides* (spurge; ❀❀❀ Z5–9)
H&S: 45 × 40cm (18 × 16in)

 O *Oenothera biennis* (evening primrose; ❀❀❀ Z4–8)
H&S: 1.2 × 0.3m (4 × 1ft)

 P *Orlaya grandiflora* (white laceflower; ❀❀❀ zone not applicable)
H&S: 60 × 55cm (24 × 22in)

 Q *Calendula officinalis* (pot marigold; ❀❀❀ zone not applicable)
H&S: 30 × 60cm (1 × 2ft)

R *Atriplex hortensis* var. *rubra* (red orache; ❀ Z7–9)
H&S: 1.2 × 0.3m (4 × 1ft)

Contemporary cottage

Everyone loves a romantic cottage garden (see pp94–97). In recent years this style, with its informal aesthetic, has been updated for the 21st century. Modern interpretations have a strong structure, and shrubs don't dominate as they once might have; instead clipped hedges that define beds and borders, or topiary specimens repeated throughout, perform this role. Cottage classics such as mallow (*Lavatera × clementii* 'Barnsley'), alternate-leaved butterfly bush (*Buddleja alternifolia*) and roses (*Rosa*) do appear for their flower power or as a backdrop, but it's the perennials that are the stars.

Tricks of the trade

- **Natural influences:** The naturalistic look is key to the modern cottage garden. Arrange plants in drifts, mingling accents with strong forms such as quamash (*Camassia*), *Iris* and foxglove (*Digitalis*) throughout. A pared-down plant palette is important too, so increase the numbers of each plant rather than including little groups of everything.

- **Mind the gap:** While wisdom suggests spacing plants at an appropriate distance, the more bare soil you leave for plants to grow into, the more weeds you'll get in the first few years. Use slender annuals or perennials synonymous with cottage gardens such as granny's bonnet (*Aquilegia*) to fill the gaps temporarily. These shouldn't become a nuisance, as they self-seed only where they find room to do so.

- **Off with their heads:** While some self-seeders should be encouraged, don't let vigorous plants such as love-in-a-mist (*Nigella*) run amok. Snip off spent flowerheads before they burst open and spread seed everywhere. Do however save a few to sprinkle in gaps the following year – where you want them, of course.

- **Cover up:** Groundcover perennials such as cranesbill (*Geranium*) keep the soil moist and bring just as much colour as their tall, more glamorous cousins. Usefully they'll help cut weeding time down too.

Euphorbia characias subsp. *wulfenii* (spurge)

Foeniculum vulgare (fennel)

Choisya × dewitteana 'Aztec Pearl' (Mexican orange blossom)

Papaver orientale 'Patty's Plum' (oriental poppy)

Nepeta racemosa 'Walker's Low' (dwarf catmint)

Allium hollandicum 'Purple Sensation' (ornamental onion)

Iris 'Superstition'

Sedum 'Matrona' (orpine)

In this bee-friendly, modern cottage border, backed by a 2m (6½ft) high wall (or hedge), a second boundary features on the left-hand side. This could represent the front of a cottage or house (plants that might block windows should be rearranged accordingly). While traditional cottage favourites such as oriental poppies (*Papaver*) feature strongly, many 'new' perennials also sit informally alongside. Together they are repeated throughout the foreground to help tie the scheme together. Reliable evergreen shrubs and tightly clipped box (*Buxus*) balls provide the support structure.

(H) *Anemone × hybrida* 'Honorine Jobert' (Japanese anemone): Popular back-of-the-border perennial with white flowers in mid- to late summer. Give some sun and moist but well-drained soil. Dislikes being moved.

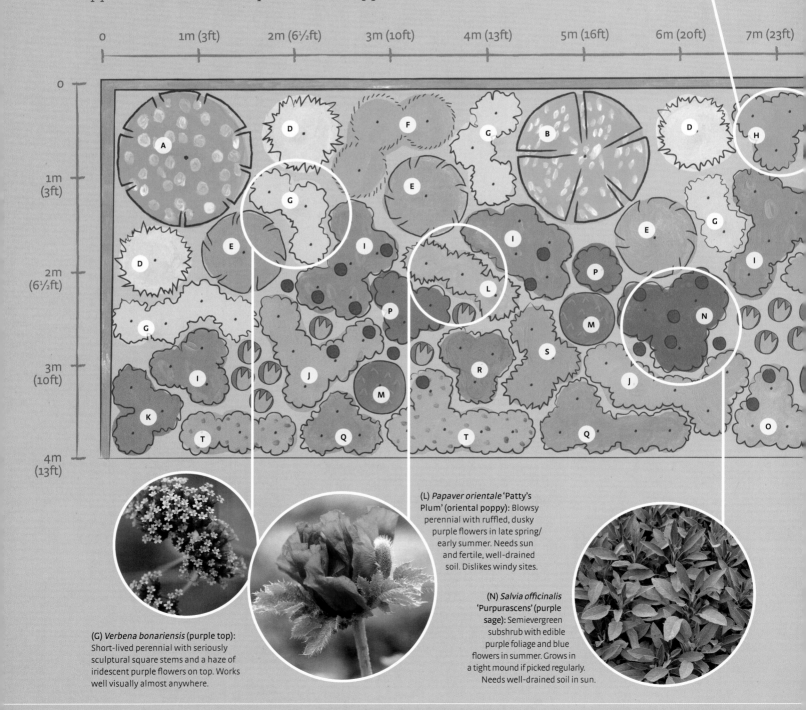

(G) *Verbena bonariensis* (purple top): Short-lived perennial with seriously sculptural square stems and a haze of iridescent purple flowers on top. Works well visually almost anywhere.

(L) *Papaver orientale* 'Patty's Plum' (oriental poppy): Blowsy perennial with ruffled, dusky purple flowers in late spring/ early summer. Needs sun and fertile, well-drained soil. Dislikes windy sites.

(N) *Salvia officinalis* 'Purpurascens' (purple sage): Semievergreen subshrub with edible purple foliage and blue flowers in summer. Grows in a tight mound if picked regularly. Needs well-drained soil in sun.

The fine detail

Aspect: South- or west-facing. Requires shelter from strong winds.

Soil type: Relatively free-draining.

pH: Acid to neutral to alkaline.

Peak period of interest: Late spring to autumn. Common box (M) balls provide sculptural form in autumn/winter, as do the skeletal shapes of purple top (G), giant hyssop (I), orpine (J) and coneflower (K).

Flower colour: Blue, pink, mauve, purple and yellow.

Foliage colour & texture: Green and silver. Coarse to medium.

Maintenance: Low to medium. Fennel (F) and purple top may need staking. Common box balls need trimming once a year. Purple top, coneflower and Macedonian scabious (P) are relatively short-lived, so replant when necessary and allow self-sown seedlings. The three evergreen shrubs at the back of the border – A, B and C – will eventually need trimming to control their size.

Other notes: Attractive to bees and butterflies, especially in mid- and late summer.

Design decisions

With a wall behind, this planting is layered from three shrubs at the back, including delavay osmanthus (A) and tosa spirea (B), to low ground cover in front. Accompanied by spurge (E), these shrubs also split the bed up into little 'bays', to draw in the eye. As with all the designs in this chapter, this plan can be easily adapted. In a narrow front garden with a path down the middle, flip the border over to the other side as a mirror image. Perhaps change the shrubs at the back for variety, but work with the same parameters size-wise. If shade is cast on sun-lovers in front by doing this, choose alternatives where appropriate. This planting would also work as a segment of a longer border. Perhaps flip the plan over on end and repeat. Again, perhaps change the shrubs.

8m (25ft)

 Euphorbia characias subsp. *wulfenii* (spurge; ✺✺✺ Z7–10) H&S: 1.2 × 1.2m (4 × 4ft)

 Foeniculum vulgare (fennel; ✺✺✺ Z4–9) H&S: 1.8m × 45cm (6ft × 18in)

 Verbena bonariensis (purple top; ✺✺ Z7–11) H&S: 1.8m × 45cm (6ft × 18in)

 Anemone × *hybrida* 'Honorine Jobert' (Japanese anemone; ✺✺✺ Z4–8) H&S: 1.2m × 80cm (4ft × 32in)

 Agastache 'Blackadder' (giant hyssop; ✺✺✺ Z6–9) H&S: 90 × 40cm (36 × 16in)

 Sedum 'Matrona' (orpine; ✺✺✺ Z4–9) H&S: 60 × 40cm (24 × 16in)

 Echinacea purpurea 'Magnus' (coneflower; ✺✺✺ Z3–9) H&S: 80 × 40cm (32 × 16in)

 Papaver orientale 'Patty's Plum' (oriental poppy; ✺✺✺ Z3–9) H&S: 80 × 50cm (32 × 20in)

 Buxus sempervirens 'Faulkner' (common box; ✺✺✺ Z6–9) H&S (when clipped): 60 × 60cm (2 × 2ft)

 Salvia officinalis 'Purpurascens' (purple sage; ✺✺✺ Z5–8) H&S: 70 × 70cm (28 × 28in)

 Geranium × *oxonianum* 'Wargrave Pink' (cranesbill; ✺✺✺ Z4–8) H&S: 60 × 50cm (24 × 20in)

 Knautia macedonica (Macedonian scabious; ✺✺✺ Z5–9) H&S: 75 × 40cm (30 × 16in)

 Nepeta racemosa 'Walker's Low' (dwarf catmint; ✺✺✺ Z4–8) H&S: 60 × 50cm (24 × 20in)

 Penstemon 'Sour Grapes' (✺✺✺ Z7–10) H&S: 70 × 50cm (28 × 20in)

 Stachys byzantina 'Big Ears' (lambs' tongues; ✺✺✺ Z4–8) H&S: 50 × 50cm (20 × 20in)

 Astrantia 'Roma' (masterwort; ✺✺✺ Z4–7) H&S: 60 × 40cm (24 × 16in)

 Iris 'Superstition' (✺✺✺ Z5–10) H&S: 90 × 50cm (36 × 20in)

 Allium hollandicum 'Purple Sensation' (ornamental onion; ✺✺✺ Z4–9) H&S: 90 × 10cm (36 × 4in)10cm

 Osmanthus delavayi (delavay osmanthus; ✺✺✺ Z7–9) H&S: 3 × 2.75m (10 × 9ft)

 Spiraea nipponica 'Snowmound' (tosa spirea; ✺✺✺ Z4–8) H&S: 2 × 2.5m (6½ × 8ft)

Choisya × *dewitteana* 'Aztec Pearl' (Mexican orange blossom; ✺✺✺ Z8–10) H&S: 2.5 × 2.5m (8 × 8ft)

Cynara cardunculus 'Cardy' (cardoon; ✺✺✺ Z7–10) H&S: 1.5 × 1.2m (5 × 4ft)

Walk on the wildside

An 'intermingled matrix planting' inspired by the dynamic natural patterns of plants in the meadow-like tradition isn't easy to design, even for experienced gardeners. As discussed on p190, there's a lot to think about that will affect the success of the scheme. Picking four or five sociable plants of similar spreads, but different heights, is one option already looked at. However, there's an even easier (and certainly cheaper) way to achieve an exciting intermingled meadow-like effect using annuals, perennials and grasses: seed.

Tricks of the trade

- **Contemporary thinking:** Traditional wildflower mixes have been around for ages but recent research in the UK, mainland Europe and North America has resulted in new blends that are better for gardens. Many include colourful non-natives, added to extend the display. Among the notable suppliers are Pictorial Meadows (www.pictorialmeadows.co.uk), Perennimix (www.perennimix.com), American Meadows (www.americanmeadows.com) and Perennemix (www.prof-kircher.de). The last is based on research by the German naturalistic planting design authority Wolfram Kircher.

- **Match the mix:** For traditional meadows with native wild flowers, a relatively poor soil is necessary to stop grasses taking over. Many modern blends however perform best in rich soil. Usefully, there are many mixes available, so you're bound to find one that works well, whether your soil is acid or alkaline, thick clay or free-draining sand.

- **The bigger the area the better:** In tiny gardens, intermingled meadow-style plantings look out of place and aren't practical. In larger suburban gardens, it's usually possible to sacrifice some lawn.

- **Resow?** Annual mixes flower very quickly but need replacing each year, whereas perennial ones take longer to establish (two years or more) but they don't need resowing.

'Pictorial Meadow' with *Allium* 'Globemaster' (ornamental onion) and *Viscaria oculata* (rose of heaven)

Pictorial Meadow 'Candy' annual mix with *Coreopsis tinctoria* (tickseed), *Linaria maroccana* (fairy toadflax), *Eschscholzia californica* (California poppy) and *Xanthophthalmum segetum* (corn marigold)

British native meadow mix with *Leucanthemum vulgare* (ox-eye daisy)

North American prairie-style meadow mix with *Rudbeckia fulgida* var. *deamii* (black-eyed Susan), *R. maxima* (giant coneflower) and New England aster (*Symphyotrichum novae-angliae* 'Septemberrubin') and *S. oblongifolium*

British native meadow mix with *Papaver rhoeas* (field poppy) and *Silene dioica* (red campion)

British native meadow mix with *Polygala vulgaris* (common milkwort) and *Rhinanthus minor* (yellow rattle)

The great advantage of this plan is that there isn't one – at least not in the traditional sense. Here the choices are yours. Only two plants have been specifically placed. Wrapping around and underneath is a meadow mix of your choosing, selected with your specific soil type and aspect in mind. Mother Nature then does the main design work by determining what grows where, in a dynamic planting that will change year after year. This idea would work well in suburban gardens where there is room to sacrifice some lawn. Enlarge or shrink it depending on the size of the space.

(A) *Amelanchier × grandiflora* 'Robin Hill' (juneberry): Another hardworking juneberry with rosy red berries, attractive leaves and orange-red autumn leaf tints. This cultivar stands out for its fine, broadly conical form and white flowers, which are pink in bud.

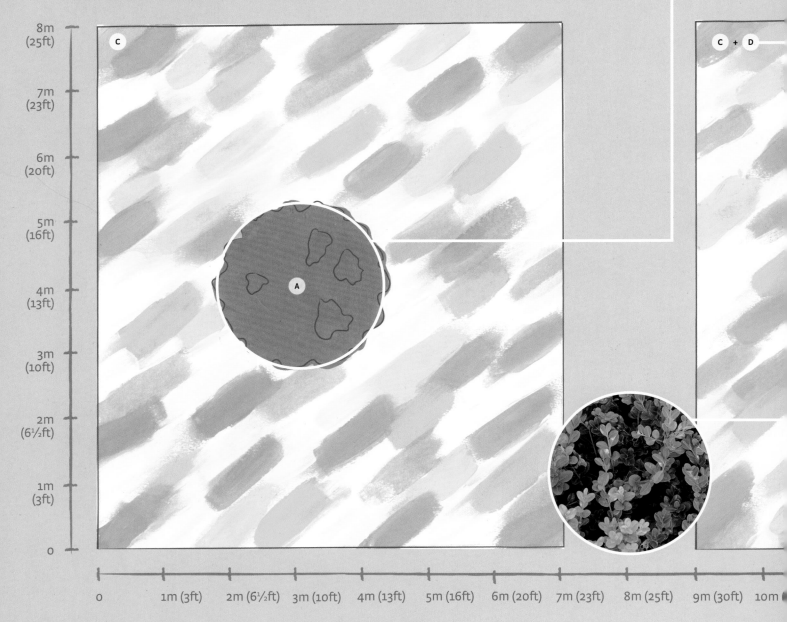

The fine detail

Aspect: Sun or semishade.

Soil type: Moderately fertile but free-draining.

pH: Acid to neutral to alkaline; choose an appropriate mix, depending on your soil texture and pH.

Peak period of interest: All meadows peak in summer, some blooming as early as late spring, others lasting well into autumn.

Flower colour: Various – you choose.

Foliage colour & texture: Typically fine to very fine.

Maintenance: Depends on your selected mix but generally low. Weed control before and after sowing is important – so too is regular watering at the germination and young seedling stages.

Other notes: All meadow mixes attract wildlife and beneficial insects. If you decide to model your own design on this one, buy a large-sized box (B) and juneberry (A) for instant impact.

(D) *Narcissus poeticus* var. *recurvus* (old pheasant's eye): Truly beautiful, slightly fragrant daffodil, ideal for naturalising in grass. Suitable for all soils as long as they're well drained. Sun/semishade preferred.

(B) *Buxus microphylla* 'Rococo' (box): Slow-growing cultivar which, like all box species, can be clipped into all manner of quirky shapes. Notably, this relatively recent introduction is said to be tolerant of box blight disease.

Design decisions

Although nature lends a big hand here, not everything is left to chance. A multistemmed deciduous juneberry (A) on the left-hand side and three big box balls (B) on the right are included. Together with crisp mown edges and a path down the middle, they add a formal note to proceedings and look good year-round – in the case of the juneberry, with or without leaves. Placed like this, both plants also have a sculptural quality, maintaining interest while whatever mix you've chosen underneath gears up for its summer show. An even simpler option here is to let the lawn grass grow long, which can look beautiful. For flowers, plant a few wildflower plugs into the sward after mowing. Perhaps include drifts of spring bulbs that are suitable for naturalising too.

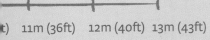

t) 11m (36ft)   12m (40ft)   13m (43ft)

 A *Amelanchier × grandiflora* 'Robin Hill' (juneberry; ❀❀❀ Z3–7) H&S: 4–8 × 4–8m (13–25 × 13–25ft)

 B *Buxus microphylla* 'Rococo' (box; ❀❀❀ Z6–9) H&S (when clipped): 80 × 80cm (32 × 32in)

C Meadow 'mix' (specific to soil type, aspect and geographical location) H&S: n/a

 D *Narcissus poeticus* var. *recurvus* (old pheasant's eye; ❀❀❀ Z3–9) – naturalised throughout H&S: 35 × 10cm (14 × 4in)

On the waterfront

All gardens regardless of size or style need a focal point to catch the eye or to act as a full stop in the space. Water, whether a still reflective pool or a sparking fountain, is ideal and little can compete with its allure and mesmeric quality. It also presents some fantastic planting opportunities, regardless of size or shape (see p70). Even an old bath, butler's sink or wooden barrel has room for a small waterlily such as *Nymphaea* 'Pygmaea Helvola'. Larger ponds and pools, especially those bordered with clay soil, support all manner of 'Jurassic Park' giants.

Sanguisorba 'Red Thunder' (burnet)

Matteuccia struthiopteris (shuttlecock fern)

Tricks of the trade

- **Damp or dry?** Moisture-loving marginal and bog plants will not thrive around a pool set into dry soil. For a natural transition, either bury a butyl liner beyond the water's edge (with punctured holes for drainage) or pick plants that visually mimic marginals but don't mind dry conditions.

- **Controlling vigour:** Many water plants and marginals (those that need their roots submerged in 5–30cm (2–12in) of water, depending on the species – see p70) are very vigorous. In small ponds, grow plants in aquatic baskets to control them. Or choose one or two but place them where they won't intertwine easily; both can then be separated with a spade when need be.

- **Planting prowess:** Conventional planting techniques don't work in waterlogged soil next to pools; deep digging in particular just makes a mess. Instead dig shallow holes tailored for each plant and gently press plants into place, rather than cultivating the whole area.

- **Problem solved:** An old leaky pond filled with soil can make a fine bog garden. It's also a safe option for a family with young children, who may be anxious about large pools of standing water.

- **Support wildlife:** Cover half a wildlife pond with plants and always allocate space around it for bog plants, shrubs and even small trees for cover and protection.

Rodgersia pinnata (featherleaf rodgersia) in the foreground

Lythrum salicaria
(purple loosestrife)

Geum rivale
(water avens)

Astilbe 'Deutschland'

Waterside plantings are noted for their big, brazen, lush leaves and tall flowers, and this design offers no exception. Evergreen oaks at the back cast light shade, stopping short of the water itself. To make good use of space, a cantilevered deck juts out just over the edge so older children and adults alike can dangle their feet or dip for wildlife.

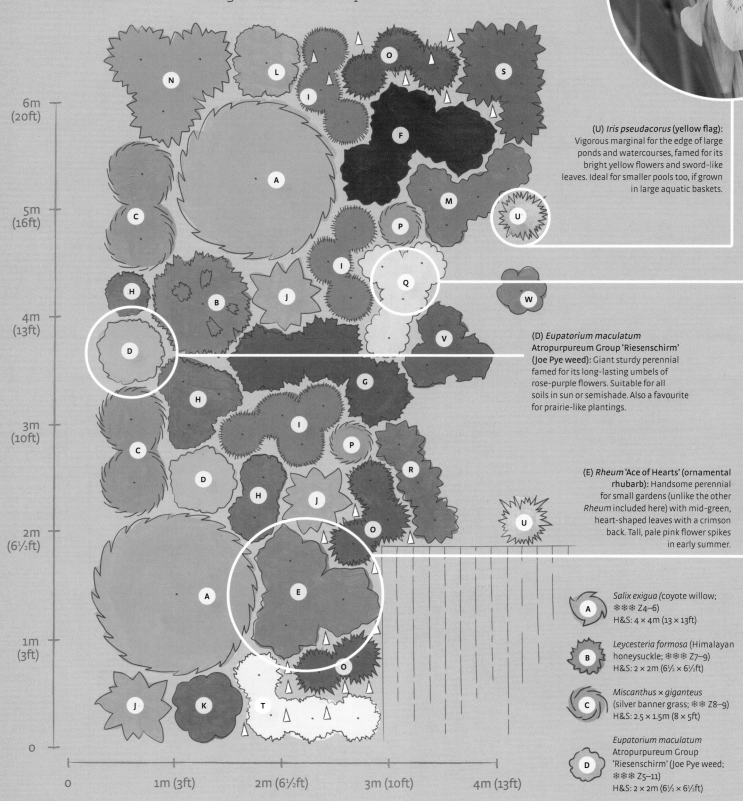

(U) *Iris pseudacorus* (yellow flag): Vigorous marginal for the edge of large ponds and watercourses, famed for its bright yellow flowers and sword-like leaves. Ideal for smaller pools too, if grown in large aquatic baskets.

(D) *Eupatorium maculatum* Atropurpureum Group 'Riesenschirm' (Joe Pye weed): Giant sturdy perennial famed for its long-lasting umbels of rose-purple flowers. Suitable for all soils in sun or semishade. Also a favourite for prairie-like plantings.

(E) *Rheum* 'Ace of Hearts' (ornamental rhubarb): Handsome perennial for small gardens (unlike the other *Rheum* included here) with mid-green, heart-shaped leaves with a crimson back. Tall, pale pink flower spikes in early summer.

A *Salix exigua* (coyote willow; ❋❋❋ Z4–6)
H&S: 4 × 4m (13 × 13ft)

B *Leycesteria formosa* (Himalayan honeysuckle; ❋❋❋ Z7–9)
H&S: 2 × 2m (6½ × 6½ft)

C *Miscanthus × giganteus* (silver banner grass; ❋❋ Z8–9)
H&S: 2.5 × 1.5m (8 × 5ft)

D *Eupatorium maculatum* Atropurpureum Group 'Riesenschirm' (Joe Pye weed; ❋❋❋ Z5–11)
H&S: 2 × 2m (6½ × 6½ft)

The fine detail

Aspect: Full sun to semishade.

Soil type: Moist, damp (clay).

pH: Acid to neutral. All except Japanese water iris (O) will tolerate alkaline conditions although Chinese rhubarb (F), featherleaf rodgersia (G), shuttlecock fern (J), yellow flag (U), giant cowslip (Q) and plaintain lilies (R, S) may struggle at high pHs.

Peak period of interest: Spring to late summer.

Flower colour: Pink, pale pink and white in late spring/ early summer. Yellow, orange, red, violet and purple-pink in mid- to late summer and autumn.

Foliage colour & texture: Green (in various tints and shades) and purple. Very coarse to coarse to medium.

Maintenance: Low. Cut out spent flower spikes and clear last season's stems and foliage from perennials in spring. If large perennials start to swamp others, use a spade to keep them in check; swap spare clumps with your friends and neighbours.

Other notes: Choose your willows (A) carefully as some grow BIG in damp soil.

(Q) *Primula florindae* (giant cowslip): Big cowslip with long-stalked, sulphur-yellow, nodding, fragrant flowers atop low-growing rosettes of oblong leaves. Sun or semishade.

Design decisions

Two feathery, well-behaved coyote willows (A), partnered with a Himalayan honeysuckle (B), structure this planting, and their slender leaves are a flattering textural foil to the big and bold perennials around them. Although deciduous, both are also a reliable presence in winter, when everything else dies down. Tipping into the water's edge, where the soil is wet, are colourful marginal plants including yellow flag (U) and bog arum (V). Further back, the damp soil means beautiful bog plants such as Japanese water iris (O) should thrive; were the bed to be permanently wet, more marginals would be a better option. Behind these, where the soil is moist but drains more freely, purple loosestrife (I) and burnet (H) are included to smooth the transition visually.

 H *Sanguisorba* 'Red Thunder' (burnet; ✳✳✳ Z3–8) H&S: 1.2 × 0.6m (4 × 2ft)

 I *Lythrum salicaria* (purple loosestrife; ✳✳✳ Z4–9) H&S: 1m × 50cm (3ft × 20in)

 J *Matteuccia struthiopteris* (shuttlecock fern; ✳✳✳ Z2–8) H&S: 1.5m × 90cm (5ft × 36in)

 K *Ligularia dentata* 'Othello' (leopard plant; ✳✳✳ Z4–8) H&S: 1m × 75cm (3 × 2½ft)

 L *Darmera peltata* (umbrella plant; ✳✳✳ Z5–9) H&S: 1.5m × 80cm (5 × 2½ft)

 M *Geum rivale* (water avens; ✳✳✳ Z3–8) H&S: 45 × 45cm (18 × 18in)

 E *Rheum* 'Ace of Hearts' (ornamental rhubarb; ✳✳✳ Z3–9) H&S: 1.2m × 90cm (4ft × 36in)

 F *Rheum palmatum* 'Atrosanguineum' (Chinese rhubarb; ✳✳✳ Z5–9) H&S: 2 × 1.2m (6½ × 4ft)

 G *Rodgersia pinnata* (featherleaf rodgersia; ✳✳✳ Z3–7) H&S: 1.2 × 0.75m (4 × 2½ft)

 N *Persicaria amplexicaulis* 'Firetail' (bistort; ✳✳✳ Z3–8) H&S: 1.2m × 80cm (4 × 2½ft)

 O *Iris ensata* (Japanese water iris; ✳✳✳ Z3–9) H&S: 80 × 40cm (32 × 16in)

 P *Schoenoplectus lacustris* subsp. *tabernaemontani* (grey club-rush; ✳✳✳ Z6–9) H&S: 1 × 0.6m (3 × 2ft)

 Q *Primula florindae* (giant cowslip; ✳✳✳ Z3–8) H&S: 90 × 80cm (36 × 32in)

 R *Hosta* 'Halcyon' (Tardiana Group) (plantain lily; ✳✳✳ Z3–9) H&S: 40 × 60cm (16 × 24in)

 S *Hosta* 'Krossa Regal' (plantain lily; ✳✳✳ Z3–9) H&S: 70 × 70cm (28 × 28in)

 T *Astilbe* 'Deutschland' (✳✳✳ Z4–9) H&S: 70 × 40cm (28 × 16in)

 U *Iris pseudacorus* (yellow flag; ✳✳✳✳ Z5–8) H&S: 1.2 × 1.2m (4 × 4ft)

 V *Calla palustris* (bog arum; ✳✳✳ Z4–8) H&S: 25 × 60cm (10 × 24in)

 W *Nymphaea* 'Gonnère' (waterlily; ✳✳✳ Z3–11) H&S: 10cm × 1.2m (4in × 4ft)

 Leucojum aestivum (summer snowflake; ✳✳✳ Z3–9) H&S: 50 × 10cm (20 × 4in)

Formality out front

The planting potential of many front gardens is often unrealised; we tend to put our energies into the back garden and do just the bare minimum in the front. Although low maintenance is important and functionality should always come first, this doesn't mean you can't be creative, particularly with plants. Even in a front garden used for off-street parking, there's room for a tidy scented shrub in every corner (see pp158–161). Walls and fences support beautiful climbers and wall shrubs. Even a big summer basket hanging by the front door makes all the difference.

Sedum Herbstfreude Group 'Herbstfreude' (stonecrop)

Geranium 'Brookside' (cranesbill)

Allium cristophii (star of Persia)

Tricks of the trade

- **Interest year-round:** For front gardens, always pick plants with as many seasons of interest as possible. A reliable evergreen backbone also helps. Topiary is one option, but repetitive groups of airy grasses such as Mexican feather grass (*Stipa tenuissima*) also work well. Low knot gardens are popular, especially in small terraced gardens, often replacing a lawn.

- **Security conscious:** Use big plants for privacy or to screen a parking space. But watch out you don't create corners where intruders could work away undetected. Ensure trees don't block light to the home either.

- **Control the car:** Where a parking space dominates a front garden, use plants to 'control' the car so it doesn't become the main focus, especially where there isn't a set path to the front door. A couple of colourful half-barrels will help. So too will a simple green central strip under the parked car; this should be of tough, shade-tolerant ground-huggers such as *Waldsteinia ternata*, Irish moss (*Minuartia verna*) and bugle (*Ajuga reptans*).

- **Creative containers:** If the whole garden is paved, grow plants in large, heavy-to-shift pots. Big containers also help keep maintenance to a minimum, as plants won't need watering or feeding so often. Colourful, semi-permanent displays of tidy shrubs, grasses and perennials are best; these don't need replacing annually.

Nepeta racemosa 'Walker's Low'
(dwarf catmint) and *Salvia verticillata*
'Purple Rain' (whorled clary)

Narcissus 'Topolino'
(daffodil)

Anemone × hybrida
'September Charm'
(Japanese anemone)

A touch of formality helps to forge all-important links between house and garden. Clipped topiary is a perennial favourite, complementing modern and traditional architecture. In this border, designed to line the path to the front door of a typical suburban garden, three evergreen standard balls bring structure to the simple perennial planting underneath. They also have a sculptural quality.

(C) *Aster × frikartii* 'Mönch' (Michaelmas daisy): Sometimes-floppy perennial daisy with luminous, lavender-blue flowers. Needs full sun to thrive and benefits from support in early spring (grow-through grids are ideal).

(I) *Monarda* 'Beauty of Cobham' (bergamot): Tidy clump-former with whorls of purple flowers in summer and autumn. Humus-rich, well-drained soil essential. Full sun or semishade. A favourite for prairie-like plantings too.

(G) *Erysimum* 'Bowles's Mauve' (perennial wallflower): Bushy evergreen perennial with narrow, grey-green leaves and incredibly long-lasting, mauve flowers from spring until autumn. Well-drained soils in full sun.

(D) *Bergenia* 'Silberlicht' (elephant's ears): Tough evergreen clump-former with erect white flowers in spring. Sun or semishade. Supposedly dislikes dry soils, yet is ideal for dry gravel gardens.

The fine detail

Aspect: Full sun to semishade.

Soil type: Moist, fertile but free draining.

pH: Neutral to alkaline. All except perennial wallflowers (G) grow well in acidic conditions.

Peak period of interest: Summer.

Flower colour: White and yellow in spring, changing to mauve, pink and purple from late spring to late summer.

Foliage colour & texture: Green (in various tints and shades) and silvery grey. Medium to fine.

Maintenance: Low. Clip the delavay privet (A) in late spring to maintain its globular shape. Tidy spent perennials after flowering. Michaelmas daisies (C) might need staking in exposed spots.

Other notes: Consider buying large specimens of the delavay privet because they are important structural plants here but slow-growing. All perennials are attractive to pollinating insects including bees and butterflies.

Design decisions

Seasonal interest is provided by long-flowering, low-maintenance perennials, graduated in height from front to back. Each season is observed. In spring white elephant's ears (D) and two trumpet daffodils (triangles and inverted triangles) welcome the new growing season. A blue cranesbill (F), dwarf catmint (E) and whorled clary (B) are among those that bloom in late spring and summer. Mid- to late summer/autumn sees a pink Japanese anemone (H), lavender-blue Michaelmas daisy (C) and purple bergamot (I) join in. Together they will hide the stems of the delavay privet (A), so the balls will seemingly float on a sea of late summer flowers.

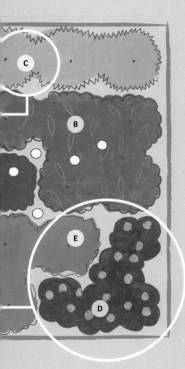

5m (16ft)   6m (20ft)

 A
Ligustrum delavayanum (delavay privet; ✳✳✳ Z8–9) H&S (when clipped): 1.65 × 0.6m (5½ × 2ft)

 B
Salvia verticillata 'Purple Rain' (whorled clary; ✳✳✳ Z6–8) H&S: 75 × 40cm (30 × 16in)

 C
Aster × frikartii 'Mönch' (Michaelmas daisy; ✳✳✳ Z5–8) H&S: 90 × 40cm (36 × 16in)

 D
Bergenia 'Silberlicht' (elephant's ears; ✳✳✳ Z3–8) H&S: 40 × 50cm (16 × 20in)

 E
Nepeta racemosa 'Walker's Low' (dwarf catmint; ✳✳✳ Z4–8) H&S: 60 × 50cm (24 × 20in)

 F
Geranium 'Brookside' (cranesbill; ✳✳✳ Z5–9) H&S: 60 × 40cm (24 × 16in)

G
Erysimum 'Bowles's Mauve' (perennial wallflower; ✳✳✳ Z6–10) H&S: 75 × 60cm (30 × 24in)

 H
Anemone × hybrida 'September Charm' (Japanese anemone; ✳✳✳ Z4–8) H&S: 90 × 55cm (36 × 22in)

 I
Monarda 'Beauty of Cobham' (bergamot; ✳✳✳ Z4–9) H&S: 90 × 45cm (36 × 18in)

 J
Origanum laevigatum 'Herrenhausen' (oregano; ✳✳✳ Z7–10) H&S: 55 × 45cm (22 × 18in)

 K
Sedum Herbstfreude Group 'Herbstfreude' (stonecrop; ✳✳✳ Z3–10) H&S: 60 × 50cm (24 × 20in)

▽ *Narcissus* 'Topolino' (daffodil; ✳✳✳ Z4–8) H&S: 20 × 10cm (8 × 4in)

△ *Narcissus* 'W P Milner' (daffodil; ✳✳✳ Z4–8) H&S: 35 × 10cm (14 × 4in)

○ *Allium cristophii* (star of Persia; ✳✳ Z5–8) H&S: 45 × 20cm (18 × 8in)

A modern herbal

Today herbs are appreciated as much for their scent, colourful flowers and contrasting foliage as they are for their culinary qualities. No longer restricted to a traditional patch, herbs are now a key part of modern, often low-maintenance, mixed plantings alongside other shrubs, conifers, perennials and bulbs. Common to both formal and informal designs – regardless of the style or theme – this approach is particularly popular in small gardens, where plants that reward in more ways than one are most invaluable.

Rosa Gertrude Jekyll = 'Ausbord' (rose)

Tricks of the trade

- **Ornamental arrangement:** To avoid the 'spotty' look synonymous with traditional culinary collections, place plants in the same way as you would other ornamentals, that is in blocks or drifts of three or more, repeating certain ones throughout to help unify the scheme.

- **Focus in:** Fastigiate Irish juniper (*Juniperus communis* 'Hibernica') or trimmed bay laurel (*Laurus*) balls make attractive, but edible, focal points. Partner them with contrasting forms or space them in a way that shows off their bold shape. Olive (*Olea*) trees are also useful.

- **Medicinal quality:** Many ornamental herbs have medicinal qualities or can be used in cooking; choose these, or similar cultivars, if you want to stay true to herb garden tradition. Colourful perennials such as coneflower (*Echinacea purpurea*) and evening primrose (*Oenothera biennis*) are more familiar, but border favourites, including lady's mantle (*Alchemilla*) and giant hyssop (*Agastache*), are also said to cure various ailments.

- **Space apart:** Many herbs grow quickly so avoid planting too densely. Regularly pull out vigorous seedlings too. Certain mints (*Mentha*) in particular have invasive roots. Grow each one in a pot then sink this into the ground (leaving the lip just above the soil surface) to stop the runners going wild.

Atriplex hortensis var. *rubra* (red orache) and *Allium schoenoprasum* (chive)

Agastache foeniculum
(anise hyssop)

Iris 'Blue Rhythm'

Thymus vulgaris
(common thyme)

Origanum majorana
(sweet marjoram)

Lavandula angustifolia
'Twickel Purple' (lavender)

The plants in this modern herbal design, sandwiched as they are between two gravel paths alongside a formal lawn, were picked both for their good looks as well as for their flavoursome foliage or flowers. Even those plants which are not edible, are typical of herb gardens. Many of their close relatives are used to create homeopathic remedies to treat various ills.

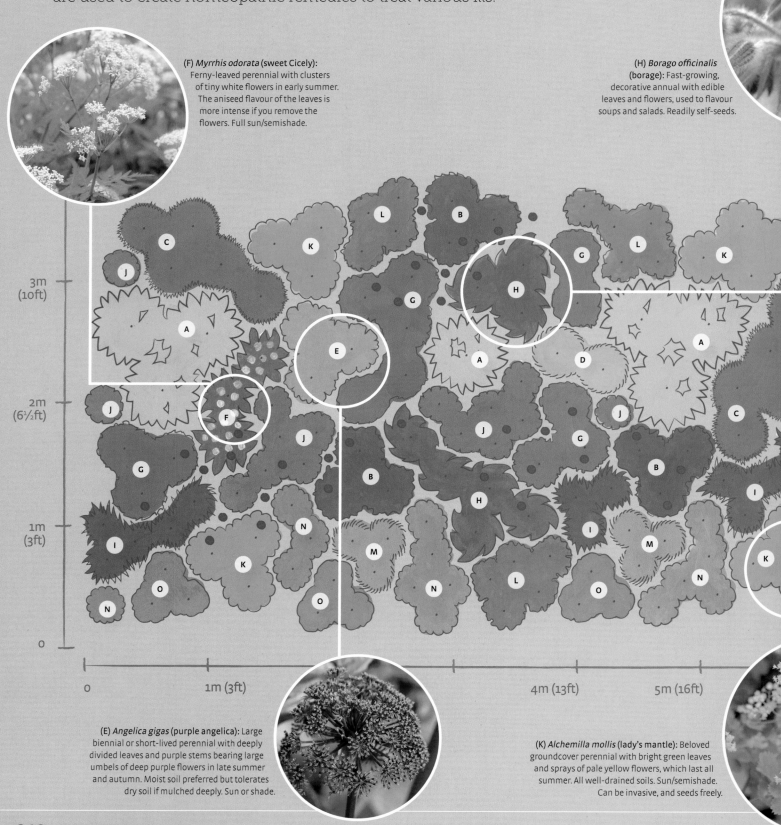

(F) *Myrrhis odorata* (sweet Cicely): Ferny-leaved perennial with clusters of tiny white flowers in early summer. The aniseed flavour of the leaves is more intense if you remove the flowers. Full sun/semishade.

(H) *Borago officinalis* (borage): Fast-growing, decorative annual with edible leaves and flowers, used to flavour soups and salads. Readily self-seeds.

3m (10ft)

2m (6½ft)

1m (3ft)

0

0   1m (3ft)   4m (13ft)   5m (16ft)

(E) *Angelica gigas* (purple angelica): Large biennial or short-lived perennial with deeply divided leaves and purple stems bearing large umbels of deep purple flowers in late summer and autumn. Moist soil preferred but tolerates dry soil if mulched deeply. Sun or shade.

(K) *Alchemilla mollis* (lady's mantle): Beloved groundcover perennial with bright green leaves and sprays of pale yellow flowers, which last all summer. All well-drained soils. Sun/semishade. Can be invasive, and seeds freely.

The fine detail

Aspect: Full sun.

Soil type: Fairly fertile but free-draining.

pH: Acid to neutral to alkaline.

Peak period of interest: Midsummer; late spring and early autumn too.

Flower colour: Blue, pink, purple, yellow and white.

Foliage colour & texture: Green (various), golden yellow and purple. Medium to fine.

Maintenance: Medium. Deadhead when necessary and clear spent foliage, particularly in spring. In summer, borage (H), lady's mantle (K), sweet marjoram (L) and chives (M) might require a light trim to keep them in check. Watch for prolific self-seeders. Fennel (D), purple angelica (E) and sweet Cicely (F) need staking early in the year, whereas borage and red orache (J) need replacing annually. Mulch the roses (A), purple angelica (E) and sweet Cicely with compost every spring.

Other notes: When they flower, all the herbs included here attract bees, butterflies and other beneficial insects that help control pests such as whitefly and blackfly.

Design decisions

A fragrant pink shrub rose (A), repeated in the middle, adds reliable height and a steady formal rhythm to this informal island bed. Around them, favourites such as fennel (D), borage (H) and sweet Cicely (F) drift lazily down the centre, but are well within easy reach. Low-growing culinary classics such as common sage (B) and thyme (O) flow out into the gravel on either side. One strip of common thyme (P), bordered by two strips of golden wild marjoram (Q) attract the eye and add an asymmetric modernist touch. This partnership could be repeated in various ways if the planting were extended. Both marjoram and thyme can be trimmed to remove flowers (which intensifies the flavour of the leaves) without affecting the composition.

7m (23ft)

 Rosa Gertrude Jekyll = 'Ausbord' (rose; ❋❋❋ Z5–9) H&S: 1.2 × 1m (4 × 3ft)

 Salvia officinalis (common sage; ❋❋❋ Z5–8) H&S: 80 × 80cm (32 × 32in)

 Lavandula angustifolia 'Twickel Purple' (lavender; ❋❋❋ Z5–8) H&S: 50 × 50cm (20 × 20in)

 Foeniculum vulgare (fennel; ❋❋❋ Z4–9) H&S: 1.8m × 45cm (6ft × 18in)

 Angelica gigas (purple angelica; ❋❋❋ Z4–9) H&S: 1.35 × 1m (4½ × 3ft)

 Myrrhis odorata (sweet Cicely; ❋❋❋ Z3–7) H&S: 1.8 × 1.2m (6 × 4ft)

 Agastache foeniculum (anise hyssop; ❋❋ Z4–11) H&S: 1.1m × 35cm (3½ft × 14in)

 Borago officinalis (borage; ❋❋❋ zone not applicable) H&S: 80 × 40cm (32 × 16in)

 Iris 'Blue Rhythm' (❋❋❋ Z5–10) H&S: 1.1m × 45cm (3½ft × 18in)

 Atriplex hortensis var. *rubra* (red orache; ❋ Z7–9) H&S: 1.2 × 0.3m (4 × 1ft)

 Alchemilla mollis (lady's mantle; ❋❋❋ Z4–7) H&S: 60 × 60cm (2 × 2ft)

 Origanum majorana (sweet marjoram; ❋❋ Z4–9) H&S: 60 × 45cm (24 × 18in)

 Allium schoenoprasum (chive; ❋❋❋ Z5–11) H&S: 40 × 5cm (16 × 2in)

 Geranium 'Nimbus' (cranesbill; ❋❋❋ Z5–8) H&S: 45 × 45cm (18 × 18in)

 Thymus Coccineus Group (thyme; ❋❋❋ Z4–9) H&S: 30 × 10cm (12 × 4in)

 Thymus vulgaris (common thyme; ❋❋❋ Z4–9) H&S: 40 × 40cm (16 × 16in)

 Origanum vulgare 'Aureum' (golden wild marjoram; ❋❋❋ Z4–9) H&S: 30 × 40cm (12 × 16in)

 Allium hollandicum 'Purple Sensation' (ornamental onion; ❋❋❋ Z4–11) H&S: 90 × 20cm (36 × 8in)

Packed with perfume

Every plant group, from tall trees to tiny bulbs, has many fragrant species and there are numerous wonderful choices to be made regardless of the style or theme, the time of year or the size of the space to be planted. Scent also has a powerful effect on our emotions and can evoke long-lost memories and childhood summer holidays. But don't get carried away; lots of scented plants pumping out perfume all at the same time can be too much of a good thing. Many of the plants here, for example, suit the cottage design on pp250–251 but are not scented for that very reason.

Syringa meyeri 'Palibin' (Korean lilac)

Tricks of the trade

- **Try before you buy:** What is sweet to one nose may be nauseous to another. Powerful free scents (see p81) such as from regal lilies (*Lilium regale*) are often the worst culprits, sometimes causing problems for asthma sufferers. Smell the flowers at the garden centre before you buy.

- **Scent sense:** While continuity of scent is important, ask yourself when you use the garden most, especially where space in it is tight. Focus on spring scents if you're away all summer. Plants such as night phlox (*Zaluzianskya ovata*), which release their fragrance on warm summer evenings, are ideal if you use the garden mainly after work.

- **Winter interest:** Scented plants are invaluable in winter and early spring. Many tough, somewhat unassuming shrubs fill the air with strong scents at these times of year. Favourites include wintersweet (*Chimonathus*), witch hazel (*Hamamelis*) and *Viburnum*. Even if cold weather keeps you inside, situate them close to the house so the scent can waft through an open door or window.

- **Scent seeker:** Delicate fragrances on the air tickle the nose just enough to encourage you to seek out the source. Position such plants so they're not only within easy reach but also lead you from one garden area to another.

Astrantia 'Roma' (masterwort)

Phlox paniculata 'Blue Evening'
(perennial phlox)

Nectaroscordum siculum
subsp. bulgaricum
(Bulgarian honey garlic)

Cosmos bipinnatus
Sonata Series Mixed

Scabiosa 'Butterfly Blue'
(pincushion flower)

Allium hollandicum
(ornamental onion)

In a warm, protected cottage courtyard, this narrow, L-shaped border partially wraps around a seating space in front. Shrubs and perennials fill the air with sweet and spicy scent from early spring to late summer. But, while scented plants are key here, the cottage context (see pp94–97) and a harmonious colour palette (see pp142–143) of pink, mauve, purple and blue, with white, are also important.

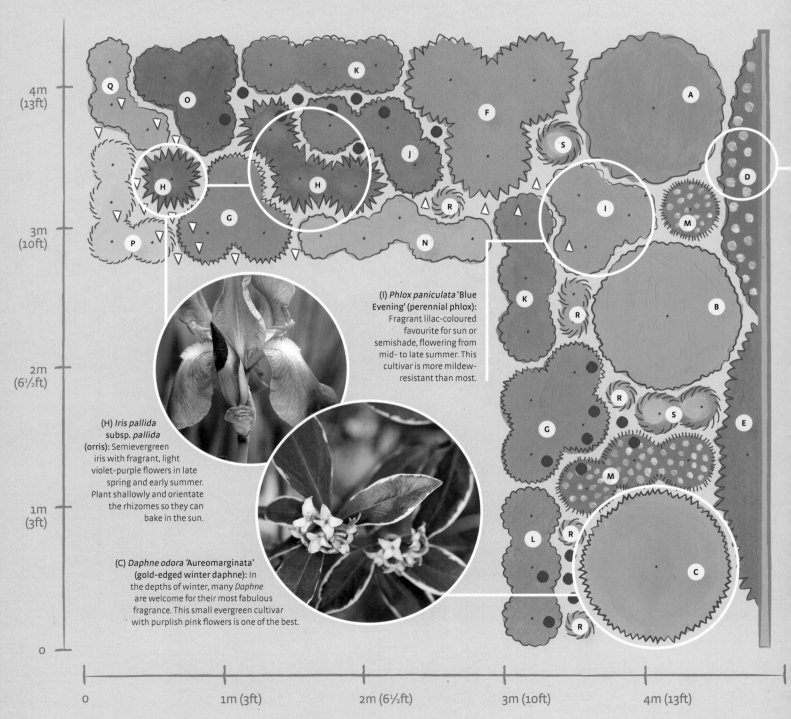

(I) *Phlox paniculata* 'Blue Evening' (perennial phlox): Fragrant lilac-coloured favourite for sun or semishade, flowering from mid- to late summer. This cultivar is more mildew-resistant than most.

(H) *Iris pallida* subsp. *pallida* (orris): Semievergreen iris with fragrant, light violet-purple flowers in late spring and early summer. Plant shallowly and orientate the rhizomes so they can bake in the sun.

(C) *Daphne odora* 'Aureomarginata' (gold-edged winter daphne): In the depths of winter, many *Daphne* are welcome for their most fabulous fragrance. This small evergreen cultivar with purplish pink flowers is one of the best.

The fine detail

Aspect: Full sun. Some shelter is necessary too.

Soil type: Moist, fertile but free-draining.

pH: Neutral to alkaline.

Peak period of interest: Spread evenly between spring and mid- to late summer.

Flower colour: Pink, pale pink and yellow in early spring, turning white, blue, deep pink, lilac, rose-purple and purple in late spring and on into autumn.

Foliage colour & texture: Green (in various tints and shades), silvery grey, some yellow variegation. Medium to fine.

Maintenance: Low. Tie in the two wall shrubs – tree anemone (D) and rose (E) – throughout the year. Deadhead when necessary. Tidy spent perennials after flowering. White cosmos (S) might need staking.

Other notes: Being members of the onion family, both the ornamental onion (black spots) and Bulgarian honey garlic (triangles) have garlic-scented leaves when crushed.

(D) *Carpenteria californica* (tree anemone): Evergreen shrub famed for its fragrant white flowers centred with yellow stamens. Being a Californian native, it relishes the protection of a hot, south-or west-facing wall.

Design decisions

To take advantage of every centimetre, a warm wall on the right-hand side supports a summer-fragrant evergreen tree anemone (D) and a scented pink rose (E), behind three small shrubs – *Viburnum* (A), Korean lilac (B), gold-edged winter daphne (C) – each famed for its late winter or spring scent. In front, lavender (G) and thyme (Q) are placed within easy reach, accompanied by a strongly coloured pink (P) – no cottage planting is complete without one. But you can have too much of a good thing. Elsewhere, cottage classics such as *Cosmos* (R, S), cranesbill (K, L), *Gaura* (M) and pincushion flower (O) have been included specifically because they're not scented.

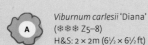 **A** *Viburnum carlesii* 'Diana' (❁❁❁ Z5–8) H&S: 2 × 2m (6½ × 6½ft)

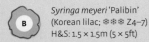 **B** *Syringa meyeri* 'Palibin' (Korean lilac; ❁❁❁ Z4–7) H&S: 1.5 × 1.5m (5 × 5ft)

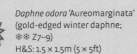 **C** *Daphne odora* 'Aureomarginata' (gold-edged winter daphne; ❁❁ Z7–9) H&S: 1.5 × 1.5m (5 × 5ft)

D *Carpenteria californica* (tree anemone; ❁❁ Z8–9) H&S (when wall-trained): 2m × 50cm (6½ft × 20in)

E *Rosa* 'Souvenir du Docteur Jamain' (rose; ❁❁❁ Z5–9) H&S (when wall-trained): 3m × 50cm (10ft × 20in)

F *Rosa* Heather Austin = 'Auscook' (rose; ❁❁❁ Z5–9) H&S: 1.35m × 90cm (4½ft × 36in)

 G *Lavandula × intermedia* 'Sussex' (lavender; ❁❁❁ Z5–8) H&S: 65 × 60cm (26 × 24in)

 H *Iris pallida* subsp. *pallida* (orris; ❁❁❁ Z1–9) H&S: 1.2 × 0.3m (4 × 1ft)

 I *Phlox paniculata* 'Blue Evening' (perennial phlox; ❁❁❁ Z4–8) H&S: 80 × 40cm (32 × 16in)

 J *Lychnis coronaria* (rose campion; ❁❁❁ Z3–8) H&S: 75 × 40cm (30 × 16in)

 K *Geranium* 'Nimbus' (cranesbill; ❁❁❁ Z5–9) H&S: 45 × 45cm (18 × 18in)

L *Geranium pyrenaicum* 'Bill Wallis' (cranesbill; ❁❁❁ Z5–9) H&S: 30 × 40cm (12 × 16in)

 M *Gaura lindheimeri* 'Whirling Butterflies' (❁❁❁ Z6–9) H&S: 75 × 45cm (30 × 18in)

 N *Astrantia* 'Roma' (masterwort; ❁❁❁ Z4–7) H&S: 60 × 40cm (24 × 16in)

 O *Scabiosa* 'Butterfly Blue' (pincushion flower; ❁❁❁ Z3–8) H&S: 40 × 40cm (16 × 16in)

 P *Dianthus* 'Doris' (pink; ❁❁❁ Z5–9) H&S: 40 × 40cm (16 × 16in)

 Q *Thymus* 'Porlock' (thyme; ❁❁❁ Z5–9) H&S: 20 × 30cm (8 × 12in)

 R *Cosmos bipinnatus* Sonata Series Mixed (❁ zone not applicable) H&S: 50 × 25cm (20 × 10in)

 S *Cosmos bipinnatus* 'Purity' (white cosmos; ❁ zone not applicable) H&S: 1.2 × 0.3m (4 × 1ft)

 Allium hollandicum (ornamental onion; ❁❁❁ Z4–11) H&S: 90 × 20cm (36 × 8in)

 Nectaroscordum siculum subsp. *bulgaricum* (Bulgarian honey garlic; ❁❁❁ Z6–10) H&S: 1.2 × 0.3m (4 × 1ft)

 Narcissus 'Baby Moon' (jonquil; ❁❁❁ Z3–9) H&S: 25 × 5cm (10 × 2in)

Bees' needs

Gardens are vital for bees, butterflies and other pollinating insects – urban gardens more than most, as these form an invaluable part of the wildlife corridors crossing our cities. But encouraging bees and butterflies to help support biodiversity is only part of the picture; these essential pollinators also assist us in growing bigger and better crops. For many people they make the garden more exciting. Fortunately there are plenty of bee-plants you can choose, regardless of your style or theme. The 'RHS Perfect for Pollinators' lists will help (www.rhs.org.uk/science/).

Rosa rubiginosa
(eglantine rose)

Penstemon 'Raven'

Tricks of the trade

- **Golden rule No 1:** Don't use pesticides. If you feel you have to, choose those based on natural products that state they don't harm bees. And never spray near plants in flower.

- **Instant attraction:** Flowering fruit trees, traditional shrubs and perennials such as *Buddleja* and catmint (*Nepeta*) are most attractive to pollinating insects. Native flowers such as Jacob's ladder (*Polemonium caeruleum*) and field scabious (*Knautia arvensis*) are better still.

- **Seasonal thinking:** Spring flowers are vital for waking bees: aubretia (*Aubrieta*) and honesty (*Lunaria*) are all good early pollen and nectar sources. Autumn is important too. Stonecrop (*Sedum*), Michaelmas daisy (*Aster* and *Symphyotrichum*) and ivy (*Hedera*) flowers are desirable at this time and help insects build up reserves for winter.

- **Easy access:** The more flower forms the better, as different insect species have individual preferences. But avoid double-flowered cultivars, which are bred for bigger and better flowers – the pollen and nectar aren't easy to reach. They're usually sterile too.

- **Bee colour wise:** Purple, mauve and violet flowers are most attractive to bees, followed by blue, white and yellow. Butterflies like red and orange too. Include them all, perhaps.

Salvia nemorosa 'Caradonna'
(Balkan clary)

Ammi majus
(bullwort)

Verbena bonariensis
(purple top)

Anthemis tinctoria
'Sauce Hollandaise'
(oxeye chamomile)

Agastache 'Blackadder'
(giant hyssop)

Chamaenerion angustifolium 'Album'
(white rosebay willowherb)

Valeriana officinalis
(common valerian)

This deep informal border, filled with traditional cottage or country garden classics and backed by an evergreen yew hedge, is a magnet for pollinating insects. The plants not only make a colourful spectacle but also provide pollen and nectar right through the year. This border is both sunny and sheltered and this is important; bees and butterflies aren't as active in shade and they struggle in strong winds.

(I) *Valeriana officinalis* (common valerian): Tall, tough perennial with erect flower stems topped with sweetly scented, pink or white flowers in summer. Ideal for the back of deep borders.

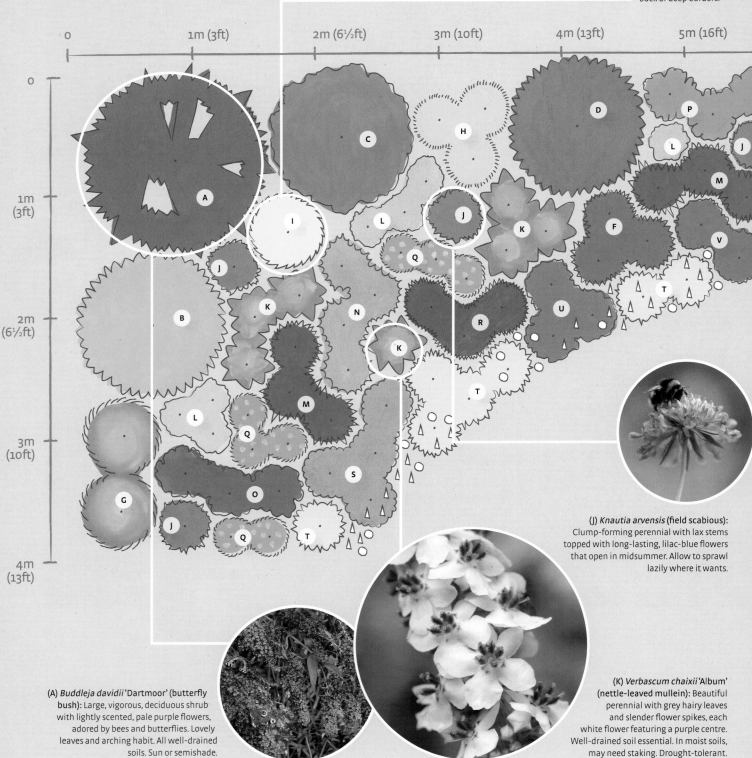

(J) *Knautia arvensis* (field scabious): Clump-forming perennial with lax stems topped with long-lasting, lilac-blue flowers that open in midsummer. Allow to sprawl lazily where it wants.

(A) *Buddleja davidii* 'Dartmoor' (butterfly bush): Large, vigorous, deciduous shrub with lightly scented, pale purple flowers, adored by bees and butterflies. Lovely leaves and arching habit. All well-drained soils. Sun or semishade.

(K) *Verbascum chaixii* 'Album' (nettle-leaved mullein): Beautiful perennial with grey hairy leaves and slender flower spikes, each white flower featuring a purple centre. Well-drained soil essential. In moist soils, may need staking. Drought-tolerant.

The fine detail

Aspect: Full sun.

Soil type: Moist, fertile but free-draining.

pH: Neutral to alkaline. All except butterfly bush (A), field scabious (J), nettle-leaved mullein (K) and great bellflower (M) tolerate acid soils.

Peak period of interest: Summer.

Flower colour: Blush-pink, white, yellow, mauve and blue in early spring, changing to deep blue, sky-blue, yellow, mauve, purple and white in late spring/summer until late summer/autumn.

Foliage colour & texture: Green (in various tints and shades), silvery grey and bronze. Medium to fine.

Maintenance: Medium. Hard prune the butterfly bush in spring to promote new flowers. Some staking of perennials, particularly yarrow (H), nettle-leaved mullein, purple top (L) and Michaelmas daisy (P) may well be required. Deadhead regularly to encourage more flowers for visitors. Bullwort (Q) is an annual so needs replacing every year.

Other notes: Many plants are scented but laurustinus (C), rose (D), mock orange (E) and common valerian (I) are the best of the bunch.

6m (20ft)

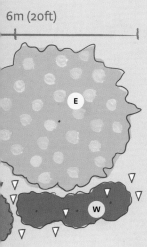

Key:
Sp: Spring flowering
Su: Summer flowering
A: Autumn flowering
W: Winter flowering

Design decisions

A big, purple-flowered butterfly bush (A) is the main focal point, supported by an evergreen, early spring-flowering laurustinus (C), late spring-flowering mock orange (E) and two species roses (B, D) – both chosen for their simple, bee-friendly flowers. In front, a variety of attractive perennials intermingle, all arranged with height in mind and partnered so that gaps after flowering aren't too obvious. There are plenty of different flower forms too, from globular globe thistles (N) to the erect spires of white rosebay willowherb (G). Contrast is important in perennial plantings, and different forms entice different pollinators too. While this display peaks in summer, importantly, plants have been included to provide pollen and nectar for bees at other times (see the key, above left).

 A *Buddleja davidii* 'Dartmoor' (butterfly bush – Su; ✳✳✳ Z6–9) H&S: 3 × 3m (10 × 10ft)

 B *Rosa rubiginosa* (eglantine rose – Su; ✳✳✳ Z4–9) H&S: 2.5 × 2.5m (8 × 8ft)

 C *Viburnum tinus* 'Gwenllian' (laurustinus – W/Sp; ✳✳✳ Z8–10) H&S: 2 × 2m (6½ × 6½ft)

 D *Rosa forrestiana* (rose – Su; ✳✳✳ Z4–9) H&S: 1.8 × 1.8m (6 × 6ft)

 E *Philadelphus* 'Belle Étoile' (mock orange – Sp/Su; ✳✳✳ Z5–8) H&S: 1.5 × 2m (5 × 6½ft)

 F *Lavandula angustifolia* 'Hidcote' (lavender – Su; ✳✳✳ Z5–8) H&S: 50 × 50cm (20 × 20in)

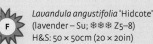 **G** *Chamaenerion angustifolium* 'Album' (white rosebay willowherb – Su; ✳✳✳ Z3–7) H&S: 1.5m × 50cm (5ft × 20in)

 H *Achillea filipendulina* 'Cloth of Gold' (yarrow – Su/A; ✳✳✳ Z3–9) H&S: 1.2m × 45cm (4ft × 18in)

 I *Valeriana officinalis* (common valerian – Su; ✳✳✳ Z4–9) H&S: 1.5m × 0.6m (5 × 2ft)

 J *Knautia arvensis* (field scabious – Su; ✳✳✳ Z5–9) H&S: 1.35 × 0.3m (4½ × 1ft)

 K *Verbascum chaixii* 'Album' (nettle-leaved mullein – Su; ✳✳✳ Z5–9) H&S: 1m × 45cm (3ft × 18in)

 L *Verbena bonariensis* (purple top – Su/A; ✳✳ Z7–11) H&S: 1.8m × 45cm (6ft × 18in)

 M *Campanula latiloba* 'Highcliffe Variety' (great bellflower – Su; ✳✳✳ Z5–7) H&S: 80 × 50cm (32 × 20in)

 N *Echinops ritro* 'Veitch's Blue' (globe thistle – Su/A; ✳✳✳ Z3–9) H&S: 90 × 45cm (36 × 18in)

 O *Agastache* 'Blackadder' (giant hyssop – Su/A; ✳✳✳ Z8–11) H&S: 90 × 40cm (36 × 16in)

 P *Symphyotrichum novi-belgii* 'Schöne von Dietlikon' (Michaelmas daisy – A; ✳✳✳ Z4–8) H&S: 1.2 × 0.6m (4 × 2ft)

 Q *Ammi majus* (bullwort – Su; ✳✳✳ zone not applicable) H&S: 90 × 30cm (36 × 12in)

 R *Penstemon* 'Raven' (Su; ✳✳ Z9–11) H&S: 80 × 35cm (32 × 14in)

 S *Geranium* 'Blue Cloud' (cranesbill – Su/A; ✳✳✳ Z5–8) H&S: 50 × 50cm (20 × 20in)

 T *Anthemis tinctoria* 'Sauce Hollandaise' (oxeye chamomile – Su; ✳✳✳ Z3–8) H&S: 50 × 50cm (20 × 20in)

 U *Salvia nemorosa* 'Caradonna' (Balkan clary – Su; ✳✳✳ Z5–9) H&S: 50 × 35cm (20 × 14in)

 V *Nepeta racemosa* 'Walkers' Low' (dwarf catmint – Su/A; ✳✳✳ Z4–8) H&S: 60 × 50cm (24 × 20in)

 W *Ajuga reptans* 'Braunherz' (bugle – Sp; ✳✳✳ Z3–9) H&S: 15 × 60cm (6 × 24in)

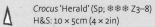 *Crocus* 'Herald' (Sp; ✳✳✳ Z3–8) H&S: 10 × 5cm (4 × 2in)

○ *Crocus tommasinianus* (Sp; ✳✳✳ Z3–8) H&S: 10 × 5cm (4 × 2in)

 Colchicum autumnale 'Album' (autumn crocus – Sp; ✳✳✳ Z4–9) H&S: 15 × 5cm (6 × 2in)

Growing in gravel

A wonderful way to keep maintenance to a minimum is to grow plants in gravel, and it is the ideal alternative to an unloved lawn, especially in sunny front gardens (see pp122–125). What's more, gravel is cheap, especially if you choose local stone (which always looks better anyway). Gravel gardens work well almost anywhere, the gravel itself being the perfect foil to a huge range of plants. That said, in large areas, plants originating from hot Mediterranean climates or dry arid ones look best, as gravel is their natural partner in the wild.

Verbena bonariensis (purple top)

Anthemis Susanna Mitchell = 'Blomit' (mayweed) together with *Geranium* Rozanne = 'Gerwat' (cranesbill). The plant in the centre is *Stipa tenuissima* (Mexican feather grass)

Tricks of the trade

- **A helping hand:** Once established, many classic gravel garden plants thrive on neglect. However some help is necessary initially. Cultivate the soil prior to planting as normal, forking in a little organic matter to relieve compaction and gently raise background fertility levels. Irrigate in dry spells during the first year.

- **The right option?** By itself a gravel mulch won't solve drainage problems (although it will stop the base of succulent species from rotting). If your garden soil is constantly damp, adding grit to improve drainage is expensive and, over a large area, hard work. In this situation, perhaps choose another style of planting.

- **Complete cover?** Covering every centimetre with gravel is again expensive, and also unnecessary. Instead, just gravel the paths and those sections where the planting is intentionally sparse. Where the planting is particularly dense, don't bother.

- **Weed control:** For paths, use permeable landscape fabric to help keep weeds down. Overlap each edge by 30cm (12in) to stop weeds before pinning down with U-shaped wire staples. Do not lay the fabric on beds and borders, as it inhibits surface spreaders and self-seeders.

- **Size & shape:** Small gravel (of 10–15mm/½in diameter) is best for small plants, the wheels of prams and tiny feet. Cats tend to dislike angular gravel.

Kniphofia caulescens
(red hot poker) and *Nepeta
racemosa* 'Walker's Low'
(dwarf catmint)

Eryngium bourgatii
'Picos Blue' (sea holly)

Geranium Rozanne = 'Gerwat'
(cranesbill)

This informal island bed mulched in gravel in the Beth Chatto tradition (see p122) is a departure from formal Mediterranean planting (see pp224–227). All plants included are drought-tolerant once established. Low maintenance is also a key characteristic. This proposal would work well replacing part of a large lawn, with the massing of each species to be increased according to the size of the area.

(G) *Perovskia* 'Blue Spire' (Russian sage): Small, erect, silver-leaved subshrub famed for its long-lasting, violet-blue flowers, which bloom in midsummer. Hardy to -15°C (5°F).

(O) *Achillea filipendulina* 'Cloth of Gold' (yarrow): Tall, tough, back-of-the-border favourite with feathery foliage and large, flat plate-like, sunshine-yellow flowers, which open in summer and last well into autumn.

The fine detail

Aspect: Full sun, partial exposure to wind.

Soil type: Dry; or free-draining but moist.

pH: Acid to neutral to alkaline.

Peak period of interest: Spring to late summer.

Flower colour: Yellow, blue, orange and white from early spring to late summer.

Foliage colour & texture: Green (in various tints and shades), silvery green, yellow-green/straw. Medium to fine.

Maintenance: Very low to low. Tall perennials might need staking in very exposed spots. Clear spent stems and foliage from perennials in spring. Avoid doing this earlier, as most have attractive winter seedheads. Watch for aggressive self-seeding and remove seedlings as required.

Other notes: Both white rose campion (P) and purple top (J) bloom for ages, but are also short-lived so might need replacing every three to four years, unless they self-seed.

(I) *Stipa gigantea* (golden oats): Big and beautiful evergreen grass with oatmeal-coloured flowers, which turn gold as the season progresses. All except waterlogged soils. Full sun essential.

Design decisions

Arranged in a loose pyramid, the apex formed by a fastigiate juniper (A), this design features many colourful, drought-tolerant perennials such as globe thistles (K) and sea kale (X); many of these feature in the foreground and are repeated for impact and to unify the scheme. But it's the flowering shrubs – daisy bush (B), California lilac (C), broom (D), rock rose (E) and rosemary (H) that are most noteworthy. Together with two floriferous subshrubs – Russian sage (G) and Jerusalem sage (F) – and the juniper, of course, these structure the planting and together divide up the area into a series of pockets, each partially screened from the next. As you walk around the outside of the planting, the different colourful combinations of perennials and bulbs within each one are revealed.

 A *Juniperus scopulorum* 'Skyrocket' (Rocky Mountain juniper; ✳✳✳ Z3–7) H&S: 4–8 × 1m (13–25 × 3ft)

 B *Olearia* × *haastii* (daisy bush; ✳✳✳ Z9–10) H&S: 2 × 3m (6½ × 10ft)

 C *Ceanothus* 'Skylark' (California lilac; ✳✳ Z8–10) H&S: 2 × 2m (6½ × 6½ft)

 D *Cytisus* × *praecox* 'Allgold' (broom; ✳✳✳ Z6–9) H&S: 1.2 × 1.2m (4 × 4ft)

 E *Cistus* × *cyprius* (rock rose; ✳✳ Z8–11) H&S: 1.2 × 1.2m (4 × 4ft)

 F *Phlomis fruticosa* (Jerusalem sage; ✳✳✳ Z8–9) H&S: 1 × 1.2m (3 × 4ft)

 G *Perouskia* 'Blue Spire' (Russian sage; ✳✳✳ Z6–8) H&S: 1m × 80cm (3ft × 32in)

 H *Rosmarinus officinalis* 'Tuscan Blue' (rosemary; ✳✳ Z8–11) H&S: 1.35 × 1.1m (4½ × 3½ft)

 I *Stipa gigantea* (golden oats; ✳✳✳ Z8–15) H&S: 2 × 1m (6½ × 3ft)

 J *Verbena bonariensis* (purple top; ✳✳ Z7–11) H&S: 1.8m × 45cm (6ft × 18in)

 K *Echinops ritro* 'Veitch's Blue' (globe thistle; ✳✳✳ Z3–9) H&S: 90 × 45cm (36 × 18in)

 L *Leucanthemum* × *superbum* 'T E Killin' (✳✳✳ Z5–8) H&S: 90 × 60cm (36 × 24in)

 M *Agastache* 'Blue Fortune' (giant hyssop; ✳✳✳ Z6–9) H&S: 90 × 40cm (36 × 16in)

 N *Kniphofia caulescens* (red hot poker; ✳✳✳ Z6–9) H&S: 1.2 × 0.6m (4 × 2ft)

 O *Achillea filipendulina* 'Cloth of Gold' (yarrow; ✳✳✳ Z3–9) H&S: 1.2m × 45cm (4ft × 18in)

 P *Lychnis coronaria* 'Alba' (white rose campion; ✳✳✳ Z3–8) H&S: 75 × 40cm (30 × 16in)

 Q *Anthemis* Susanna Mitchell = 'Blomit' (mayweed; ✳✳✳ Z–9) H&S: 60 × 60cm (2 × 2ft)

 R *Geum* 'Prinses Juliana' (avens; ✳✳✳ Z5–9) H&S: 60 × 50cm (24 × 20in)

 S *Achillea* 'Moonshine' (yarrow; ✳✳✳ Z3–8) H&S: 60 × 45cm (24 × 18in)

 T *Nepeta racemosa* 'Walker's Low' (dwarf catmint; ✳✳✳ Z4–8) H&S: 60 × 50cm (24 × 20in)

 U *Eryngium bourgatii* 'Picos Blue' (sea holly; ✳✳✳ Z5–9) H&S: 50 × 55cm (20 × 22in)

 V *Geranium* Rozanne = 'Gerwat' (cranesbill; ✳✳✳ Z4–9) H&S: 50 × 50cm (20 × 20in)

 W *Alchemilla mollis* (lady's mantle; ✳✳✳ Z4–8) H&S: 60 × 60cm (2 × 2ft)

 X *Crambe maritima* (sea kale; ✳✳✳ Z6–9) H&S: 60 × 35cm (24 × 14in)

 Y *Euphorbia cornigera* (horned spurge; ✳✳✳ Z5–10) H&S: 80 × 80cm (32 × 32in)

 Z *Allium sphaerocephalon* (roundheaded leek; ✳✳✳ Z5–10b) H&S: 90 × 5cm (36 × 2in)

Prairie play

Good garden designers know that family-friendly gardens need to be all things to all people. For parents, easy-care plants that look beautiful yet withstand a wayward goal kick are important. Children, on the other hand, desire big, colourful, tactile plants, which can be picked continuously or made into a den, without them being scolded for doing so. Satisfying these different criteria might seem tricky but there are plenty of plants that work well. Certain planting design styles are particularly appropriate; prairie-like plantings (see pp118–121) for example seem to please everyone.

Narcissus lobularis (daffodil)

Pennisetum alopecuroides 'Cassian's Choice' (fountain grass)

Tricks of the trade

- **Speed is of the essence:** Fast-growing species that are larger than life are best. Annuals such as sunflowers (*Helianthus*) are popular, but can be time-consuming to look after. Instead perhaps choose similar perennials – tall coneflowers such as *Rudbeckia maxima* or *R. laciniata* – that return readily year after year.

- **Football friendly:** Ornamental grasses, many shrubs, ground cover and floriferous but sturdy perennials such as cranesbill (*Geranium*) and day lily (*Hemerocallis*) are good, as they recover quickly from superficial damage. Always position thorny plants out of reach, and if there are young children, avoid anything poisonous.

- **Something to sniff:** Scented plants are always appealing. Sweet peas (*Lathyrus odoratus*), stocks (*Matthiola*) and chocolate cosmos (*Cosmos atrosanguineus*) grow quickly and respond well to overenthusiastic picking. Touchy-feely scents such as thyme (*Thymus*) and lavender (*Lavandula*) are good too. Position plants within easy reach of fingers or feet.

- **Dividing interests:** All children (and adults!) need their own, partially screened play space. Freestanding trellis covered with climbers or drifts of veil-like grasses and perennials are tall enough to hide behind, yet open enough for parents to see through.

Sesleria autumnalis (moor grass) and *Sedum* 'Matrona' (orpine)

Cotinus 'Grace' (smoke bush)

Aster amellus 'King George' (Italian aster) and *Rudbeckia fulgida* var. *deamii* (black-eyed Susan)

Prairie plantings embrace tough, low-maintenance, often big, colourful perennials and grasses, making this style ideal for family gardens. This prairie-inspired strip splits part of a larger lawn, subtly screening a play area behind, while also giving the rest of the garden protection from flying footballs. But being football friendly wasn't the only caveat. The planting here is also attractive to bees and other wildlife and provides opportunities for drawing and painting too.

(F) *Rudbeckia maxima* (giant coneflower): Tall but robust, yellow coneflower with large, waxy, blue-grey leaves. Never needs staking. Full sun.

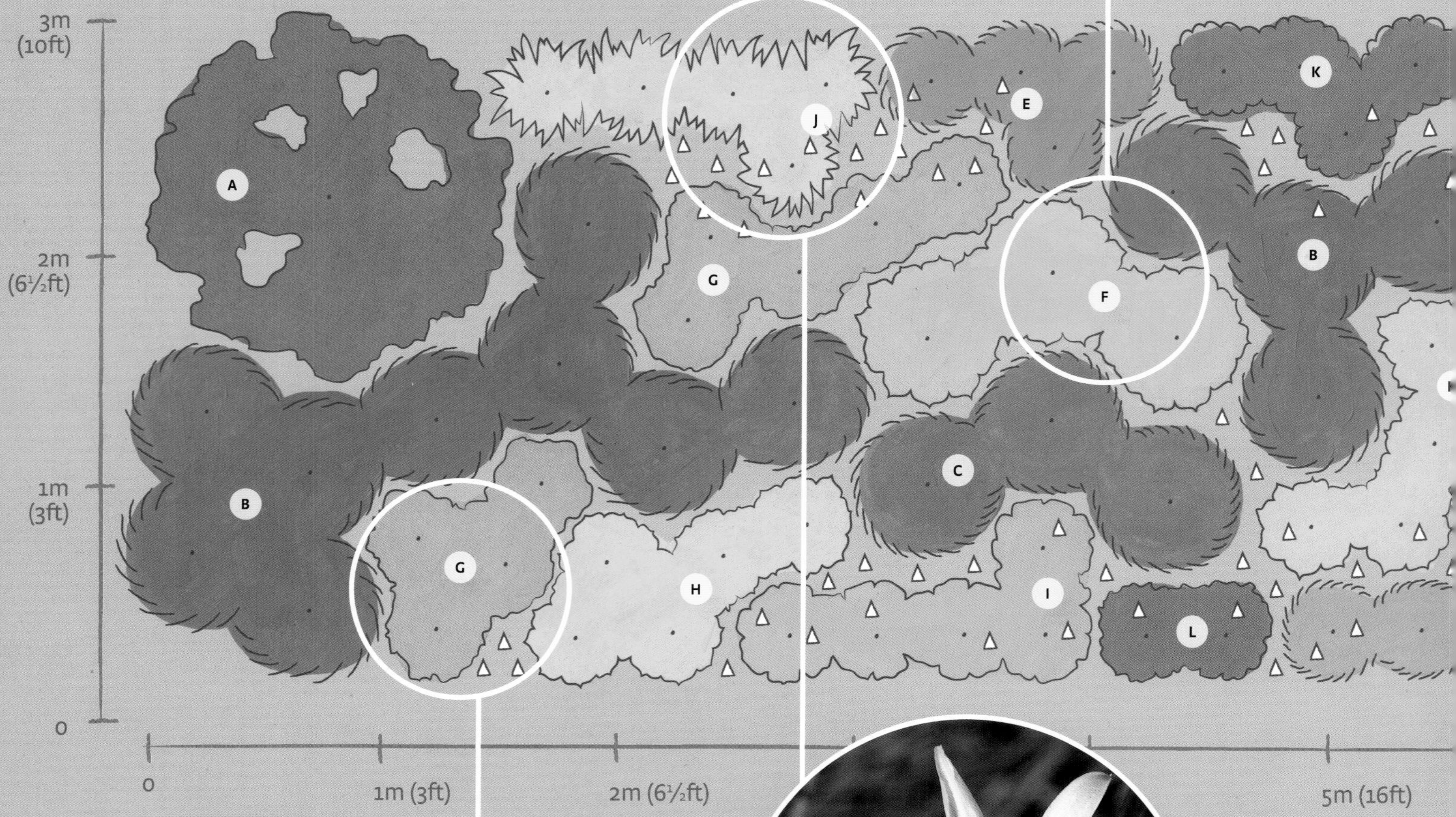

3m (10ft)

2m (6½ft)

1m (3ft)

0

0 1m (3ft) 2m (6½ft) 5m (16ft)

(G) *Echinacea purpurea* (coneflower): Tough, rose-purple perennial (given the right conditions) that won't require staking. Likes all but dry soils. Watch out for slugs during spring.

(J) *Hemerocallis lilioasphodelus* (lemon day lily): Reliable semievergreen clump-former with early, fragrant, sunshine-yellow flowers. Deadhead regularly.

The fine detail

Aspect: Full sun.

Soil type: Moist but free-draining.

pH: Alkaline to neutral. All except the Italian aster (L) tolerate acidic soil conditions.

Peak period of interest: A sea of daffodils (triangles) provides spring interest; the main flowering season is from mid- to late summer.

Flower colour: Creamy white/yellow flowers in spring, followed by rose-red, bronze, silver, lemon-yellow, orange-yellow and lavender-blue.

Foliage colour & texture: Green (in various tints and shades), silver, blue-grey, bronze and reddish purple in autumn. Coarse to medium to fine.

Maintenance: Very low to low. Cut back deciduous perennials and grasses in spring, unless they've already flopped over in wet weather. With these plants it's an easy job – get children to help.

Other notes: Lambs' tongues (M) are loved for their soft, velvety leaves.

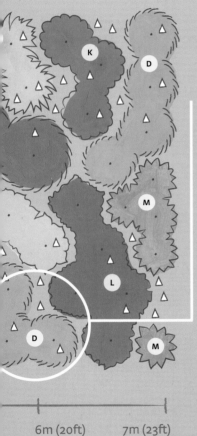

(D) *Sesleria autumnalis* (moor grass): Clump-forming, evergreen grass. Happy in sun/part shade. Silvery grey/white, summer flowers shimmer in the slightest breeze. Tolerant of all well-drained soils, but prefers alkaline conditions.

6m (20ft)   7m (23ft)

Design decisions

The star here is a deciduous but fast-growing feather reed grass (B), which runs down the middle. This has both the main structural and screening role. Switch grass (C), moor grass (D) and fountain grass (E) – each notable for flowers and autumn foliage – are also included. Arranged in drifts around them are popular prairie perennials, the colour scheme soft red, blue and yellow. Robust species such as meadow cranesbill (K) face the play space behind. Others such as an Italian aster (L), which suits the style but won't tolerate rough treatment, are protected on the other side. The deciduous grasses and perennials in this scheme have fantastic dead foliage, flowers and seedheads; don't be too quick to remove them.

 A *Cotinus* 'Grace' (smoke bush; ❋❋❋ Z5–9)
H&S: to 6 × 4m (20 × 13ft)

 B *Calamagrostis* × *acutiflora* 'Karl Foerster' (feather reed grass; ❋❋❋ Z5–9)
H&S: 1.65 × 0.6m (5½ × 2ft)

 C *Panicum virgatum* 'Rehbraun' (switch grass; ❋❋❋ Z5–9)
H&S: 1 × 0.75m (3 × 2½ft)

 D *Sesleria autumnalis* (moor grass; ❋❋❋ Z5–8)
H&S: 60 × 60cm (2 × 2ft)

 E *Pennisetum alopecuroides* 'Cassian's Choice' (fountain grass; ❋❋ Z6–9)
H&S: 70 × 70cm (28 × 28in)

 F *Rudbeckia maxima* (giant coneflower; ❋❋❋ Z4–8)
H&S: 2m × 80cm (6½ft × 32in)

 G *Echinacea purpurea* (coneflower; ❋❋❋ Z3–9)
H&S: 1.2m × 45cm (4ft × 18in)

 H *Rudbeckia fulgida* var. *deamii* (black-eyed Susan; ❋❋❋ Z4–9)
H&S: 70 × 45cm (28 × 18in)

 I *Sedum* 'Matrona' (orpine; ❋❋❋ Z4–9)
H&S: 60 × 40cm (24 × 16in)

 J *Hemerocallis lilioasphodelus* (lemon day lily; ❋❋❋ Z3–10)
H&S: 80 × 60cm (32 × 24in)

 K *Geranium pratense* (meadow cranesbill; ❋❋❋ Z4–8)
H&S: 70 × 60cm (28 × 24in)

 L *Aster amellus* 'King George' (Italian aster; ❋❋❋ Z5–8)
H&S: 55 × 40cm (22 × 16in)

 M *Stachys byzantina* 'Big Ears' (lambs' tongues; ❋❋❋ Z4–8)
H&S: 50 × 50cm (20 × 20in)

 △ *Narcissus lobularis* (daffodil; ❋❋❋ Z3–9)
H&S: 25 × 10cm (10 × 4in)

8.

Getting it into the Ground

Introducing new plants, especially to a border you've designed yourself, is one of the joys of gardening and garden design. I don't know of any gardener or garden designer who doesn't drool at the thought of getting their hands dirty. In this chapter I won't dwell on the physical planting process though – many books, such as *The RHS Encyclopedia of Gardening*, already cover this in detail – but we'll focus on where to get plants for your new scheme, what to look for, whether to buy big or small and how to calculate the number required to get your design into the ground. These are the practical considerations you need to embrace before picking up a spade or fork.

Sourcing: Where to go

Plants for a new scheme often come from various places. Some – notably annuals and biennials – you might propagate yourself, which is quite rewarding to do. Friends, family and neighbours will often help out with spare seedlings or clumps of perennials that they've split. But most plants will need to be bought in. Garden centres and big DIY stores are the most obvious places to go. However specialist nurseries and mail order companies are also well worth considering.

Garden centres

For small plantings, an afternoon trip to a big garden centre might be all that's necessary, especially in spring when the most plants are in stock. While a café and a children's playground make for a pleasurable family experience, you should always check the plant sales area closely. It should be clean, tidy and weed-free, and each sales bench should be packed with healthy-looking plants. If plants are in poor condition (with yellow, wilting leaves, for example) and unlabelled and the whole area basically looks unloved, buy fertiliser and dog treats perhaps, but get your plants somewhere else. Some garden centres are brilliant for plants, but others are not.

DIY stores & supermarkets

These can be useful, but don't expect a big range at such outlets. Most are geared up for seasonal impulse sales – for example only selling plants when they are in flower – and can't be relied on as a source for specific plants. Always check plant quality carefully. Specialist nurseries will have grown the plants offered for sale, but after sitting on a trolley devoid of natural light for a few weeks, the plants might be looking the worse for wear and may not establish well.

Left: Garden centres are an obvious port of call to purchase plants. But with so many delights on offer, it's easy to get distracted. Always go armed with a list, to avoid buying plants on impulse that may well be inappropriate for your garden!

Specialist nurseries

Garden designers and keen gardeners favour specialist nurseries run by the people who have nurtured the plants themselves. Most specialise in, and hold a huge range of, a certain plant type – trees, ornamental grasses or plants for shade for example – rather than stock a little of everything as garden centres do. Many nurseries often specialise further still in one plant genus such as *Iris* or snowdrops (*Galanthus*), something the owner particularly cherishes.

If you're planning to plant a large area requiring more than just a few plants, this is the most cost-effective option, as specialist nurseries are invariably cheaper and may offer a discount on large numbers. The quality of the plants is also often superior to anywhere else, as is the advice available.

To identify specialist nurseries and growers nearby, check the classified advertisements in good gardening magazines or search online. Trips to both local and national flower shows will also help; so too will the latest edition of the *RHS Plant Finder*, which features an exhaustive list of who sells what, and where (UK only).

Mail order

Many specialist nurseries (and good garden centres) also sell plants and bulbs by mail order. It's a great way to acquire rarities or favourites that aren't available locally, and to access brilliant growers that can't be easily visited.

Most suppliers offer quick delivery using trusted couriers. Good ones also label boxes 'live plants' so that delivery drivers know they're handling perishable cargo. On arrival, you should unpack purchases as quickly as possible and give the compost or roots a thorough soaking if appropriate. Don't worry if plants look a bit squashed; they'll soon recover. Ideally, plant them as soon as possible, although tender plants will need hardening off to conditions outside and planting out only once all danger of frost has passed.

When looking for plants, a simple, attractive, easy-to-navigate website packed with clearly presented information bodes well. So too does a good range of plants, each with growing instructions and tips on aftercare. Evidence of medals on the horticultural shows circuit or endorsement by a local gardening society/association is also a good sign. The size and price should be clear so you can compare like for like with other suppliers. Don't forget to factor in delivery costs (and taxes, if relevant).

Not all growers offer a mail order service year-round – it depends on the availability of plants and the best time to pack, post and plant them. Some planning in advance is therefore necessary. In the UK for example spring bulbs will be delivered only from August to November, and bare-root fruit trees and hedging (see pp270–271) from October to March.

Above: Specialist growers carry large quantities of their particular plants and are ideal if you're massing big groups of the same plant over a large area. It's possible that plants will be the cheapest there too.

Left, above: For semimature specimen plants, use an experienced grower every time, unless you're buying just one or two plants. Plants as big as these aren't cheap or easy to handle. There's also provenance to consider – have plants imported from warmer climates been properly acclimatised to your region? A quick search online will reveal suppliers nearby; type in 'specimen plants'.

Left, below: Specialist nurseries may not have the bright lights and colourful livery of big garden centres but they are first choice for keen gardeners and garden designers. The range is usually better, so too is advice on appropriate substitutes. For many of us, it's also important to 'buy local' and support our local economy.

The root of it all

Plants are sold in all shapes and sizes, but when it comes to the roots, each plant falls into one of three groups. Container-grown (and containerised) plants are the most common and the easiest to work with, while bare-root, and rootballed (also known as balled and burlapped) plants are also available. Each one has advantages and disadvantages related to cost, handling, the range sold and the time of year they can be planted.

Containers

Container plants can be planted year-round provided the ground isn't frozen or waterlogged, although planting in hot summers isn't recommended. Spring and autumn are therefore the ideal times.

To obtain the best plants, assess each one before buying. Top growth should be bushy, evenly spread out and pest- and disease-free. Ignore plants, particularly trees, which have deep grazes or gouges on their trunks. Pots full of weeds are not a good sign either. Tug plants gently from their containers to check that they're not pot-bound. If there's nothing but matted roots with little soil visible, choose another plant. The same applies if there are lots of thick roots poking through the drainage holes in the bottom of the container. Both are signs that the plant has been in its pot for too long. There are two exceptions however. Vigorous fibrous-rooted perennials such as Michaelmas daisies (*Aster* and *Symphyotrichum*) and spreading ground cover fill their pots quickly. Many gardeners buy these and divide them into fist-sized clumps at home, in turn making two, perhaps even three, plants from one. And tender annuals always grow fast – for me, the more roots the better here, provided the top growth isn't too tall and leggy.

Sizes

In the UK, Europe and Australia, containers are measured in litres (abbreviated to L or Lt) or sized in centimetres. In the US, they're measured in gallons and quarts, or in inches. As a guide, a coffee-mug-sized pot (for young perennials, ground cover and bigger bedding plants) is about 0.5 litres (half a quart). A pot the size of a standard builder's bucket is 15 litres (about 4 gallons) – usual for young standard trees. The bigger the pot the bigger the plant, and the more expensive it will be – some specimen plants are grown in pots the size of a small car, with a similar price tag!

Bare-root

In temperate climates, the traditional way to buy deciduous trees, shrubs, roses and field-grown perennials is bare-root, between autumn and early spring. At this time, deciduous plants are dormant and don't mind being dug up without any soil around their roots and then replanted. While this means you have to hit what is a very precise timing window, the big advantage of bare-root plants is that they're a lot cheaper than container-grown plants. This makes them ideal for long runs of hedging. Plus the range of trees and roses available is much bigger too.

Check plants when you buy, paying close attention to the roots. They should have been plunged in compost or bagged to keep them moist, so reject plants with roots that have dried out. Roots forming a neat circular pattern are a good sign. Avoid roots that have obviously been mangled by a machine. With mail order, the downside is that you can't check the roots beforehand, so always source from a reputable supplier.

The No 1 rule with bare-root plants is to keep the roots covered at all times so they don't dry out; if you can't plant straightaway, always place some moist soil or potting compost over the roots until you can.

Planting bare-root plants is little different from planting those in containers. Set each at the same depth the plant was grown in the nursery. Look for the old soil mark at the bottom of the main stem to guide you.

Rootballed/Balled & burlapped

Evergreens and conifers never go truly dormant and therefore need to be treated differently. All field-grown stock, except small hedging plants such as yew (*Taxus*) and holly (*Ilex*), should come supplied with a firm rootball, tightly wrapped in hessian to hold the soil around the roots. Larger, deciduous, field-grown trees and shrubs will also come packaged this way, the aim being to minimise transplanting shock and help establishment. Keep the rootball covered before planting and plant to the same depth as before. To maintain the integrity of the rootball, some specialist nurseries don't recommend removing the hessian and wire from big plants, but for smaller ones it's normally taken off.

Top: White bags allow a little light to reach the root zone, which helps prevent root girdling – the bags encourage roots to grow downwards or inwards rather than wind around the inside edge of the container.

Above: Large rootballs are often covered with wire or chainlink, to provide additional support.

Top: Reputable mail order suppliers of bare-root plants will always wrap the roots carefully for protection and also to stop them drying out.

Above: Container trees are readily available and, unlike rootballed or bare-root specimens, can be planted year-round, if weather conditions permit.

Above: Giant plants such as this one need careful handling using machinery. If access is tight at home, this will be an additional cost to consider, unless you have some seriously strong relations!

Size matters

Do you have the patience to wait for small plants to grow or do you want the instant impact of larger plants? Your budget will have an impact here. A bit of both is the most common and cost-effective solution, but big isn't always best. Small plants are cheaper than large ones, and they establish more readily, especially in exposed spots, where those with a big 'sail' area in particular will struggle without protection. However big specimens do have their place if they're planted and looked after properly.

Size wise

While it's possible to purchase a large specimen of almost anything, some plants are more worth buying than others. For instant privacy and screening, trees should come top of the list. Close behind are woody structural plants including palms, conifers, bamboos and shrubs, particularly slow-growing species; just one or two will give any new planting an immediate sense of maturity and proportion. Instant hedges are also popular and although they cost a lot, they are still cheaper than a brick wall. Huge perennials and grasses are available too. However, I'd buy these as small plants, especially if you are planting a large area – after a year or so, there's not a lot of difference size-wise, and small plants are much more cost-effective. The same goes for vigorous climbers and shrubs such as *Buddleja*, which bulk up rapidly.

Buying big: Factors to consider

- **Sourcing:** While garden centres stock some large plants nowadays, specialist growers are the most useful source. They're cheaper, give good, free advice, stock a wider range of different sizes and will deliver oversized specimens carefully. Most offer a planting service too, which might be useful for peace of mind.

- **Price:** This depends on height and spread, age, origin and the pot size, if appropriate. With trees, the thickness or girth of the trunk is also important.

- **Access:** Measure passageways (or the hallway in a terraced house) before you buy, to check that plants will go through. For extra-large plants (in pots bigger than 200L, or 44 gallons) a crane to manoeuvre them into position might be necessary – a cost that is prohibitively expensive for only one or two plants.

- **Handling:** Plants in big pots or tall, bare-root trees are difficult to handle and plant by only one person. Ask friends and family to help.

- **Guarantee:** Many growers offer a guarantee, provided plants have been planted and cared for correctly. Always ask.

- **Aftercare & establishment:** Mature plants need more care and attention than small ones. The 'establishment phase' (where plants require most support) for a 2L (½ gallon) shrub is no more than a year. For the same species in a 120L (26 gallon) pot, this could be three years. Drought is the most common cause of failure – drip irrigation systems are helpful here. So too is a thick mulch and an 'earth dam' around plants, which acts as a reservoir and keeps water where it's needed.

Quantities & spacing: How many plants?

Determining how many plants you need depends on the vigour, competitiveness, size and spread of each one. The role of each plant in the design also comes into play. Of particular importance is how long you're willing to wait for the scheme to bloom into something beautiful. While many people don't desire or cannot afford an 'instant' garden, few of us want to wait a long time to see results. But, before we look at the detail, do note that plant spacing is not an exact science; growing conditions have a huge impact, and you'll find different books contradict each other too. Common sense is therefore key, and never do you need to be measurement perfect.

Far apart or up close?

Spacing plants according to their size when mature is the traditional method, and is still perfectly acceptable. However with slow-growing shrubs and conifers in particular, this can result in lots of bare soil and a 'spotty' look for years as plants bulk up. On the flip side, cramming plants together (particularly vigorous perennials) in an effort to create an instant effect isn't advisable either. Too close and each plant will perform poorly, and some will need to be sacrificed later on to make room for the remainder to mature, so wasting time and money. Instead most gardeners and designers now trade off between the two options, spacing some plants closer for a mature look more quickly, but not so close that they'll struggle and compete for water, light and nutrients. The guide on pp274–275 will help.

Suitable spacings

No standardised rules exist on plant spacing, so garden designers and keen gardeners create their own, based on knowledge they've gathered from research, personal observation and experience. Depending on where people are gardening or working, there are inevitably some subtle differences but most recommended spacings are pretty similar to what you see on pp274–275. The featured spacings should create a relatively close-knit or 'full' appearance in three to five years' time – the timeframe within which most of us want to see some results. With these spacings, it's really the perennials that will mature in three years, while the shrubs will take five or more.

Do note this is a guide only and doesn't factor in local and regional differences when it comes to soil type and climate. Nor does it consider large specimen plants, which should be planted wider apart (specialist suppliers will advise here). Tweak things as you see fit too. You may decide to space perennials at the back of the border slightly further apart, if you're working to a tight budget. Alternatively, you might space a tall shrub slightly closer to a shorter one, so it arches over the top. You may also disagree with me and set vigorous species much further apart, or slow-growing ones closer together – here your own experience counts.

Left: Plant vigour, size at maturity, your budget and how long you want to wait for a 'mature look' will influence how far apart you space your plants. Unfortunately, it isn't an exact science, although the table on pp274–275 should help.

Plant spacings

GROUP	EXAMPLES	SPACING	NUMBER OF PLANTS PER SQ M (SQ YD)
Small bulbs, corms and tubers	*Crocus* 'Jeanne d'Arc', *Narcissus jonquilla* (jonquil), *Hyacinthoides non-scripta* (English bluebell), *Anemone nemorosa* (wood anemone)	5–10cm (2–4in)	50–60
Large bulbs, corms and tubers	*Lilium regale* (regal lily), *Narcissus* 'Salome' (trumpet daffodil), *Allium* 'Globemaster' (ornamental onion), *Tulipa* 'Apeldoorn' (tulip)	15–25cm (6–10in)	20–40 (depending on height)
Hardy annuals, half-hardy annuals and small/slender biennials	*Nigella damascena* (love-in-a-mist), *Centaurea cyanus* (cornflower), *Papaver somniferum* (opium poppy), *Orlaya grandiflora* (white laceflower), *Cosmos bipinnatus* 'Purity' (white cosmos), *Dianthus barbatus* 'Noverna Purple' (sweet William)	20–30cm (8–12in)	15–25 (depending on height and spread)
Large biennials, vigorous alpines, small, clump-forming herbaceous perennials and grasses	*Festuca glauca* 'Elijah Blue' (blue fescue), *Bergenia* 'Silberlicht' (elephant's ears), *Nepeta racemosa* 'Walker's Low' (dwarf catmint), *Digitalis purpurea* (foxglove)	25–35cm (10–14in)	5–9
Medium-sized and/or spreading grasses, ferns and herbaceous perennials (including ground cover)	*Miscanthus sinensis* 'Silberfeder' (silver grass), *Lysimachia clethroides* (loosestrife), *Macleaya microcarpa* 'Kelway's Coral Plume' (plume poppy), *Acanthus mollis* (bear's breeches)	50–60cm (20–24in)	1–3
Small shrubs, conifers and roses (H&S: 45cm–1m/1½–3ft)	*Pittosporum tobira* 'Nanum' (dwarf Japanese mock orange), *Cistus* × *hybridus* (rock rose), *Juniperus squamata* 'Blue Star' (flaky juniper), *Rosa* Munstead Wood = 'Ausbernard' (rose)	50–65cm (20–26in)	2–3
Medium shrubs, conifers and roses (H&S: 1–2m/3–6½ft); small, clump-forming bamboos	*Rosa* Falstaff = 'Ausverse' (rose), *Rosa* × *odorata* 'Mutabilis' (rose), *Fargesia murielae* (umbrella bamboo), *Choisya* × *dewitteana* 'Aztec Pearl' (Mexican orange blossom)	1–1.2m (3–4ft)	1–2
Large shrubs and bamboos (H&S: 2m+/6½ft+)	*Viburnum* × *bodnantense* 'Dawn' (arrowwood), *V. tinus* (laurustinus), *Cotinus* 'Grace' (smoke bush), *Buddleja davidii* 'Dartmoor' (butterfly bush)	1.35–1.8m (4½–6ft)	0.5

GROUP	EXAMPLES	SPACING	NUMBER OF PLANTS PER SQ M (SQ YD)
Slow-growing wall shrubs and small–medium spreading climbers	*Clematis* 'Niobe', *Hydrangea anomala* subsp. *petiolaris* (climbing hydrangea), *Itea ilicifolia* (holly-leaved sweetspire), *Trachelospermum jasminoides* (star jasmine)	2m (6½ft)	n/a
Medium–large, vigorous climbers	*Clematis* 'Apple Blossom', *Parthenocissus tricuspidata* 'Veitchii' (Boston ivy), *Wisteria floribunda* 'Alba' (Japanese wisteria), *Solanum laxum* 'Album' (potato vine)	3m (10ft)	n/a
Small ornamental trees (H&S: 6–10m/20–33ft)	*Sorbus* 'Joseph Rock' (rowan), *Amelanchier × grandiflora* 'Ballerina' (juneberry), *Malus* 'Evereste' (crab apple), *Prunus* 'Accolade' (cherry), *Cornus kousa* var. *chinensis* (Chinese dogwood), *Acer griseum* (paper-bark maple)	4m (13ft) or more	n/a

Calculating quantities

If you have followed the sequence on pp202–203 of plotting the mature sizes of plants on paper when creating a design, you can now use the guide above, together with a circle template, to calculate how many plants are actually needed to turn your scheme into reality.

1. Lay a sheet of tracing paper over your plan and fix the edges together with masking tape.

2. Pick one of the plants from your plan and identify which group it comes under, with reference to the description and the examples given in the table (left and above).

3. Working to the same scale as before, now find the appropriate circle on your template, considering the spacing given in the table. For example, a small shrub such as dwarf Japanese mock orange (*Pittosporum tobira* 'Nanum') should be spaced 50–65cm (20–26in) apart. On your circle template, working at a scale of 1:20, this would be circle size 30 (30mm/1in). Working at 1:50, this would be circle size 12 (12mm/½in). It helps here to see the centre of the circle on the template as being the centre of a plant; the diameter represents the spacing between plants.

4. With the template, now draw circles over the relevant blob, drift or sausage shape on your plan, making the edges only just touch. Repeat until you fill the area allocated for each plant with circles. The distance from the centre of one circle to the centre of the next will be the same as the diameter of each circle – the planting distance.

5. Repeat this process for each of the different plants included on your plan. Try to fill gaps as you go, slightly overlapping a few if need be; those you can't overlap can be plugged with a temporary filler (see p180).

6. Count up the number of circles drawn over every plant to determine the total quantity of plants needed to implement the design. This overlay sketch becomes the final plan. And, because you now know how many plants of each species you require, you can use it to cost the scheme. For big shrubs, in particular, you'll probably find you want three or more plants to fill the space allocated for a 'full' look in five years or so.

Note: The circles on each plan in Chapter 7 were created exactly in this way, using the guide above.

Choosing substitutes

Good garden centres and specialist nurseries will suggest other local growers if they don't stock your requirements. If you have a long list, some might even source these plants from their pool of suppliers, gathering a large order together so that everything can be planted at the same time – a common service offered to professional gardeners and designers at some trade-only nurseries. However it's inevitable there will be something you can't get – a rare species perhaps or something of a specific size. Although the latest edition of *RHS Plant Finder* may help, even this is no guarantee. Instead do appreciate that choosing appropriate alternatives is all part of putting a new planting together.

Decisions, decisions

Even professional gardeners and designers, who are experienced in what's commonly available and what's not, will occasionally have problems. Fortunately there is always something appropriate, if not better, than your original selection that can be used instead.

To find a good alternative, note the characteristics of the plant you can't source. Consider its appearance (colour, shape etc), size and spread at maturity, necessary growing conditions, role in the design and any specific reasons it was included originally – scented leaves for example. Now refer to your initial list, the one made before trimming it to your final selection. Is there an appropriate substitute there? If not, look to the same plant group – another maple (*Acer*) or lavender (*Lavandula*) for example; some will look noticeably different, but many won't.

Lateral thinking

Choosing substitutes becomes more time-consuming when you're forced to opt for a different plant altogether. However you should apply the same process, that is, comparing the characteristics of the original to any alternatives, ticking off the criteria (see opposite for an example). On occasion, it's likely that sacrifices will have to be made – lavender-blue flowers as opposed to mauve for example. Just make sure that the most important criteria – growing conditions being top priority – are met.

To help you, seek advice from specialist growers or trained horticulturists at garden centres, who can often suggest appropriate alternative plants. Otherwise select one from specific supplier catalogues or, better still, 'current availability lists', to guarantee that alternatives are on sale.

Left: If plants can't be sourced in one form – containers for example – they might be available in another that you can fall back on. However, with bare-root plants in particular, you will have to wait until winter, which could radically affect the schedule of seeing your scheme into the ground.

Left: Shade-tolerant box (*Buxus*) balls are much loved and readily available. But they do require regular clipping, and mature specimens aren't cheap, plus there's box blight disease to consider. Might one of the alternatives below be a viable substitute?

Below: Dwarf Japanese mock orange (*Pittosporum tobira* 'Nanum') needs sun but no pruning and suffers little from disease.

Left: Dwarf mountain pine (*Pinus mugo* Pumilio Group) is tough and needs no clipping but it is slow growing and prefers sun.

Below, right: *Hebe* 'Emerald Gem' tolerates all well-drained soils and partial shade. It is similar to box (*Buxus*) in outline appearance but grows to only 30cm (12in) tall.

Below: Kohuhu (*Pittosporum tenuifolium* 'Silver Queen') is simple to clip into a spherical shape, but keeping plants at this size isn't easy. Best in sun or partial shade.

Hardiness ratings/zones

Hardiness ratings/zones are a tool that gardeners can use to determine which plants will survive winter temperatures in any one location. There are two systems used in this book and they both feature at the end of each full plant name. The first is the Royal Horticultural Society (RHS) 'snowflake' rating, while the second is the United States Department of Agriculture (USDA) map and coding system of hardiness zones.

The snowflake system (see key, opposite) features first, followed by the USDA system, where the two numbers – preceded with a capital 'Z'– signify the particular zones on the maps (see below) where that plant will survive. For example, common sage (*Salvia officinalis*) is rated Z5–8. In zones 4 and below, the plant might die because it's too cold, yet it might not be cold

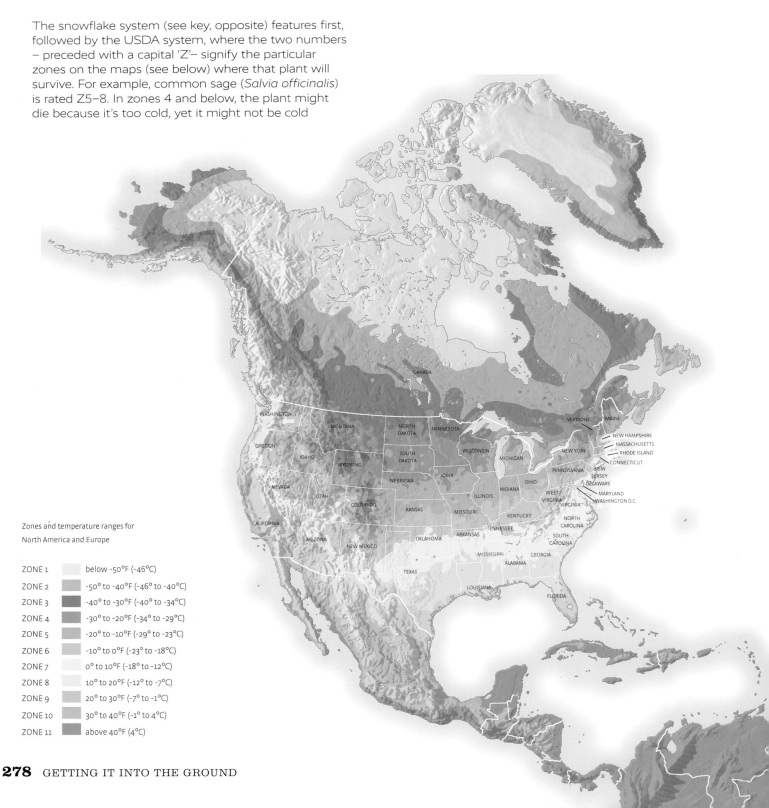

Zones and temperature ranges for
North America and Europe

ZONE 1		below -50°F (-46°C)
ZONE 2		-50° to -40°F (-46° to -40°C)
ZONE 3		-40° to -30°F (-40° to -34°C)
ZONE 4		-30° to -20°F (-34° to -29°C)
ZONE 5		-20° to -10°F (-29° to -23°C)
ZONE 6		-10° to 0°F (-23° to -18°C)
ZONE 7		0° to 10°F (-18° to -12°C)
ZONE 8		10° to 20°F (-12° to -7°C)
ZONE 9		20° to 30°F (-7° to -1°C)
ZONE 10		30° to 40°F (-1° to 4°C)
ZONE 11		above 40°F (4°C)

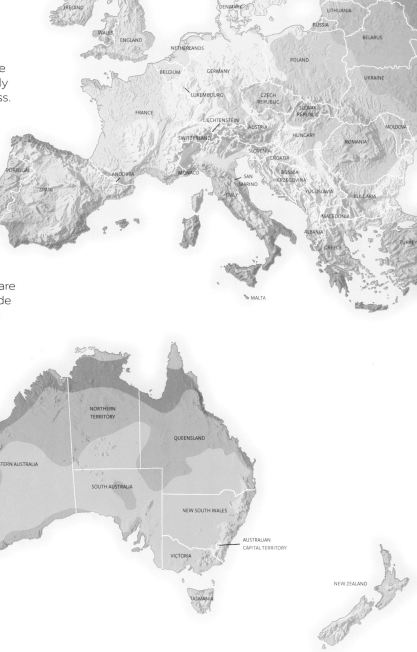

RHS 'snowflake' system

❁ Frost-tender: plant may be damaged by temperatures below 5°C (41°F)

❄ Half-hardy: plant can withstand temperatures down to 0°C (32°F)

❄❄ Frost-hardy: plant can withstand temperatures down to -5°C (23°F)

❄❄❄ Fully hardy: plant can withstand temperatures down to -15°C (5°F)

enough – for example for it to flower (a process called vernalisation) – in zones higher than 8.

As the USDA system is based only on average annual minimum temperatures, it should be used simply as a guide. It doesn't take into account severe winters, local conditions or other factors – particularly high temperatures that also influence plant hardiness. This means that areas with the same average minimum temperature in winter, but distinctly different summer temperatures, are often given the same rating. In particularly hot regions – Texas, Arizona or Florida for example – it's well worth considering the American Horticultural Society's Plant Heat Zones as well as the USDA ratings given here (see www.ahs.org for all the details).

Australasia has a slightly different system. Because the average winter minimum temperatures experienced on this continent are generally warmer than North America, just 7 zones are used there; see the chart below. On the left-hand side you'll also see the USDA zones for comparison. Use the Australasian system in exactly the same way as you would the North American and European one.

Zones and temperature ranges for Australia and New Zealand (in comparison to North America and Europe)

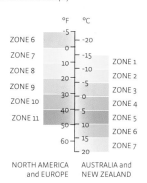

	°F	°C	
ZONE 6	-5	-20	
ZONE 7	0	-15	ZONE 1
ZONE 8	10	-10	ZONE 2
ZONE 9	20	-5	ZONE 3
ZONE 10	30	0	ZONE 4
ZONE 11	40	5	ZONE 5
	50	10	ZONE 6
	60	15	ZONE 7
		20	

NORTH AMERICA and EUROPE   AUSTRALIA and NEW ZEALAND

Further reading

A list of favourite books you might also find useful. Some will help you to choose appropriate plants; others are ideal if you'd like to delve more deeply into certain areas. All should be easy to obtain.

Giant Perennials: Star Performers for the Garden by Susan Berry (Collins & Brown, 2003).

RHS Encyclopedia of Plants and Flowers edited by Christopher Brickell (Dorling Kindersley, 2010).

RHS Encyclopedia of Gardening (4th Ed) edited by Christopher Brickell (Dorling Kindersley, 2012).

Beth Chatto's Gravel Garden by Beth Chatto (Frances Lincoln, 2000).

Late Summer Flowers by Marina Christopher (Frances Lincoln, 2011).

The Well-Designed Mixed Garden: Building Beds and Borders with Trees, Shrubs, Perennials, Annuals, and Bulbs by Tracy DiSabato-Aust (Timber Press, 2009).

The Dry Gardening Handbook: Plants and Practices for a Changing Climate by Olivier Filippi (Thames & Hudson, 2008).

A New Naturalism by Catherine Heatherington & Juliet Sargeant (Packard Publishing Limited, 2005).

Encyclopedia of Exotic Plants for Temperate Climates by Will Giles (Timber Press, 2007).

Gardening with Woodland Plants by Karan Junker (Timber Press, 2007).

The RHS Companion to Scented Plants by Stephen Lacey (Frances Lincoln, 2014).

Perfect Plant, Perfect Place by Roy Lancaster (Dorling Kindersley, 2010).

Creative Vegetable Gardening by Joy Larkcom (Mitchell Beazley, 2014).

Succession Planting for Adventurous Gardeners by Christopher Lloyd (BBC Books, 2005).

Jekka's Complete Herb Book by Jekka McVicar (Kyle Cathie, 2007).

Designing With Grasses by Neil Lucas (Timber Press, 2011).

Dream Plants for the Natural Garden by Piet Ouldolf & Henk Gerristsen (Frances Lincoln, 2013).

Planting Design: Gardens in Time & Space by Piet Ouldolf & Noel Kingsbury (Timber Press, 2005).

Planting: A New Perspective by Piet Ouldolf & Noel Kingsbury (Timber Press, 2013).

RHS What Plant When by the Royal Horticultural Society (Dorling Kindersley, 2011).

RHS What Plant Where Encyclopedia by the Royal Horticultural Society (Dorling Kindersley, 2013).

Planting the Dry Shade Garden: The Best Plants for the Toughest Spot in Your Garden by Graham Rice (Timber Press, 2011).

RHS Garden Plants and Flowers Through the Year (2nd Ed) by Ian Spence (Dorling Kindersley, 2009).

RSPB Gardening for Wildlife: A Complete Guide to Nature-friendly Gardening by Adrian Thomas (A & C Black Publishers Ltd, 2010).

The Self-Sustaining Garden: The Guide to Matrix Planting by Peter Thompson (Timber Press, 2007).

On the Wildside: Experiments in New Naturalism by Keith Wiley (Timber Press, 2004).

Contemporary Colour in the Garden: Top Designers, Inspiring Ideas & New Combinations by Andrew Wilson (Timber Press, 2011).

Index

Picture credits

The publisher would like to thank the following sources for their kind permission to reproduce the photographs in this book:

HELEN DILLON 91b.

HELEN FICKLING des: Andy Sturgeon 198–199.

GAP PHOTOS 136bc, 156 image 7, 225bc, 240a; **Amy Vonheim** 161 image 9; **Carol Casselden** 78 image 5, 108, 206–207b; **Carole Drake** 10–11, Bosvigo/Owner: Wendy Perry 162, Courtesy Mrs T Lewis 26–27; 161 image 1, Courtesy The Sir Harold Hillier Gardens/ Hampshire County Council 214a, 224a; **Charles Hawes** The Cancer Research UK Garden/Andy Sturgeon 180–181, 234b, 239b, 271al; **Chris Burrows** 66 image 8; **Christa Brand** 57r, **Clive Nichols** Des: Clare Matthews 78 image 8, 148–149; **Dave Zubraski** 139br, 258a; **Elke Borkowski** 126–127, 131b, 143br, 154 image 5, Des: Robert Myers 181r, 236b, The Botanic Nursery, Atworth, Wiltshire 269r, 273; **FhF Greenmedia** 66 Image 6, 161 image 2; **Fiona Lee** 114–115a, Des: Graham Hardman 277bl; **Fiona McLeod** 139ac, 142–143b, 156 image 4; **Fiona Rice** 136ar, 159 image 3, 160 image 3; **Friedrich Strauss** 155 image 5, 271ar; **Gary Smith** 222bl; **Gillian Plummer** 254r; **Graham Strong** 271br; **Heather Edwards** 21, 226bc, 242bl; **Howard Rice** 10bl, 14l, c and r, 15l and c, 30–31, 38–39b, 70, 247a; **J S Sira** Des: Arne Maynard, Chelsea Flower Show 2012 95b, 167ar 230br, 237 background; **Jan Smith** 80 image 7, 244–245i, 257b; **Jason Ingram** 155 image 7; **Jason Smalley** 154 image 2; **Jerry Harpur** 72–73; Des: Vladimir Sitta 83a, Des: Christopher Bradley-Hole 140–141; **Jo Whitworth** 80 image 4, 160 image 6, 205ar, 205cr, Des: Piet Oudolf 242ar, Des: Tom Stuart-Smith 246b, 262br; **Joanna Kossak** 44 image 8, 136al, 161 image 10, 230bl; **John Glover** 88cr, 154 image 4, 159 image 4, 254c, 268–269b, 277cl; **John Swithinbank** 15br; **Jonathan Buckley** 20, Des: Orlando Murrin 109a, Des: Tom Stuart-Smith 130r, Des: Carol Klein 137, 233br, 249cr; **Jonathan Need** 230a, 244a; **Julie Dansereau** 258al; **Lee Avison** 277br; **Lucy Griffiths** 154 image 8, 161 image 3; **Lynn Keddie** 253b, Des: Laurie Chetwood and Patrick Collins 244bl; **Maddie Thornhill** 75r; **Marcus Harpur** 80 image 3, 160 image 7; **Marg Cousens** 202 image 1, 206bl; **Mark Bolton** 154 image 6, 156 image 9, 173b, 245ar; **Martin Shaffler** 205bl; **Martin Staffler** 161 image 5, 202 image 2; **Matt Anker** 144a, 204cl, 233cl; **Matteo Carassale** 24l, 271bl; **Maxine Adcock** 136ac, 161 image 7; **Neil Holmes** 214br, 245b; **Nicola Stocken** 248–249 background; **Pernilla Berg dahl** 221a; **Rachel Warne** 128–129; **Richard Bloom** Scampston Hall Garden/Piet Oudolf 114–115b, 248a; **Rob Whitworth** 35, 147bl, 159 image 6, 159 image 7, 242al; **Robert Mabic** 155 Image 3; **Ron Evans** 170–171, 242br; **S&O** 160 image 4, 206–207a, 252i; **Sue Heath** 161 image 8; **Suzie Gibbons** 268–269a; **Thomas Alamy** 17 image 1, 159 image 5; **Victoria Firmston** 136bl; **Visions** 44 image 7, 135b, 221cr, 238a; **Zara Napier** 168l.

HARLEQUIN FABRICS AND WALLCOVERINGS LTD 89ar.

MATT JAMES 88al and cl, 89al and c, 136 br, 156 image 8, Tendercare Nurseries. Denham, Middlesex 272, Thornhayes Nursery, Dulford, Devon 276.

MMGI 106; **Andrew Lawson** 17 image 9, 80 image 6, Des: Anthony Noel 81, 89br, Pensthorpe Millennium Garden/Pensthorpe Waterfowl Park 138b, 254l; **Bennet Smith** 152, 155 image 6, 214bl, 226, 247b, Lip na Cloiche, Isle of Mull/Lucy Mackenzie Panizzon 212b, Pembury House, West Sussex 223, The B&Q Garden, RHS Chelsea Flower Show 2011/Laurie Chetwood and Patrick Collins 244–245 background, The Cancer Research UK garden, RHS Chelsea Flower Show 2011/Robert Myers 180l, The Largest Room in the House, RHS Chelsea Flower Show 2008/Denise Preston 67, 128al, The QVC Garden, Chelsea Flower Show 2008/Patrick Clarke & Sarah Price 147ar, Vital Earth The Night Sky Garden, RHS Chelsea Flower Show 2014/David and Harry Rich 130l, Walker's Pine Cottage Garden, RHS Chelsea Flower Show 2013/ Graham Bodle 204–205 background; **Bob Gibbons** 155 Image 2; **Heather Edwards** 44 image 1; **J S Sira** 88br, The Laurent Perrier Garden, RHS Chelsea

Flower Show 2011/Luciano Giubbilei 192–193b, **Marianne Majerus** 17 image 2, 33cl, 44 image 2, 3 4 5 and 6, 44–45b, 65r, 66 image 4 and 7, 78 image 2 and 6, 80 image 1, 154 images 1, 3, 7, 9 and 10, 155 images 4, 8, 9 and 10, 156 images 2, 3, 5, 9 and 10, 159 images 1, 2 and 10, 160 images 1, 5 and 8, 161 images 4 and 6, 202 image 5, 204bl, 209al, 209ac, 210a, 211, 213ar, 215l, 216a and b, 217ar, 218r, 225ar, 226a, 228b, 229b, 230bc, 235, 236a, 236c, 240br, 246a, 248b, 249ac and bc, 250 b, 257al, 257ar, 260b, Acres Wild 163, 194–195, 260–261 background, Aldenhaeve, The Netherlands 218l, 220br, Alzheimer's Society Remember to Reflect Garden, RHS Tatton Park Flower Show 2013/Louise Harrison-Holland, 118bl, Bates Green 241br, Beech Court, Kent 78 images 3 and 4, Beth Chatto Gardens, Essex 60, 69, 124–125, 125r, 216–217 background, 217br, 220–221 background, 221bl, Bramdean House, Hampshire 233bl, Brent and Becky's Bulbs, Gloucester, VA, USA 241bc, 260a, Brian and Dawn Dunn 17 image 3, Brook Cottage, Glos. 213br, Bryan's Ground, Herefordshire/Simon Dorrell and David Wheeler 43, 232–233 background, Carine Reckinger-Thill 49a, 239cl, Catherine Heatherington 17 image 6, Chelsea Flower Show 2001/Tom Stuart-Smith 145ar, Clinton Lodge 159 image 8, 252a, Cloudy Bay Sensory Garden, RHS Chelsea Flower Show 2014/Andrew Wilson and Gavin McWilliam 46–47, 166a, Debbie Roberts and Ian Smith/Acres Wild 8–9, 79, Denmans, Sussex/John Brookes 80 image 8, 224–225 background, Des: Alison Wear 225cr, Des: Amir Schlezinger/MyLandscapes 11br, 113r, Des: Ann Godfrey 134ar, Des: Ann Mollo 24–25, 213bc, Des: Annie Pearce 28a, 61, Des: Bernard Hickie, Dublin, Ireland 109 b, Des: Bunny Guinness 104b, Des: Carolyn Dunster 46l, Des: Charlotte Rowe 12–13, 84–85, 90, 104a, 105b, 134al, 196, 240–241 background, 277a, Des: Chris Ghyselen, Belgium 40, Des: Christopher Bradley-Hole 118–119, 129r, 131c, 141r, 156 image 11, Des: Claire Mee Designs 64–65, 168ar, Des: Declan Buckley 4, 55br, 107, 128bl, 212–213 background, Des: del Buono Gazerwitz Landscape Architecture 30l, 33a, 38–39a, 74–75, 86–87, 91a, 121, 133a, 157, 197a, Des: Emma Griffin 18a, Des: Graham Lloyd-Brunt 94, 241l, Des: Ian Kitson 177b, Des: James Alexander-Sinclair 150–151, Des: Jane Brockbank 23a, 256bl, Des: Jilayne Rickards 77ar, Des: Jo Thompson 11ar, Des: John Bailey Gardens 175c, Des: Julie Toll 53, 80 image 5, 169, 217bl, Des: Lynne Marcus 197b, 202 image 3, Des: Maurizio Vegini, Studio GPT, Italy 176b, Michael Taubenheim and Christopher Moore 253c, Des: Noel Kingsbury 222al, Des: Rachel James 50a, 138bl, Des: Rita Streitz 143bcr, 160 image 9, 240bl, Des: Sam Martin 156 image 1, Des: Sean Walter 23b, 102–103, 105a, 176–177a, Des: Stephen Crisp 201, Des: Stuart Craine 58, Des: Sue Townsend 17 image 7, 51a, 54–55a, 139b, 148l, 153a, 228–229 background, 256–257 background, 264–265, Des: Tom Stuart-Smith 29, 37a, 52, 56–57, 120a, 134b, 160 image 11, 189b, Des: Tom Stuart-Smith, James Hitchmough 2,120b, 233cr, Des: William Moore and John Wilson 17 image 8, Dove Cottage/Des: Stephen Rogers 168br, 175b, 249al, Dyffryn Fernant Garden, Wales/Christina Shand 209ar, 209cl, East Lambrook Manor/Design: Margery Fish 39br, Eccleston Square, London 17 image 5, Elton Hall, Herefordshire 54–55b, 139a, Feeringbury Manor 16 image 5, Gaard um Titzebierg, Luxembourg 66 image 5, Gilbert Folschette 10al, Grafton Cottage, Staffs/ Margaret and Peter Hargreaves 96–97, 143ar, 219, Gravetye Manor, West Sussex/Tom Coward 249ar, Great Comp, Kent 217al, Great Dixter, East Sussex 97a, Green Island Gardens, Essex 155 image 11, Haddon Lake House/Phillippa Lambert 208–209 background, Hadspen Garden 144bl, Hare Court, Inner Temple/Des: Andrea Brunsendorf 225al 261br, Hauser and Wirth/Des: Piet Oudolf 261al, Hermannshof, Weinheim, Germany/Cassian Schmidt 50–51b, Hollycroft Cottage/Emma Duncan 259, Homebase Teenage Cancer Trust Garden, RHS Chelsea Flower Show 2012/Joe Swift 133b, 277cr, 'Hortus Conclusus', RHS Chelsea 2004/Christopher Bradley-Hole 89bc, Inner Temple Gardens 66 Image 3, Jeannine Sponville 160 image 10, Jordans Mill/Julie Toll and Ian Kitson 100–101, Jordans Wildlife Garden, RHS Hampton Court Flower Show 2014/Selina Botham 142bl, 252b, Josceline Dimbleby, Chelsea Physic Garden,

London 210bl, Julie Dansereau 221bc, 95a, Knoll Gardens, Dorset/ Des: Neil Lucas 34a, Longacre, Kent 66 image 1, 138ac, Lowder Mill 76al, Marchants Hardy Plants, East Sussex/Graham Gough 209br, Mindrum 251, 'Nature Ascending', RHS Chelsea Flower Show 2009/ Jane Brockbank 71, No Man's Land: ABF The Soldier's Charity, RHS Chelsea Flower Show 2014/Charlotte Rowe 178, Norman's Farm 33bl, Norney Wood/Acres Wild 161 image 11, Old Bladbean Stud, Kent 62, Oliver's, Essex 204b, 'Passage', Gardens of Gothenburg Festival, Sweden 2008/Philip Nixon 132, RBC Blue Water Roof Garden, RHS Chelsea Flower Show 2013/Nigel Dunnett 191b, RHS Garden Hyde Hall 210br, RHS Floral Celebration 2008, Inner Temple 147al, RHS Garden Wisley 16 images 1, 2, 3, 6, 7 and 8, 17 image 4, 78 image 7, 82, 138a, al and bc, 202 image 4, 204a, 229a, 234a, RHS Garden Wisley/James Hitchmough 190–191a, Robert Myers/A Cadogan Garden, RHS Chelsea Flower Show 2008 116–117, Rosemary Lindsay 213al, Royal Botanical Gardens, Kew, London 28b, Rymans, Sussex 36–37, Sandhill Farm House, Hampshire/Des: Rosemary Alexander 172a, Sarah Price, Patrick Wynniatt-Husey and Patrick Clarke/The QVC Garden, Chelsea Flower Show 2008 88bl, Satoyama Life, RHS Chelsea Flower Show 2012/Kazuyuki Ishihara 110–111, 174a, Sezincote Garden, Gloucestershire 135al, Sheffield Park, East Sussex 16 image 4, 139bc, Sir Harold Hillier Gardens, Hampshire 160 image 2, Sissinghurst Castle, Kent 45br, 66 image 2, Smallwood Farmhouse/Widget Finn 175a, Spencer Viner 59, Stockton Bury Gardens 146a, Summer Solstice, Daylesford Organic Garden, RHS Chelsea Flower Show 2008/del Buono Gazerwitz Landscape Architecture 99br, Susan Bennett & Earl Hyde 63, Sussex Prairies/ Paul and Pauline McBride 166b, 262a, Sussex Prairies/Paul and Pauline McBride 156 image 6, The Arthritis Research UK Garden, RHS Chelsea Flower Show 2012/Thomas Hoblyn 112, 225br, 225bl, 226–227b, The Arthritis Research UK Garden, RHS Chelsea Flower Show 2013/Chris Beardshaw 92–93, 182–183b, The B&Q Garden, RHS Chelsea Flower Show 2011/Laurie Chetwood and Patrick Collins 98a, 100al, The Brewin Dolphin Garden, RHS Chelsea Flower Show 2012/Cleve West 145br, 174b, The Brewin Dolphin Garden, RHS Chelsea Flower Show 2014 /Matthew Childs 80 image 2, The Copella Bee Garden, RHS Hampton Court Flower Show 2010/Sadie May Stowell 253 background and a, The Coutts Skyline Garden, London 158, The Daily Telegraph Garden, RHS Chelsea Flower Show 2009/Ulf Nordfjell 179, The Daily Telegraph Garden, RHS

Chelsea Flower Show 2010/Andy Sturgeon 122–123, The Daily Telegraph Garden, RHS Chelsea Flower Show 2011/Cleve West 144–145a, The Daily Telegraph Garden, RHS Chelsea 2006/Tom Stuart-Smith 188–189a, The Ecover Garden, RHS Hampton Court Flower Show 2013 /Matthew Child 142al, The Laurent-Perrier Bicentenary Garden, RHS Chelsea Flower Show 2012/Arne Maynard 49b, 184– 185, The Laurent-Perrier Garden, RHS Chelsea Flower Show 2008/ Tom Stuart-Smith 186–187, The Laurent-Perrier Garden, RHS Chelsea Flower Show 2010/Tom Stuart-Smith 183a, 213bl, The Laurent-Perrier Garden, RHS Chelsea Flower Show 2013/Ulf Nordfjell 135ar, The Laurent-Perrier Garden, RHS Chelsea Flower Show 2014/Luciano Giubbilei 188b, The Laurent-Perrier Harpers & Queen Garden, RHS Chelsea Flower Show 2003/Tom Stuart-Smith 192–193a, The M&G Centenary Garden – Windows through Time, RHS Chelsea Flower Show 2013/Roger Platts 186l, The Manor, Hemingford Grey 146b, The Merrill Lynch Garden, RHS Chelsea Flower Show 2005/Andy Sturgeon 88ar, The Old Rectory, Sudborough 99a, The Old Vicarage, East Ruston, Norfolk 233c, The Place For Plants 78 image 1, The Queen Elizabeth Olympic Park, London/Design: Nigel Dunnett and James Hitchmough 232i, The Sadolin Nature to Nurture Garden, RHS Hampton Court Flower Show 2009/Philippa Pearson 147br, The Savill Garden, Surrey 34b, 115ar, The Telegraph Garden, RHS Chelsea Flower Show 2012/Sarah Price 153b, Marianne Majerus/The Telegraph Garden, RHS Chelsea Flower Show 2014/del Buono Gazerwitz Landscape Architecture 32, 131a Todd Longstaffe-Gowan 68, 212a, Together Again – D-shape garden, RHS Hampton Court Flower Show 2010/Victoria Pustygina and Ludovica Ginanneschi 142–143a, Ulting Wick 144–145b, Urban Jungle 155 image 1, Wollerton Old Hall, Shrops. 42, 96a, Yews Farm, Somerset/Louise Dowding 7.

OCTOPUS PUBLISHING GROUP Marianne Majerus 6.

SERPENTINE GALLERY Hufton & Crow 119a.

SHUTTERSTOCK Arina P Habich 266–267; **Em7** 89bl; **Igor Stramyk** 15ar; **Imageman** 222br; **Ottochka** 262b inset; **Skorpionik00** 202 image 6.

THE GARDEN COLLECTION David Burton/FLPA 18b; **Flora Press** 83b; **Liz Eddison** 113l; **Nicola Stoken Tomkins** 22, **Steven Wooster** 76–77, 77b.

Author acknowledgements

I would like to express my sincere thanks to the following for their valued help and support in the creation of this book.

All at Mitchell Beazley, but in particular Alison Starling, Juliette Norsworthy and Leanne Bryan, for their commitment and enthusiasm. Thank you to designer Lizzie Ballantyne for another great-looking book, Emily Hedges for her tireless encouragement and exacting eye for an image, plus Joanna Chisolm, along with Helen Ridge, for their persistence and meticulous attention to detail. Thanks also to Lesley O'Hanlon and Grace Helmer for their help with the illustrations, Abigail Read and Naomi Edmondson for design assistance, and Nell Coffey for the calendar design, which I have always loved so much.

Thanks to Rae Spencer-Jones, Simon Maughan and Chris Young at the Royal Horticultural Society for their advice and guidance. Thanks also to the designers, gardeners and photographers (particularly Marianne Majerus) whose beautiful work we have used.

Lastly, thanks to Gordon Wise and Jacquie Drewe at Curtis Brown. And to my family, particularly Andria, Ellie, Frankie and Rosie (my two gorgeous gardeners) for their encouragement and uncanny ability to make me giggle, just when I needed to.

Author biography

Matt James is a garden designer, broadcaster and senior lecturer teaching on horticulture degree programmes at the Eden Project, Cornwall, where he also manages a respected HND in Garden & Landscape Design.

Channel 4's *The City Gardener* introduced Matt to the gardening public; the series was later broadcast around the globe. Two series about urban garden design in the US followed. He continues to make regular appearances on television and radio today.

Matt has several books to his credit, including *RHS The Urban Gardener* (also Mitchell Beazley), and also runs a design practice based in Cornwall, working in the UK and abroad.

www.mattjamesgardens.com

Royal Horticultural Society

The Royal Horticultural Society (RHS) is the UK's largest gardening charity, dedicated to advancing horticulture and promoting good gardening. Its charitable work includes providing expert advice and information, training the next generation of gardeners and promoting the ecological, aesthetic and psychological benefits of gardening in an urban environment.

For more information visit www.rhs.org.uk or call 0845 130 4646

An Hachette UK Company
www.hachette.co.uk

First published in Great Britain in 2016 by Mitchell Beazley, an imprint of Octopus Publishing Group Ltd, Carmelite House, 50 Victoria Embankment, London EC4Y 0DZ
ww.octopusbooks.co.uk

Published in association with the Royal Horticultural Society, London.

Distributed in the US by Hachette Book Group, 1290 Avenue of the Americas, 4th and 5th Floors, New York, NY 10020

Distributed in Canada by Canadian Manda Group, 664 Annette St, Toronto, Ontario, Canada M6S 2C8

Design and layout copyright © Octopus Publishing Group Ltd 2016
Text copyright © Matt James 2016

ISBN: 978 1 84533 984 5

A CIP record for this book is available from the British Library.

Printed and bound in China.

Publisher Alison Starling
Senior Editor Leanne Bryan
Art Director Juliette Norsworthy
Designer Lizzie Ballantyne
Picture Research Manager Giulia Hetherington
Picture Researcher Emily Hedges
Copy Editor Joanna Chisholm
Proofreader Helen Ridge
Indexer Helen Snaith
Assistant Production Manager Caroline Alberti

RHS Publisher Rae Spencer-Jones
RHS Consultant Editor Simon Maughan